Laborato

for use with

MW01110222

Java Program Design

James Cohoon
University of Virginia

Jack Davidson
University of Virginia

Prepared by

Robert P. Burton
Brigham Young University

Lara Burton
North Slope Systems

 **Higher Education**

Boston   Burr Ridge, IL   Dubuque, IA   Madison, WI   New York
San Francisco   St. Louis   Bangkok   Bogotá   Caracas   Kuala Lumpur
Lisbon   London   Madrid   Mexico City   Milan   Montreal   New Delhi
Santiago   Seoul   Singapore   Sydney   Taipei   Toronto

The **McGraw·Hill** Companies

Laboratory Manual for use with
JAVA PROGRAM DESIGN
JAMES COHOON, JACK DAVIDSON

Published by McGraw-Hill Higher Education, an imprint of The McGraw-Hill Companies, Inc.,
1221 Avenue of the Americas, New York, NY 10020. Copyright © 2004 by The McGraw-Hill
Companies, Inc. All rights reserved.

This book will be printed on acid-free paper.

1 2 3 4 5 6 7 8 9 0 BKM BKM 0 9 8 7 6 5 4 3

ISBN 0-07-294865-5

www.mhhe.com

Table of Contents

Preface

Introduction

This laboratory manual is intended to be used as a companion to the text *Java Program Design* by James A. Cohoon and Jack W. Davidson, published by McGraw-Hill, 2003.

Most laboratory manuals are designed to be self-study aids for mastering syntax or for providing students with straightforward, self-guided activities to be completed in an "open" laboratory at times and places of the students' choosing. This laboratory manual is different. This manual is designed for use in a "closed" laboratory. A closed laboratory session meets at an assigned time and place with a laboratory instructor, and, depending upon the number of students in the laboratory, laboratory assistants. A closed laboratory activity illustrates concepts from lectures by using examples, implementations, and problems designed to enhance the students' understanding of the concepts. A closed laboratory environment provides students with the opportunity to try various options and approaches and to receive immediate feedback. Similarly, when a student makes a mistake or needs clarification of a concept, help is available immediately.

The authors of the textbook associated with this laboratory manual have used closed laboratories in conjunction with their introductory computer science course for the past ten years. They have been extremely pleased with the results. Standardized tests show that their students leave the course with a much better mastery of the material than they did prior to the use of closed laboratories. Just as important, student evaluations show that students believe the closed laboratory activities are major contributors to their understanding of course material. Students cite the laboratory activities as the most interesting, useful, and fun part of the course. Another indicator of the high level of acceptance of the closed laboratory is the large number of students who volunteer as laboratory assistants in subsequent offerings of the course.

Using this manual

Each week of the course anticipates formal lectures and student participation in the accompanying two-hour laboratory activity provided in this manual. Labs in this manual are designed to illustrate and explore concepts from the week's lectures. Thus, the lectures and the laboratory activities proceed in synchrony.

A typical laboratory session might involve twenty to forty students, with two supervising laboratory instructors and at least two undergraduate laboratory assistants. Every student should have access to a personal computer. We have found that it can be useful to have students work together in groups of two or three—students help each other and share the responsibilities of teaching and learning. At any point during the laboratory session, students should be encouraged to seek assistance from other students or from a laboratory assistant or instructor, when needed.

Individual laboratory activities are not intended to be graded, but attendance is recorded and becomes a factor in the final grade. This approach allows students to have an opportunity to explore and learn without time or grade pressures. Some of the laboratory activities are designed so that an average student is challenged to finish in the allotted time. Students who do not complete a laboratory activity are encouraged to finish it independently.

Each laboratory activity consists of a set of experiments for the student to perform. This model is similar to the familiar closed laboratory models of biology, chemistry, and physics courses. Associated with each laboratory activity is a write up, a check-off sheet, and an experimental "apparatus." Each chapter in this manual provides space for the write-up. The back of this manual contains tear-out check-off sheets for each laboratory activity. The experimental apparatus is a set of programs and data files that the student sets up at the beginning of each laboratory activity by obtaining the appropriate files and by loading them onto the computer. The files are stored in a self-extracting archive in a location specified by the laboratory instructor. Versions of the self-extracting archives are available at our home page,

www.mhhe.com/javaprogramdesign/labs

The narratives in this manual provide the explanation of how to manipulate these files. At various points throughout each laboratory activity, students may be required to demonstrate some code, answer a question, or explain some behavior they have observed. Depending on the circumstances, the student may be asked to write an answer in the space provided or simply to provide the answer to a laboratory instructor. When a student reaches one of these "check-off" points and believes he or she is ready, the student signals a laboratory instructor and shares her or his answer. Depending on the type of question, the response, and the student involved, the laboratory instructor may simply initial the corresponding entry on the check-off sheet and proceed to the next student. If the response is incorrect or incomplete, the laboratory instructor or a laboratory instructor should help the student until the student is comfortable with the concept being explored. For some motivated students, the instructor may suggest additional experiments tailored to the student. For parts that have no right or wrong solution, the laboratory instructor may explore alternative solutions with the student to reinforce comprehension. When students complete the laboratory activity, they turn in their check-off sheets to the laboratory instructor. The check-off sheets serve as a record of attendance and student progress.

THE AUTHORS

Jim Cohoon is a Professor in the Computer Science Department at the University of Virginia and is a former Member of Technical Staff at AT&T Bell Laboratories. He joined the faculty after receiving his Ph.D. from the University of Minnesota. He has been nominated twice by the Department for the university's best-teaching award. In 1994, Professor Cohoon was awarded a Fulbright Fellowship to Germany, where he lectured on C++ and software engineering. Professor Cohoon's research interests include algorithms, computer-aided design of electronic systems, optimization strategies, and computer science education. He is the author of more than 60 papers in these fields. He is a member of the Association of Computing Machinery (ACM), the ACM Special Interest Group on Design Automation (SIGDA), the ACM Special Interest Group on Computer Science Education (SIGCSE), the Institute of Electrical and Electronics Engineers (IEEE), and the IEEE Circuits and Systems Society. He is a member of the ACM Publications and SIG Boards and is past chair of SIGDA. He can be reached at cohoon@virginia.edu. His Web homepage is http:// www.cs.virginia.edu/cohoon.

Jack Davidson is also a Professor in the Computer Science Department at the University of Virginia. He joined the faculty after receiving his Ph.D. from the University of Arizona. Professor Davidson has received NCR's Faculty Innovation Award for innovation in teaching. Professor Davidson's research interests include compilers, computer architecture, systems software, and computer science education. He is the author of more than 60 papers in these fields. He is a member of the ACM, the ACM Special Interest Group on Programming Languages (SIGPLAN), the ACM Special Interest Group on Computer Architecture (SIGARCH), SIGCSE, the IEEE, and the IEEE Computer Society. He serves as an associate editor of *Transactions on Programming Languages and Systems*, ACM's flagship journal on programming languages and systems. He was chair of the 1998 Programming Language Design and Implementation Conference (PLDI '98). He can be reached at jwd@virginia.edu. His Web homepage is http://www.cs.virginia.edu/~jwd.

Robert Burton is a Professor of Computer Science at Brigham Young University. Prior to his affiliation with the BYU faculty, he was a Member of Technical Staff at Bell Laboratories. He received a Ph.D. in Computer Science from the University of Utah. He received an Honors Degree of Bachelor of Arts in Physics from the University of Utah. As an undergraduate with dual majors in mathematics and physics, he was required, against his will and despite his best efforts to the contrary, to take an introductory programming course. The course proved to one of the most delightful of his undergraduate experience, with subject matter for which he had a natural aptitude. His programming skills together with his previous undergraduate work experience in the Department of Chemistry and the Department of Physics led immediately to employment as a programmer simulating chemical and physical systems at the Kennecott Research Center. During the '80s he developed and taught four of IBM's Programming Fundamentals courses, and participated heavily in the development of the complete Programming Fundamentals curriculum. During the '80s and '90s, he developed and taught the Computer Graphics courses for IBM's University Level Computer Science Program. On many occasions and in many locations, he taught IBM's Computer Science Fundamentals courses and Data Structures course. He has developed courses and provided consulting services for several other large corporations. Throughout the '80s and '90s, he presented an intensive, two-week introductory programming course to invited guests of Brigham Young University. He teaches several sections of BYU's introductory Java programming course each year. In 1998 he received a Computer Science Department Teacher of the Year award. In 1989 he received the Karl G. Maeser Distinguished Teaching Award, BYU's most prestigious teaching award.. In 1985 he received the Karl G. Maeser Research and Creative Arts Award, BYU's most prestigious research award. He has authored or co-authored 29 publications related to hyperdimensional computer graphics, his primary research interest. He has authored or co-authored 23 additional publications related to computer graphics, 7 additional publications related to information privacy and transborder data flows, and 10 additional publications on other computer science topics. He has supervised 32 completed master's degrees. He is a member of six honor societies.

Lara Burton has a Bachelor of Science degree in Computer Science from Brigham Young University where she worked as a teaching assistant for BYU's lower division computer science courses. Her company, North Slope Systems, offers a variety of computer contract and consultation services. She and her husband Robert have worked together on several large projects for publishers doing course text reviews and evaluations, code checking and program verification, website development, and preparation of extensive course supplements including on-line laboratories. Lara and Robert live with their sons Tom and Forrest below a cirque of an 11,000 foot mountain in Sundance, Utah. Together, they enjoy sailing, kayaking, canoeing, biking, hiking, and rock climbing during the summer, and backcountry snowshoeing, cross country skiing, and dog sledding in the winter.

ACKNOWLEDGEMENTS

Robert and Lara Burton gratefully acknowledge the substantial efforts of Jim Cohoon and Jack Davidson in the preparation and maturation of their *Laboratory Manual with Lecture Notes for use with C++ Programming Design* (© McGraw-Hill Companies, Inc., 2002, 1998), and *Java Program Design* (© McGraw-Hill Companies, Inc., 2003), which together served as a basis and springboard for this manual.

We gratefully acknowledge our friends at McGraw-Hill for the invitation extended to us to prepare this manual, for their support, for their appreciation of the value of a high standard, and for their consistently encouraging response to our work. In particular, we thank our friends Kelly Lowery and Melinda Bilecki.

Laboratory Summaries

- *Laboratory 1: Background.* Teaches students the basic skills they will need to complete future labs. These skills include copying files, deleting files, backing up files, creating directories, compiling Java programs, executing Java programs, and accessing the Java API specification.

- *Laboratory 2: Solving Our First Problem.* Provides students with their first opportunity to decompose a problem into manageable pieces and to solve it. The lab introduces the process of compiling a program that uses an API. The lab teaches how to identify and use class methods, and explains deprecated methods.

- *Laboratory 3: Investigating Objects.* Exposes students to objects, the basis of the Java language. The lab uses the `string` class to investigate how to create and to work with objects. The lab explores object references, null references, unassigned variables, and member methods.

- *Laboratory 4: Being Classy.* Introduces students to designing and working with their own classes. Students build a GUI program by creating custom classes. The lab explores information hiding, data abstraction, variables, and different types of methods.

- *Laboratory 5: Decisions, Decisions.* Familiarizes the student with truth tables, the `if` statement, Boolean logic, and program decision-making. The lab introduces common errors that a student may encounter when using these language features.

- *Laboratory 6: Looping and File Reading.* This lab explores the principal looping statements in Java. The student develops a GUI application to illustrate some of these concepts. The lab includes an introduction to input file streams.

- *Laboratory 7: All About Methods.* Provides students with an in-depth look at parameter passing and scope. The lab explores common problems associated with a misunderstanding of parameters and scope. Students learn about overriding methods, overloading methods, and static methods.

- *Laboratory 8: Arrays and Collections.* Reviews array basics and several search algorithms. The lab then introduces two examples of Java's collection classes and teaches the students how to use these classes.

- *Laboratory 9: Object-Oriented Concepts.* Introduces code reuse and organization through inheritance. The lab explores code design and inheritance hierarchies. The lab acquaints students with polymorphism. The lab explains Swing-based code design. The student demonstrates knowledge of these concepts by creating a GUI based application.

- *Laboratory 10: Exceptions.* Introduces students to several common exceptions that a beginning programmer may encounter. The lab teaches how exceptions are generated and how to "catch" them. The lab reviews the dynamics of `try-catch` blocks, paying special attention to the details of exception propagation.

- *Laboratory 11: Recursion.* Explores recursion, an elegant and powerful approach to problem solving. The lab helps students understand how recursion works and develops their abilities to think "recursively."

- Laboratory 12: *Threads.* Acquaints the student with Java's `Timer` and `TimerTask` standard classes as an introduction to threads. The lab explores fixed-rate and fixed-delay scheduling. The lab concludes by developing a Swing-based animation using threads.

Introduction

Let's begin

☐ Goal
  - ■ Teach you how to program effectively

☐ Skills and information to be acquired
  - ■ Mental model of computer and network behavior
  - ■ Problem solving
  - ■ Object-oriented design
  - ■ Java

1

Computer Organization

- ☐ Computer advertisement specification
  - ■ Intel® Pentium 4 Processor at 3.06GHz with 512K cache
  - ■ 512MB DDR SDRAM
  - ■ 200GB ATA-100 Hard Drive (7200 RPM, 9.0 ms seek time)
  - ■ 17" LCD Monitor
  - ■ 64MB NVIDIA GeForce4 MX Graphics Card®
  - ■ 16x Max DVD-ROM Drive
  - ■ 48x/24x/48x CD-RW Drive
  - ■ 56K PCI Telephony Modem
  - ■ Windows XP Home Edition®
  - ■ 10/100 Fast Ethernet Network Card

Computer Organization

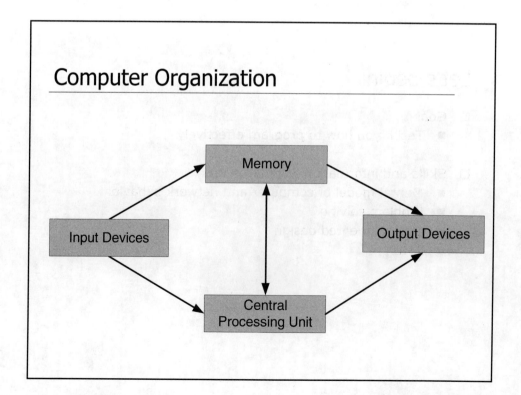

Computer Organization

☐ Computer advertisement specification
- Intel® Pentium 4 Processor
  at 3.06GHz with 512K cache
- 512MB DDR SDRAM
- 200GB ATA-100 Hard Drive
  (7200 RPM, 9.0 ms seek time)
- 17" LCD Monitor
- 64MB NVIDIA GeForce4
  MX Graphics Card®
- 16x Max DVD-ROM Drive
- 48x/24x/48x CD-RW Drive
- 56K PCI Telephony Modem
- Windows XP Home Edition®
- 10/100 Fast Ethernet Network Card

Programming

☐ Problem solving through the use of a computer system

☐ Maxim
- You cannot make a computer do something if you do not
  know how to do it yourself

Problem Solving

☐ Remember
 ■ The goal is not a clever solution but a correct solution

Problem Solving

☐ Accept
 ■ The process is iterative
  ☐ In solving the problem increased understanding might require restarting

Problem Solving

☐ Solutions
- Often require both concrete and abstract thinking
  ☐ Teamwork

Problem Solving Process

☐ What is it?
- Analysis
- Design
- Implementation
- Testing

Problem Solving Process

☐ What is it?
- *Analysis*
- Design
- Implementation
- Testing

Determine the inputs, outputs, and other components of the problem

> Description should be sufficiently specific to allow you to solve the problem

Problem Solving Process

☐ What is it?
- Analysis
- *Design*
- Implementation
- Testing

Describe the components and associated processes for solving the problem

> Straightforward and flexible

> Method – process

> Object – component and associated methods

Problem Solving Process

☐ What is it?
- ■ Analysis
- ■ Design
- ■ *Implementation*
- ■ Testing

Develop solutions for the components and use those components to produce an overall solution

Straightforward and flexible

Problem Solving Process

☐ What is it?
- ■ Analysis
- ■ Design
- ■ Implementation
- ■ *Testing*

Test the components individually and collectively

Problem Solving Process

Determine problem features → **Analysis**

Describe objects and methods → **Design**

Produce the classes and code → **Implementation**

Examine for correctness → **Testing**

Rethink as appropriate

Tips

☐ Find out as much as you can

☐ Reuse what has been done before

☐ Expect future reuse

☐ Break complex problems into subproblems

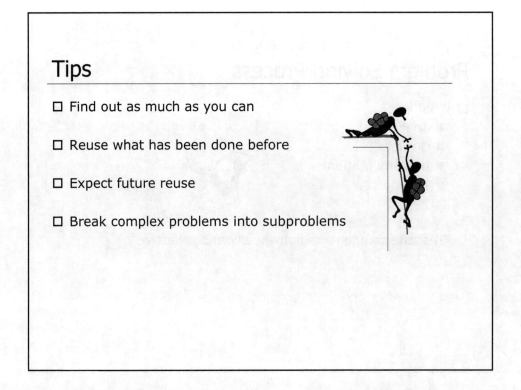

Software

- ☐ Program
  - ■ Sequence of instruction that tells a computer what to do

- ☐ Execution
  - ■ Performing the instruction sequence

- ☐ Programming language
  - ■ Language for writing instructions to a computer

- ☐ Major flavors
  - ■ *Machine language or object code*
  - ■ Assembly language
  - ■ High-level

Program to which computer can respond directly. Each instruction is a binary code that corresponds to a native instruction

Software

- ☐ Program
  - ■ Sequence of instruction that tells a computer what to do

- ☐ Execution
  - ■ Performing the instruction sequence

- ☐ Programming language
  - ■ Language for writing instructions to a computer

- ☐ Major flavors
  - ■ Machine language or object code
  - ■ *Assembly language*
  - ■ High-level

Symbolic language for coding machine language instructions

Software

- ☐ Program
  - ■ Sequence of instruction that tells a computer what to do

- ☐ Execution
  - ■ Performing the instruction sequence

- ☐ Programming language
  - ■ Language for writing instructions to a computer

- ☐ Major flavors
  - ■ Machine language or object code
  - ■ Assembly language
  - ■ *High-level*

Detailed knowledge of the machine is not required. Uses a vocabulary and structure closer to the problem being solved

---

Software

- ☐ Program
  - ■ Sequence of instruction that tells a computer what to do

- ☐ Execution
  - ■ Performing the instruction sequence

- ☐ Programming language
  - ■ Language for writing instructions to a computer

- ☐ Major flavors
  - ■ Machine language or object code
  - ■ Assembly language
  - ■ *High-level*

Java is a high-level programming language

10

Software

- Program
  - Sequence of instruction that tells a computer what to do

- Execution
  - Performing the instruction sequence

- Programming language
  - Language for writing instructions to a computer

- Major flavors
  - Machine language or object code
  - Assembly language
  - *High-level*

For program to be executed it must be translated

Translation

- Translator
  - Accepts a program written in a source language and translates it to a program in a target language

- Compiler
  - Standard name for a translator whose source language is a high-level language

- Interpreter
  - A translator that both translates and executes a source program

11

Java translation

☐ Two-step process

☐ First step
- Translation from Java to bytecodes
  ☐ Bytecodes are architecturally neutral object code
  ☐ Bytecodes are stored in a file with extension .class

☐ Second step
- An interpreter translates the bytecodes into machine instructions and executes them
  ☐ Interpreter is known a Java Virtual Machine or JVM

Task

☐ Display the forecast

I think there is a world market for maybe five computers.
Thomas Watson, IBM, 1943.

Sample output

```
C:\ Java Program Design                                    _ □ ×
cmd:  javac DisplayForecast.java

cmd:  java DisplayForecast
I think there is a world market for maybe five computers.
  Thomas Watson, IBM, 1943.

cmd:  java DisplayForecast
I think there is a world market for maybe five computers.
  Thomas Watson, IBM, 1943.

cmd:  java DisplayForecast
I think there is a world market for maybe five computers.
  Thomas Watson, IBM, 1943.

cmd:

cmd:
```

DisplayForecast.java

```java
// Authors: J. P. Cohoon and J. W. Davidson
// Purpose: display a quotation in a console window

public class DisplayForecast {

  // method main(): application entry point
  public static void main(String[] args) {
    System.out.print("I think there is a world market for");
    System.out.println(" maybe five computers.");
    System.out.println("   Thomas Watson, IBM, 1943.");
  }
}
```

13

DisplayForecast.java

```
// Authors: J. P. Cohoon and J. W. Davidson
// Purpose: display a quotation in a console window

public class DisplayForecast {

  // method main(): application entry point
  public static void main(String[] args) {
    System.out.print("I think there is a world market for");
    System.out.println(" maybe five computers.");
    System.out.println("   Thomas Watson, IBM, 1943.");
  }
}
```

Three statements make up the action of method main()

Method main() is part of class DisplayForecast

DisplayForecast.java

```
// Authors: J. P. Cohoon and J. W. Davidson
// Purpose: display a quotation in a console window

public class DisplayForecast {

  // method main(): application entry point
  public static void main(String[] args) {
    System.out.print("I think there is a world market for");
    System.out.println(" maybe five computers.");
    System.out.println("   Thomas Watson, IBM, 1943.");
  }
}
```

A method is a named piece of code that performs some action or implements a behavior

DisplayForecast.java

```java
// Authors: J. P. Cohoon and J. W. Davidson
// Purpose: display a quotation in a console window

public class DisplayForecast {

  // method main(): application entry point
  public static void main(String[] args) {
    System.out.print("I think there is a world market for");
    System.out.println(" maybe five computers.");
    System.out.println("   Thomas Watson, IBM, 1943.");
  }
}
```

An application program is required to have a
public static void method named main().

Java and the Internet

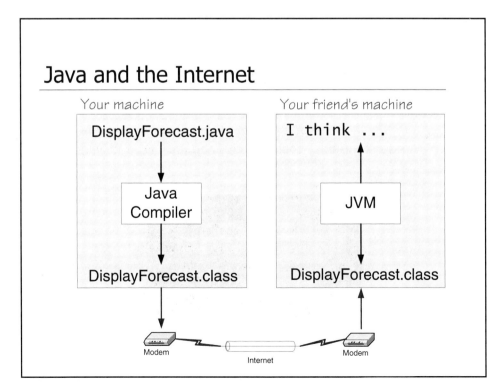

Engineering software

- ☐ Complexity of software grows as attempts are made to make it easier to use
  - ■ Rise of wizards

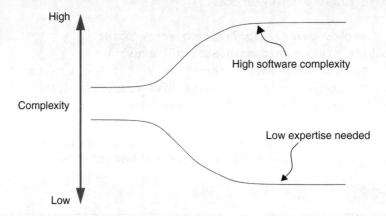

Software engineering

- ☐ Goal
  - ■ Production of software that is effective and reliable, understandable, cost effective, adaptable, and reusable

Software engineering

- ☐ Goal
  - ■ Production of software that is *effective and reliable*, understandable, cost effective, adaptable, and reusable

  - ☐ Work correctly and not fail

Software engineering

- ☐ Goal
  - ■ Production of software that is effective and reliable, *understandable*, cost effective, adaptable, and reusable

    - ☐ Because of the long lifetime many people will be involved
      - ■ Creation
      - ■ Debugging
      - ■ Maintenance
      - ■ Enhancement
    - ☐ Two-thirds of the cost is typically beyond creation

Software engineering

- ☐ Goal
  - ■ Production of software that is effective and reliable, understandable, *cost effective*, adaptable, and reusable

    - ☐ Cost to develop and maintain should not exceed expected benefit

Software engineering

- ☐ Goal
  - ■ Production of software that is effective and reliable, understandable, cost effective, *adaptable*, and reusable

    - ☐ Design software so that new features and capabilities can be added

Software engineering

- ☐ Goal
  - ■ Production of software that is effective and reliable, understandable, cost effective, adaptable, and *reusable*

    - ☐ Makes sense due to the great costs involved to have flexible components that can be used in other software

Object-oriented design

- ☐ Purpose
  - ■ Promote thinking about software in a way that models the way we think and interact with the physical word

- ☐ Object
  - ■ Properties or attributes
  - ■ Behaviors

Object-oriented design

☐ Class
- Term for a type of software object

☐ Object
- An instance of a class with
- specific properties and attributes

Java basics

Task

☐ Display the supposed forecast

I think there is a world market for maybe five computers.
Thomas Watson, IBM, 1943.

Sample output

```
C:\ Java Program Design                              _ □ ✕

cmd: javac DisplayForecast.java

cmd: java DisplayForecast
I think there is a world market for maybe five computers.
    Thomas Watson, IBM, 1943.

cmd:
```

DisplayForecast.java

```java
// Authors: J. P. Cohoon and J. W. Davidson
// Purpose: display a quotation in a console window

public class DisplayForecast {

  // method main(): application entry point
  public static void main(String[] args) {
    System.out.print("I think there is a world market for");
    System.out.println(" maybe five computers.");
    System.out.println("   Thomas Watson, IBM, 1943.");
  }
}
```

DisplayForecast.java

```
// Authors: J. P. Cohoon and J. W. Davidson
// Purpose: display a quotation in a console window

public class DisplayForecast {

  // method main(): application entry point
  public static void main(String[] args) {
    System.out.print("I think there is a world market for");
    System.out.println(" maybe five computers.");
    System.out.println("    Thomas Watson, IBM, 1943.");
  }
}
```

Three statements make up the action of method main()

Method main() is part of class DisplayForecast

DisplayForecast.java

```
// Authors: J. P. Cohoon and J. W. Davidson
// Purpose: display a quotation in a console window

public class DisplayForecast {

  // method main(): application entry point
  public static void main(String[] args) {
    System.out.print("I think there is a world market for");
    System.out.println(" maybe five computers.");
    System.out.println("    Thomas Watson, IBM, 1943.");
  }
}
```

A method is a named piece of code that performs some action or implements a behavior

DisplayForecast.java

```java
// Authors: J. P. Cohoon and J. W. Davidson
// Purpose: display a quotation in a console window

public class DisplayForecast {

  // method main(): application entry point
  public static void main(String[] args) {
    System.out.print("I think there is a world market for");
    System.out.println(" maybe five computers.");
    System.out.println("   Thomas Watson, IBM, 1943.");
  }
}
```

An application program is required to have a public static void method named main().

DisplayForecast.java

```java
// Authors: J. P. Cohoon and J. W. Davidson
// Purpose: display a quotation in a console window

public class DisplayForecast {

  // method main(): application entry point
  public static void main(String[] args) {
    System.out.print("I think there is a world market for");
    System.out.println(" maybe five computers.");
    System.out.println("   Thomas Watson, IBM, 1943.");
  }
}
```

public, static, and void are keywords. They cannot be used as names

public means the method is shareable

DisplayForecast.java

```
// Authors: J. P. Cohoon and J. W. Davidson
// Purpose: display a quotation in a console window

public class DisplayForecast {

  // method main(): application entry point
  public static void main(String[] args) {
    System.out.print("I think there is a world market for");
    System.out.println(" maybe five computers.");
    System.out.println("   Thomas Watson, IBM, 1943.");
  }
}
```
We will discuss static and void later

DisplayForecast.java

```
// Authors: J. P. Cohoon and J. W. Davidson
// Purpose: display a quotation in a console window

public class DisplayForecast {

  // method main(): application entry point
  public static void main(String[] args) {
    System.out.print("I think there is a world market for");
    System.out.println(" maybe five computers.");
    System.out.println("   Thomas Watson, IBM, 1943.");
  }
}
```
Java allows a statement to be made up of
multiple lines of text

Semicolons delimit one statement from the next

DisplayForecast.java

```
// Authors: J. P. Cohoon and J. W. Davidson
// Purpose: display a quotation in a console window

public class DisplayForecast {

  // method main(): application entry point
  public static void main(String[] args) {
    System.out.print("I think there is a world market for");
    System.out.println(" maybe five computers.");
    System.out.println("   Thomas Watson, IBM, 1943.");
  }
}
```

A class defines an object form. An object can have methods and attributes

Keyword class indicates a class definition follows

DisplayForecast.java

```
// Authors: J. P. Cohoon and J. W. Davidson
// Purpose: display a quotation in a console window

public class DisplayForecast {

  // method main(): application entry point
  public static void main(String[] args) {
    System.out.print("I think there is a world market for");
    System.out.println(" maybe five computers.");
    System.out.println("   Thomas Watson, IBM, 1943.");
  }
}
```

A class like a method must have a name

DisplayForecast.java

```java
// Authors: J. P. Cohoon and J. W. Davidson
// Purpose: display a quotation in a console window

public class DisplayForecast {

  // method main(): application entry point
  public static void main(String[] args) {
    System.out.print("I think there is a world market for");
    System.out.println(" maybe five computers.");
    System.out.println("   Thomas Watson, IBM, 1943.");
  }
}
```

Programs are read by people – make sure they are readable.

Use whitespace, comments, and indentation to aid understanding

---

DisplayForecast.java

```java
// Authors: J. P. Cohoon and J. W. Davidson
// Purpose: display a quotation in a console window

public class DisplayForecast {                    Whitespace

  // method main(): application entry point
  public static void main(String[] args) {
    System.out.print("I think there is a world market for");
    System.out.println(" maybe five computers.");
    System.out.println("   Thomas Watson, IBM, 1943.");
  }
}
```

Whitespace separates program elements

Whitespace between program elements is ignored by Java

DisplayForecast.java

```
// Authors: J. P. Cohoon and J. W. Davidson
// Purpose: display a quotation in a console window

public class DisplayForecast {

    // method main(): application entry point
    public static void main(String[] args) {
        System.out.print("I think there is a world market for");
        System.out.println(" maybe five computers.");
        System.out.println("   Thomas Watson, IBM, 1943.");
    }
}
```

Three comments

// indicates rest of the line is a comment

Comments are used to document authors, purpose, and program elements

Indentation

```
// Authors: J. P. Cohoon and J. W. Davidson
// Purpose: display a quotation in a console window

public class DisplayForecast {

    // method main(): application entry point
    public static void main(String[] args) {
        System.out.print("I think there is a world market for");
        System.out.println(" maybe five computers.");
        System.out.println("   Thomas Watson, IBM, 1943.");
    }
}
```

Method main() is part of DisplayForecast

Statements are part of method main()

Indentation indicates subcomponents

Method main()

```
public static void main(String[] args) {
   System.out.print("I think there is a world market for");
   System.out.println(" maybe five computers.");
   System.out.println("   Thomas Watson, IBM, 1943.");
}
```

☐ Class System supplies objects that can print and read values

☐ System variable out references the standard printing object
- ■ Known as the standard output stream

☐ Variable out provides access to printing methods
- ■ print(): displays a value
- ■ println(): displays a value and moves cursor to the next line

System.out

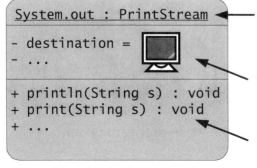

Variable System.out gives access to an output stream of type PrintStream

The printing destination attribute for this PrintStream object is the console window

The behaviors of a PrintStream object support a high-level view of printing

Selection

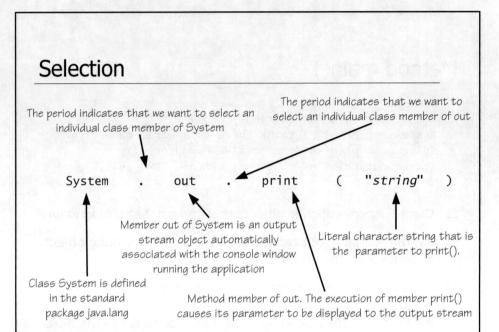

The period indicates that we want to select an individual class member of System

The period indicates that we want to select an individual class member of out

```
System    .    out    .    print    (    "string"    )
```

Member out of System is an output stream object automatically associated with the console window running the application

Literal character string that is the parameter to print().

Class System is defined in the standard package java.lang

Method member of out. The execution of member print() causes its parameter to be displayed to the output stream

Method main()

```
public static void main(String[] args) {
    System.out.print("I think there is a world market for");
    System.out.println(" maybe five computers.");
    System.out.println("   Thomas Watson, IBM, 1943.");
}
```

☐ Method print() and println() both take a string parameter

■ The parameter specifies the value that is to be used in the invocation

Method main()

```
public static void main(String[] args) {
    System.out.print("I think there is a world market for");
    System.out.println(" maybe five computers.");
    System.out.println("   Thomas Watson, IBM, 1943.");
}
```

❑ The print() statement starts the program output

I think there is a world market for■

Method main()

```
public static void main(String[] args) {
    System.out.print("I think there is a world market for");
    System.out.println(" maybe five computers.");
    System.out.println("   Thomas Watson, IBM, 1943.");
}
```

❑ The first println() statement completes the first line of output

I think there is a world market for maybe five computers
■

Method main()

```
public static void main(String[] args) {
    System.out.print("I think there is a world market for");
    System.out.println(" maybe five computers.");
    System.out.println("   Thomas Watson, IBM, 1943.");
}
```

☐ The second println() statement starts and completes the second line of output

I think there is a world market for maybe five computers
    Thomas Watson, IBM, 1943
■

Experiment

```
public static void main(String[] args) {
    System.out.print("The real problem is not whether ");
    System.out.print("machines think but whether people ");
    System.out.println("do");
    System.out.println("-- B.F. Skinner (paraphrased)");
}
```

☐ What does this method main() output?

Computation

- ☐ Programmers frequently write small programs for computing useful things

- ☐ Example – body mass index (BMI)
  - ■ Measure of fitness
    - ☐ Ratio of person's weight to the square of the person's height
      - ■ Weight in is kilograms, height is in meters
    - ☐ Person of interest is 4.5 feet and weighs 75.5 pounds

- ☐ Metric conversions
  - ■ Kilograms per pound 0.454
  - ■ Meters per foot 0.3046

Common program elements

- ☐ Type
  - ■ Set of values along with operators that can manipulate and create values from the set

- ☐ Primitive types support numeric, character, logical values
  - ■ double and float
    - ☐ Values with decimals
  - ■ byte, short, int, long
    - ☐ Integers
  - ■ char
    - ☐ Characters (considered numeric)
  - ■ boolean
    - ☐ Logical values

- ☐ Basic operators
  - ■ + addition   - subtraction
  - ■ * multiplication   / division

33

Common program elements

- □ Constant
  - ■ Symbolic name for memory location whose value does not change
    - □ KILOGRAMS_PER_POUND

- □ Variable
  - ■ Symbolic name for memory location whose value can change
    - □ weightInPounds

Program outline for BMI.java

```java
// Purpose: Compute BMI for given weight and height

public class BMI {

    // main(): application entry point
    public static void main(String[] args) {
        // define constants

        // set up person's characteristics

        // convert to metric equivalents

        // perform bmi calculation

        // display result
    }
}
```

```
public static void main(String[] args) {
    // define constants
    final double KILOGRAMS_PER_POUND = 0.454;
    final double METERS_PER_FOOT = 0.3046;

    // set up person's characteristics
    double weightInPounds = 75.5;  // our person's weight
    double heightInFeet = 4.5;     // our person's height

    // convert to metric equivalents
    double metricWeight = weightInPounds *
        KILOGRAMS_PER_POUND;
    double metricHeight = heightInFeet * METERS_PER_FOOT;

    // perform bmi calculation
    double bmi = metricWeight / (metricHeight * metricHeight);

    // display result
    System.out.println("A person with");
    System.out.println("  weight " + weightInPounds + " lbs");
    System.out.println("  height " + heightInFeet + " feet");
    System.out.println("has a BMI of " + Math.round(bmi));
}
```

```
public static void main(String[] args) {
    // define constants
    final double KILOGRAMS_PER_POUND = 0.454;
    final double METERS_PER_FOOT = 0.3046;
                                    KILOGRAMS_PER_POUND  🔒 0.454
    // set up person's characteristics
    double weightInPounds = 75.5;  // our person's weight
    double heightInFeet = 4.5;     // our person's height

    // convert to metric equivalents
    double metricWeight = weightInPounds *
        KILOGRAMS_PER_POUND;
    double metricHeight = heightInFeet * METERS_PER_FOOT;

    // perform bmi calculation
    double bmi = metricWeight / (metricHeight * metricHeight);

    // display result
    System.out.println("A person with");
    System.out.println("  weight " + weightInPounds + " lbs");
    System.out.println("  height " + heightInFeet + " feet");
    System.out.println("has a BMI of " + Math.round(bmi));
}
```

```java
public static void main(String[] args) {
    // define constants
    final double KILOGRAMS_PER_POUND = 0.454;
    final double METERS_PER_FOOT = 0.3046;
                              METERS_PER_FOOT 🔒 0.3046
    // set up person's characteristics
    double weightInPounds = 75.5;   // our person's weight
    double heightInFeet = 4.5;      // our person's height


    // convert to metric equivalents
    double metricWeight = weightInPounds *
        KILOGRAMS_PER_POUND;
    double metricHeight = heightInFeet * METERS_PER_FOOT;


    // perform bmi calculation
    double bmi = metricWeight / (metricHeight * metricHeight);


    // display result
    System.out.println("A person with");
    System.out.println("  weight " + weightInPounds + " lbs");
    System.out.println("  height " + heightInFeet + " feet");
    System.out.println("has a BMI of " + Math.round(bmi));
}
```

```java
public static void main(String[] args) {
    // define constants
    final double KILOGRAMS_PER_POUND = 0.454;
    final double METERS_PER_FOOT = 0.3046;
                                weightInPounds      75.5
    // set up person's characteristics
    double weightInPounds = 75.5;   // our person's weight
    double heightInFeet = 4.5;      // our person's height


    // convert to metric equivalents
    double metricWeight = weightInPounds *
        KILOGRAMS_PER_POUND;
    double metricHeight = heightInFeet * METERS_PER_FOOT;


    // perform bmi calculation
    double bmi = metricWeight / (metricHeight * metricHeight);


    // display result
    System.out.println("A person with");
    System.out.println("  weight " + weightInPounds + " lbs");
    System.out.println("  height " + heightInFeet + " feet");
    System.out.println("has a BMI of " + Math.round(bmi));
}
```

```
public static void main(String[] args) {
    // define constants
    final double KILOGRAMS_PER_POUND = 0.454;
    final double METERS_PER_FOOT = 0.3046;
                                        heightInFeet    4.5
    // set up person's characteristics
    double weightInPounds = 75.5;  // our person's weight
    double heightInFeet = 4.5;     // our person's height

    // convert to metric equivalents
    double metricWeight = weightInPounds *
        KILOGRAMS_PER_POUND;
    double metricHeight = heightInFeet * METERS_PER_FOOT;

    // perform bmi calculation
    double bmi = metricWeight / (metricHeight * metricHeight);

    // display result
    System.out.println("A person with");
    System.out.println("  weight " + weightInPounds + " lbs");
    System.out.println("  height " + heightInFeet + " feet");
    System.out.println("has a BMI of " + Math.round(bmi));
}
```

```
public static void main(String[] args) {
    // define constants
    final double KILOGRAMS_PER_POUND = 0.454;
    final double METERS_PER_FOOT = 0.3046;
                                        metricWeight    34.2770
    // set up person's characteristics
    double weightInPounds = 75.5;  // our person's weight
    double heightInFeet = 4.5;     // our person's height

    // convert to metric equivalents
    double metricWeight = weightInPounds *
        KILOGRAMS_PER_POUND;
    double metricHeight = heightInFeet * METERS_PER_FOOT;

    // perform bmi calculation
    double bmi = metricWeight / (metricHeight * metricHeight);

    // display result
    System.out.println("A person with");
    System.out.println("  weight " + weightInPounds + " lbs");
    System.out.println("  height " + heightInFeet + " feet");
    System.out.println("has a BMI of " + Math.round(bmi));
}
```

37

```java
public static void main(String[] args) {
    // define constants
    final double KILOGRAMS_PER_POUND = 0.454;
    final double METERS_PER_FOOT = 0.3046;
```

metricHeight   `1.3706`

```java
    // set up person's characteristics
    double weightInPounds = 75.5;   // our person's weight
    double heightInFeet = 4.5;      // our person's height


    // convert to metric equivalents
    double metricWeight = weightInPounds *
        KILOGRAMS_PER_POUND;
    double metricHeight = heightInFeet * METERS_PER_FOOT;

    // perform bmi calculation
    double bmi = metricWeight / (metricHeight * metricHeight);

    // display result
    System.out.println("A person with");
    System.out.println("  weight " + weightInPounds + " lbs");
    System.out.println("  height " + heightInFeet + " feet");
    System.out.println("has a BMI of " + Math.round(bmi));
}
```

```java
public static void main(String[] args) {
    // define constants
    final double KILOGRAMS_PER_POUND = 0.454;
    final double METERS_PER_FOOT = 0.3046;
```

bmi   `18.2439`

```java
    // set up person's characteristics
    double weightInPounds = 75.5;   // our person's weight
    double heightInFeet = 4.5;      // our person's height


    // convert to metric equivalents
    double metricWeight = weightInPounds *
                    KILOGRAMS_PER_POUND;
    double metricHeight = heightInFeet * METERS_PER_FOOT;

    // perform bmi calculation
    double bmi = metricWeight / (metricHeight * metricHeight);

    // display result
    System.out.println("A person with");
    System.out.println("  weight " + weightInPounds + " lbs");
    System.out.println("  height " + heightInFeet + " feet");
    System.out.println("has a BMI of " + Math.round(bmi));
}
```

```
public static void main(String[] args) {
    // define constants
    final double KILOGRAMS_PER_POUND = 0.454;
    final double METERS_PER_FOOT = 0.3046;
                    Operator evaluation depend upon its operands
    // set up person's characteristics
    double weightInPounds = 75.5;   // our person's weight
    double heightInFeet = 4.5;      // our person's height

    // convert to metric equivalents
    double metricWeight = weightInPounds *
                        KILOGRAMS_PER_POUND;
    double metricHeight = heightInFeet * METERS_PER_FOOT;

    // perform bmi calculation
    double bmi = metricWeight / (metricHeight * metricHeight);

    // display result
    System.out.println("A person with");
    System.out.println("  weight " + weightInPounds + " lbs");
    System.out.println("  height " + heightInFeet + " feet");
    System.out.println("has a BMI of " + Math.round(bmi));
}
```

```
public static void main(String[] args) {
    // define constants
    final double KILOGRAMS_PER_POUND = 0.454;
    final double METERS_PER_FOOT = 0.3046;

                                Math.round(bmi) is 18
    // set up person's characteristics
    double weightInPounds = 75.5;   // our person's weight
    double heightInFeet = 4.5;      // our person's height

    // convert to metric equivalents
    double metricWeight = weightInPounds *
                        KILOGRAMS_PER_POUND;
    double metricHeight = heightInFeet * METERS_PER_FOOT;

    // perform bmi calculation
    double bmi = metricWeight / (metricHeight * metricHeight);

    // display result
    System.out.println("A person with");
    System.out.println("  weight " + weightInPounds + " lbs");
    System.out.println("  height " + heightInFeet + " feet");
    System.out.println("has a BMI of " + Math.round(bmi));
}
```

```java
// Purpose: Convert a Celsius temperature to Fahrenheit

public class CelsiusToFahrenheit {

    // main(): application entry point
    public static void main(String[] args) {
        // set Celsius temperature of interest
        int celsius = 28;

        // convert to Fahrenheit equivalent
        int fahrenheit = 32 + ((9 * celsius) / 5);

        // display result
        System.out.println("Celsius temperature");
        System.out.println("    " + celsius);
        System.out.println("equals Fahrenheit temperature");
        System.out.println("    " + fahrenheit);
    }
}
```

```java
// Purpose: Demonstrate char arithmetic

public class LowerToUpper {

    // main(): application entry point
    public static void main(String[] args) {
        // set lower case character of interest
        char lowerCaseLetter = 'c';

        // convert to uppercase equivalent
        char upperCaseLetter = 'A' + (lowerCaseLetter - 'a');

        // display result
        System.out.println("Uppercase equivalent of");
        System.out.println("    " + lowerCaseLetter);
        System.out.println("is");
        System.out.println("    " + upperCaseLetter);
    }
}
```

Expressions

☐ What is the value used to initialize expression
```
int expression = 4 + 2 * 5;
```

☐ What value is displayed
```
System.out.println(5 / 2.0);
```

☐ Java rules in a nutshell
- Each operator has a precedence level and an associativity
  - ☐ Operators with higher precedence are done first
    - * and / have higher precedence than + and -
  - ☐ Associativity indicates how to handle ties
- When floating-point is used the result is floating point

Question

☐ Does the following statement compute the average of double variables a, b, and c? Why

```
double average = a + b + c / 3.0;
```

Interactive programs

☐ Programs that interact with their users through statements performing input and output

☐ BMI.java
   ■ Not interactive – weight and height are fixed

Support for interactive console programs

☐ Variable System.in
   ■ Associated with the standard input stream – the keyboard

☐ Class BufferedReader
   ■ Supports extraction of an input line as a character string

```
BufferedReader stdin = new BufferedReader(
          new InputStreamReader(System.in));
```

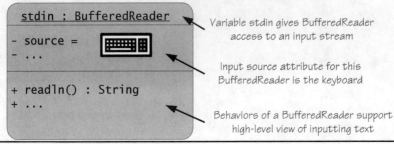

Variable stdin gives BufferedReader access to an input stream

Input source attribute for this BufferedReader is the keyboard

Behaviors of a BufferedReader support high-level view of inputting text

Accessing the standard input stream

☐ Set up

```
BufferedReader stdin = new BufferedReader(
        new InputStreamReader(System.in));
```

```
new BufferedReader(new InputStreamReader(System.in))
```

A new operation constructs a new object. The value of the operation
is a reference to the new object. This new operation constructs a
BufferedReader object out of a new InputStreamReader object that
was built using the object representing the standard input stream

Interactive program for bmi

☐ Program outline

```
// Purpose: Compute BMI for user-specified
// weight and height

import java.io.*;

public class BMICalculator {

    // main(): application entry point
    public static void main(String[] args)
            throws IOException {
        // defining constants
        // displaying legend
        // set up input stream
        // get person's characteristics
        // convert to metric equivalents
        // perform bmi calculation
        // display result
    }
}
```

```
public static void main(String[] args) throws IOException {
    final double KILOGRAMS_PER_POUND = 0.454;
    final double METERS_PER_FOOT = 0.3046;

    System.out.println("BMI Calculator\n");

    BufferedReader stdin = new BufferedReader(
            new InputStreamReader(System.in));

    System.out.print("Enter weight (lbs): ");
    double weight = Double.parseDouble(stdin.readLine());

    System.out.print("Enter height (feet): ");
    double height = Double.parseDouble(stdin.readLine());

    double metricWeight = weight * KILOGRAMS_PER_POUND;
    double metricHeight = height * METERS_PER_FOOT;

    double bmi = metricWeight / (metricHeight * metricHeight);

    System.out.println("A person with");
    System.out.println("    weight " + weight + " (lbs)");
    System.out.println("    height " + height + " (feet)");
    System.out.println("has a BMI of " + bmi);
}
```

Accessing the standard input stream

☐ Extraction

```
System.out.print("Enter weight (lbs): ");
double weight = Double.parseDouble(stdin.readLine());

System.out.print("Enter height (feet): ");
double height = Double.parseDouble(stdin.readLine());
```

Primitive variable assignment

□ Assignment operator =
  ■ Allows the memory location for a variable to be updated

$target$ = $expression$;

Name of previously   Expression to be
defined object   evaluated

□ Consider
  int j = 11;
  j = 1985;

11

Primitive variable assignment

□ Assignment operator =
  ■ Allows the memory location for a variable to be updated

$target$ = $expression$;

Name of previously   Expression to be
defined object   evaluated

□ Consider
  int j = 11;
  j = 1985;

1985

Primitive variable assignment

□ Consider
```
int a = 1;
int aSquared = a * a;
a = 5;
aSquared = a * a;
```

a | 1

aSquared | 1

□ Consider
```
int i = 0;
i = i + 1;
```

□ Consider
```
int asaRating;
asaRating = 400;
```

Primitive variable assignment

□ Consider
```
int a = 1;
int aSquared = a * a;
a = 5;
aSquared = a * a;
```

a | 5

aSquared | 1

□ Consider
```
int i = 0;
i = i + 1;
```

□ Consider
```
int asaRating;
asaRating = 400;
```

Primitive variable assignment

□ Consider
```
int a = 1;
int aSquared = a * a;
a = 5;
aSquared = a * a;
```

a   `5`

aSquared   `25`

□ Consider
```
int i = 0;
i = i + 1;
```

□ Consider
```
int asaRating;
asaRating = 400;
```

Primitive variable assignment

□ Consider
```
int a = 1;
int aSquared = a * a;
a = 5;
aSquared = a * a;
```

i   `0`

□ Consider
```
int i = 0;
i = i + 1;
```

□ Consider
```
int asaRating;
asaRating = 400;
```

Primitive variable assignment

☐ Consider

```
int a = 1;
int aSquared = a * a;
a = 5;
aSquared = a * a;
```

☐ Consider

```
int i = 0;
i = i + 1;
```

☐ Consider

```
int asaRating;
asaRating = 400;
```

i	1

Primitive variable assignment

☐ Consider

```
int a = 1;
int aSquared = a * a;
a = 5;
aSquared = a * a;
```

☐ Consider

```
int i = 0;
i = i + 1;
```

☐ Consider

```
int asaRating;
asaRating = 400;
```

asaRating	-

Primitive variable assignment

☐ Consider
```
int a = 1;
int aSquared = a * a;
a = 5;
aSquared = a * a;
```

asaRating	400

☐ Consider
```
int i = 0;
i = i + 1;
```

☐ Consider
```
int asaRating;
asaRating = 400;
```

Primitive variable assignment

☐ Consider
```
double x = 5.12;
double y = 19.28;
double rememberX = x;
x = y;
y = rememberX;
```

x	5.12

49

Primitive variable assignment

□ Consider

```
double x = 5.12;
double y = 19.28;
double rememberX = x;
x = y;
y = rememberX;
```

x	5.12

y	19.28

Primitive variable assignment

□ Consider

```
double x = 5.12;
double y = 19.28;
double rememberX = x;
x = y;
y = rememberX;
```

x	5.12

y	19.28

rememberX	5.12

Primitive variable assignment

□ Consider

```
double x = 5.12;
double y = 19.28;
double rememberX = x;
x = y;
y = rememberX;
```

x	19.28
y	19.28
rememberX	5.12

Primitive variable assignment

□ Consider

```
double x = 5.12;
double y = 19.28;
double rememberX = x;
x = y;
y = rememberX;
```

x	19.28
y	5.12
rememberX	5.12

Increment and decrement operators

☐ ++
  ■ Increments a number variable by 1
☐ --
  ■ Decrements a numeric variable by 1

☐ Consider

```
int i = 4;
++i;
System.out.println(i);
System.out.print(++i);
System.out.println(i++);
System.out.println(i);
```

Increment and decrement operators

☐ ++
  ■ Increments a number variable by 1
☐ --
  ■ Decrements a numeric variable by 1

☐ Consider

```
int i = 4;              // define
++i;
System.out.println(i);
System.out.print(++i);
System.out.println(i++);
System.out.println(i);
```

i   4

Increment and decrement operators

- [ ] ++
  - Increments a number variable by 1
- [ ] --
  - Decrements a numeric variable by 1

- [ ] Consider

```
int i = 4;
++i;                        // increment
System.out.println(i);
System.out.print(++i);
System.out.println(i++);
System.out.println(i);
```

i   `5`

Increment and decrement operators

- [ ] ++
  - Increments a number variable by 1
- [ ] --
  - Decrements a numeric variable by 1

- [ ] Consider

```
int i = 4;
++i;
System.out.println(i);   // display
System.out.print(++i);
System.out.println(i++);
System.out.println(i);
```

i   `5`

Increment and decrement operators

□ ++
   ■ Increments a number variable by 1   i | 6 |
□ --
   ■ Decrements a numeric variable by 1

□ Consider

```
int i = 4;
++i;
System.out.println(i);
System.out.print(++i);    // update then display
System.out.println(i++);
System.out.println(i);
```

Increment and decrement operators

□ ++
   ■ Increments a number variable by 1   i | 7 |
□ --
   ■ Decrements a numeric variable by 1

□ Consider

```
int i = 4;
++i;
System.out.println(i);
System.out.print(++i);
System.out.println(i++); // display then update
System.out.println(i);
```

Increment and decrement operators

- ++
  - Increments a number variable by 1
- --
  - Decrements a numeric variable by 1

- Consider

```
int i = 4;
++i;
System.out.println(i);
System.out.print(++i);
System.out.println(i++);
System.out.println(i);    // display
```

i   7

Escape sequences

- Java provides escape sequences for printing special characters
  - \b   backspace
  - \n   newline
  - \t   tab
  - \r   carriage return
  - \\   backslash
  - \"   double quote
  - \'   single quote

Escape sequences

☐ What do these statements output?

```
System.out.println("Person\tHeight\tShoe size");
System.out.println("==========================");
System.out.println("Hannah\t5'1\"\t7");
System.out.println("Jenna\t5'10\"\t9");
System.out.println("JJ\t6'1\"\t14");
```

☐ Output

```
Person   Height  Shoe size
==========================
Hannah   5'1"    7
Jenna    5'10"   9
JJ       6'1"    14
```

Objects

Getting classy

☐ Your current job
  ■ Gain experience creating and manipulating objects from the standard Java types

☐ Why
  ■ Prepares you for defining your own classes and creating and manipulating the objects of those classes

Values versus objects

- Numbers
  - Have values but they do *not* have behaviors
- Objects
  - Have attributes and behaviors
- System.in
  - References an InputStream
    - Attribute: keyboard
    - Behaviors: reading

- System.out
  - References an OutputStream
    - Attribute: monitor
    - Behaviors: printing

Other Java object types

- String

- Rectangle

- Color

- JFrame

Consider

☐ Statements
```
int peasPerPod = 8;
String message = "Don't look behind the door!"
```

☐ How show we represent these definitions according to the notions of Java?

Representation

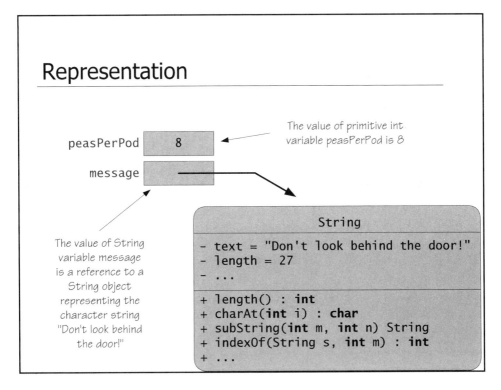

peasPerPod   8   ← The value of primitive int variable peasPerPod is 8

message

The value of String variable message is a reference to a String object representing the character string "Don't look behind the door!"

String
- text = "Don't look behind the door!"   - length = 27   - ...
+ length() : **int**   + charAt(**int** i) : **char**   + subString(**int** m, **int** n) String   + indexOf(String s, **int** m) : **int**   + ...

59

Shorthand representation

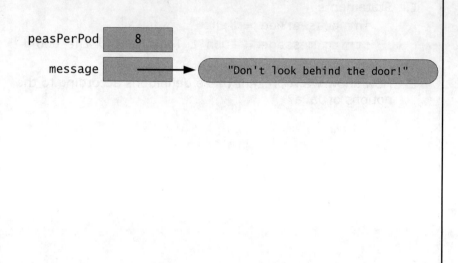

peasPerPod 8

message → "Don't look behind the door!"

Examples

☐ Consider
```
String a = "excellence";
String b = a;
```

☐ What is the representation?

Examples

☐ Consider
```
String a = "excellence";
String b = a;
```

☐ What is the representation?

Uninitialized versus null

☐ Consider
```
String dayOfWeek;
BufferedReader inStream;
```

☐ What is the representation?

Uninitialized versus null

☐ Consider
```
String dayOfWeek;
BufferedReader inStream;
```

☐ What is the representation?

Uninitialized versus null

☐ Consider
```
String fontName = null;
BufferedReader fileStream = null;
```

☐ What is the representation?

Uninitialized versus null

☐ Consider
```
String fontName = null;
BufferedReader fileStream = null;
```

☐ What is the representation?

fontName	**null**
fileStream	**null**

Assignment

☐ Consider
```
String word1 = "luminous";
String word2 = "graceful";
Word1 = word2;
```

☐ Initial representation

Assignment

☐ Consider

```
String word1 = "luminous";
String word2 = "graceful";
Word1 = word2;
```

☐ After assignment

word1 ▢ ——————➤

word2 ▢ ——————➤ ⬭ "graceful" ⬭

Using objects

☐ Consider

```
BufferedReader stdin = new BufferedReader(
    new InputStreamReader(System.in));

System.out.print("Enter your account name: ");
String response = stdin.readLine();
```

Using objects

☐ Consider
```
BufferedReader stdin = new BufferedReader(
    new InputStreamReader(System.in));

System.out.print("Enter your account name: ");
String response = stdin.readLine();
```

stdin ──────▶ BufferedReader: ⌨

Using objects

☐ Consider
```
BufferedReader stdin = new BufferedReader(
    new InputStreamReader(System.in));

System.out.print("Enter your account name: ");
String response = stdin.readLine();
```

☐ Suppose the user interaction is
```
Enter your account name: artiste
```

reponse ──────▶  "artiste"

String representation

- ☐ Consider
  - ■ String alphabet = "abcdefghijklmnopqrstuvwxyz";

- ☐ Standard shorthand representation

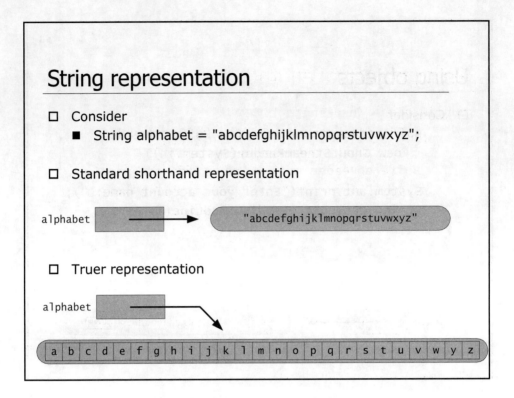

- ☐ Truer representation

String representation

- ☐ Consider
  - ■ String alphabet = "abcdefghijklmnopqrstuvwxyz";
  - ■ char c1 = alphabet.charAt(9);
  - ■ char c2 = alphabet.charAt(15);
  - ■ char c3 = alphabet.charAt(2);

- ☐ What are the values of c1, c2, and c3? Why?

    c1   'j'

    c2   'p'

    c3   'c'

Program WordLength.java

```
public class WordLength {

    public static void main(String[] args)
            throws IOException {
        BufferedReader stdin = new BufferedReader(
            new InputStreamReader(System.in));

        System.out.print("Enter a word: ");
        String word = stdin.readLine();

        int wordLength = word.length();

        System.out.println("Word " + word + " has length "
            + wordLength + ".");
    }
}
```

More String methods

☐ Consider
```
        String weddingDate = "August 21, 1976";
        String month = weddingDate.substring(0, 6);
        System.out.println("Month is " + month + ".");
```

☐ What is the output?

More String methods

☐ Consider

```
String weddingDate = "August 21, 1976";
String month = weddingDate.substring(0, 6);
System.out.println("Month is " + month + ".");
```

☐ What is the output?

```
Month is August.
```

More String methods

☐ Consider

```
String fruit = "banana";
String searchString = "an";
int n1 = fruit.indexOf(searchString, 0);
int n2 = fruit.indexOf(searchString, n1 + 1);
int n3 = fruit.indexOf(searchString, n2 + 1);

System.out.println("First search: " + n1);
System.out.println("Second search: " + n2);
System.out.println("Third search: " + n3);
```

☐ What is the output?

More String methods

☐ Consider
```
String fruit = "banana";
String searchString = "an";
int n1 = fruit.indexOf(searchString, 0);
int n2 = fruit.indexOf(searchString, n1 + 1);
int n3 = fruit.indexOf(searchString, n2 + 1);

System.out.println("First search: " + n1);
System.out.println("Second search: " + n2);
System.out.println("Third search: " + n3);
```

☐ What is the output?
```
First search: 1
Second search: 3
Third search: -1
```

More String methods

☐ Consider
```
int v1 = -12;
double v2 = 3.14;
char v3 = 'a';
String s1 = String.valueOf(v1);
String s2 = String.valueOf(v2);
String s3 = String.valueOf(v3);
```

69

Final variables

☐ Consider
```
final String POEM_TITLE = "Appearance of Brown";
final String WARNING = "Weather ball is black";
```

☐ What is the representation?

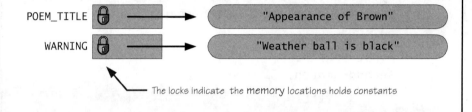

POEM_TITLE 🔒 ⟶ "Appearance of Brown"

WARNING 🔒 ⟶ "Weather ball is black"

The locks indicate the memory locations holds constants

Final variables

The reference cannot be modified once it is established

In general, these attributes can be modified through member methods

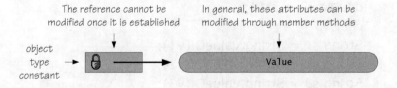

object
type ⟶ 🔒 ⟶ Value
constant

Rectangle

```
int x = 3;
int y = 4;
int width = 5;
int height = 2;
Rectangle r = new Rectangle(x, y, width, height);
```

The first two parameters of the Rectangle constructor specify the position of the upper-left-hand corner of the new Rectangle

The third and fourth parameters of the Rectangle constructor specify the dimensions of the new Rectangle

Rectangle

```
int x = 3;
int y = 4;
int width = 5;
int height = 2;
Rectangle r = new Rectangle(x, y, width, height);
```

The first two parameters of the Rectangle constructor specify the position of the upper-left-hand corner of the new Rectangle

The third and fourth parameters of the Rectangle constructor specify the dimensions of the new Rectangle

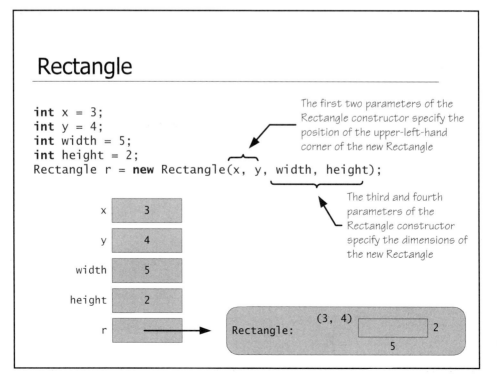

x	3
y	4
width	5
height	2

r → Rectangle: (3, 4)   2
                                5

71

Rectangle

☐ Consider
```
final Rectangle BLOCK = new Rectangle(6, 9, 4, 2);
BLOCK.setLocation(1, 4);
BLOCK.resize(8, 3);
```

BLOCK   🔒 ————▶   Rectangle: (6, 9) [ ] 2   4

Rectangle

☐ Consider
```
final Rectangle BLOCK = new Rectangle(6, 9, 4, 2);
BLOCK.setLocation(1, 4);
BLOCK.resize(8, 3);
```

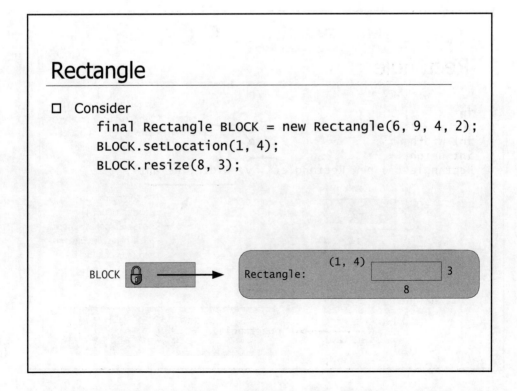

BLOCK   🔒 ————▶   Rectangle: (1, 4) [ ] 3   8

Final variables

☐ Consider
```
final String LANGUAGE = "Java";
```

The reference cannot be modified once it is established

The contents are immutable because there are no String methods that allow the contents to be changed

LANGUAGE 🔒 ⟶ "Java"

Classes

Preparation

☐ Scene so far has been background material and experience
  - Computing systems and problem solving
  - Variables
  - Types
  - Input and output
  - Expressions
  - Assignments
  - Objects
  - Standard classes and methods

Ready

☐ Experience what Java is really about
  - Design and implement objects representing information and physical world objects

Object-oriented programming

☐ Basis
  - Create and manipulate objects with attributes and behaviors that the programmer can specify

☐ Mechanism
  - Classes

☐ Benefits
  - An information type is design and implemented once
    ☐ Reused as needed
      - No need reanalysis and re-justification of the representation

First class – ColoredRectangle

☐ Purpose
  - Represent a colored rectangle in a window
  - Introduce the basics of object design and implementation

Background

☐ JFrame
  - Principal Java class for representing a titled, bordered graphical window.

  - Standard class
    ☐ Part of the swing library

    ```
    import javax.swing.* ;
    ```

Example

- ☐ Consider

```
JFrame w1 = new JFrame("Bigger");
JFrame w2 = new JFrame("Smaller");
w1.setSize(200, 125);
w2.setSize(150, 100);
w1.setVisible(true);
w2.setVisible(true);
```

Example

- ☐ Consider

```
JFrame w1 = new JFrame("Bigger");
JFrame w2 = new JFrame("Smaller");
w1.setSize(200, 125);
w2.setSize(150, 100);
w1.setVisible(true);
w2.setVisible(true);
```

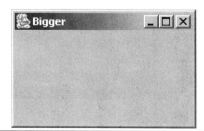

Example

□ Consider
```
JFrame w1 = new JFrame("Bigger");
JFrame w2 = new JFrame("Smaller");
w1.setSize(200, 125);
w2.setSize(150, 100);
w1.setVisible(true);
w2.setVisible(true);
```

Example

□ Consider
```
JFrame w1 = new JFrame("Bigger");
JFrame w2 = new JFrame("Smaller");
w1.setSize(200, 125);
w2.setSize(150, 100);
w1.setVisible(true);
w2.setVisible(true);
```

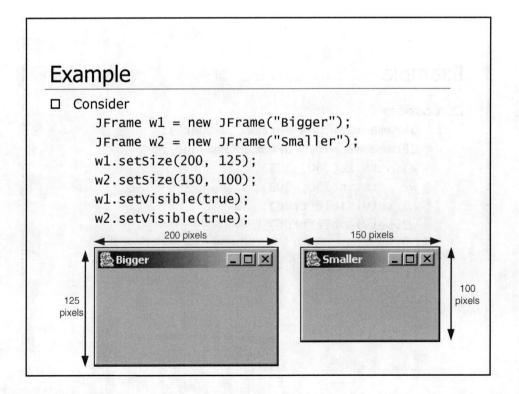

78

Class ColoredRectangle – initial version

- ☐ Purpose
  - ■ Support the display of square window containing a blue filled-in rectangle
    - ☐ Window has side length of 200 pixels
    - ☐ Rectangle is 40 pixels wide and 20 pixels high
    - ☐ Upper left hand corner of rectangle is at (80, 90)

  - ■ Limitations are temporary
    - ☐ Remember BMI.java preceded BMICalculator.java
    - ☐ Lots of concepts to introduce

ColoredRectangle in action

- ☐ Consider

  ```
  ColoredRectangle r1 = new ColoredRectangle();
  ColoredRectangle r2 = new ColoredRectangle();

  System.out.println("Enter when ready");
  System.in.read();

  r1.paint();  // draw the window associated with r1
  r2.paint();  // draw the window associated with r2
  ```

ColoredRectangle in action

☐ Consider

ColoredRectangle r1 = new ColoredRectangle();
ColoredRectangle r2 = new ColoredRectangle();

System.out.println("Enter when ready");
System.in.read();

r1.paint(); // draw the window associated with r1
r2.paint(); // draw the window associated with r2

ColoredRectangle in action

☐ Consider

ColoredRectangle r1 = new ColoredRectangle();
ColoredRectangle r2 = new ColoredRectangle();

System.out.println("Enter when ready");
System.in.read();

r1.paint(); // draw the window associated with r1
r2.paint(); // draw the window associated with r2

ColoredRectangle in action

☐ Consider

```
ColoredRectangle r1 = new ColoredRectangle();
ColoredRectangle r2 = new ColoredRectangle();

System.out.println("Enter when ready");
System.in.read();

r1.paint();  // draw the window associated with r1
r2.paint();  // draw the window associated with r2
```

ColoredRectangle object referenced by r1 is being sent a message

```
r1.paint()
           } ← The messages instruct the objects to display themselves
r2.paint()
```

ColoredRectangle object referenced by r2 is being sent a message

ColoredRectangle.java outline

```
import javax.swing.*;
import java.awt.*;
public class ColoredRectangle {
    // instance variables for holding object attributes
    private int width;
    private int height;
    private int x;
    private int y;
    private JFrame window;
    private Color color;

    // ColoredRectangle(): default constructor
    public ColoredRectangle() {  // ...
    }
    // paint(): display the rectangle in its window
    public void paint() {  // ...
    }
}
```

81

Instance variables and attributes

- Data field
  - Java term for an object attribute

- Instance variable
  - Symbolic name for a data field

  - Usually has private access
    - Assists in information hiding by encapsulating the object's attributes

  - Default initialization
    - Numeric instance variables initialized to 0
    - Logical instance variables initialized to false
    - Object instance variables initialized to null

```java
public class ColoredRectangle {

    // instance variables for holding object attributes
    private int width;            private int x;
    private int height;           private int y;
    private JFrame window;        private Color color;
    // ColoredRectangle(): default constructor
    public ColoredRectangle() {
        window = new JFrame("Box Fun");
        window.setSize(200, 200);
        width = 40;              x = 80;
        height = 20;             y = 90;
        color = Color.BLUE;
        window.setVisible(true);
    }
    // paint(): display the rectangle in its window
    public void paint() {
        Graphics g = window.getGraphics();
        g.setColor(color);
        g.fillRect(x, y, width, height);
    }
}
```

```
public class ColoredRectangle {
    // instance variables for holding object attributes
    private int width;              private int x;
    private int height;             private int y;
    private JFrame window;          private Color color;
    // ColoredRectangle(): default constructor
    public ColoredRectangle() {
        window = new JFrame("Box Fun");
        window.setSize(200, 200);
        width = 40;              x = 80;
        height = 20;             y = 90;
        color = Color.BLUE;
        window.setVisible(true);
    }
    // paint(): display the rectangle in its window
    public void paint() {
        Graphics g = window.getGraphics();
        g.setColor(color);
        g.fillRect(x, y, width, height);
    }
}
```

ColoredRectangle default constructor

```
public class ColoredRectangle {
    // instance variables to describe object attributes
    ...

    // ColoredRectangle(): default constructor
    public ColoredRectangle() {

        ...

    }
    ...
}
```

The name of a constructor always matches the name of its class

A constructor does not list its return type. A constructor always returns a reference to a new object of its class

```
public class ColoredRectangle {

    // instance variables for holding object attributes
    private int width;              private int x;
    private int height;             private int y;
    private JFrame window;          private Color color;
    // ColoredRectangle(): default constructor
    public ColoredRectangle() {
        window = new JFrame("Box Fun");
        window.setSize(200, 200);
        width = 40;               x = 80;
        height = 20;              y = 90;
        color = Color.BLUE;
        window.setVisible(true);
    }
    // paint(): display the rectangle in its window
    public void paint() {
        Graphics g = window.getGraphics();
        g.setColor(color);
        g.fillRect(x, y, width, height);
    }
}
```

Color constants

- ☐ Color.BLACK
- ☐ Color.BLUE
- ☐ Color.CYAN
- ☐ Color.DARK_GRAY
- ☐ Color.GRAY
- ☐ Color.GREEN
- ☐ Color.LIGHT_GRAY
- ☐ Color.MAGENTA
- ☐ Color.ORANGE
- ☐ Color.PINK
- ☐ Color.RED
- ☐ Color.WHITE
- ☐ Color.YELLOW

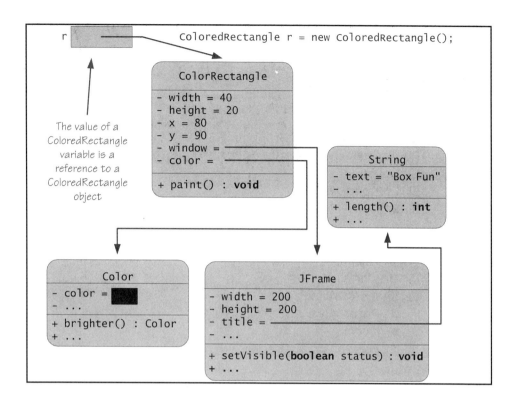

```
ColoredRectangle r = new ColoredRectangle();
```

r

The value of a
ColoredRectangle
variable is a
reference to a
ColoredRectangle
object

ColorRectangle

- width = 40
- height = 20
- x = 80
- y = 90
- window =
- color =

+ paint() : **void**

String

- text = "Box Fun"
- ...

+ length() : **int**
+ ...

Color

- color =
- ...

+ brighter() : Color
+ ...

JFrame

- width = 200
- height = 200
- title =
- ...

+ setVisible(**boolean** status) : **void**
+ ...

```
public class ColoredRectangle {

    // instance variables for holding object attributes
    private int width;              private int x;
    private int height;             private int y;
    private JFrame window;          private Color color;
    // ColoredRectangle(): default constructor
    public ColoredRectangle() {
        window = new JFrame("Box Fun");
        window.setSize(200, 200);
        width = 40;          x = 80;
        height = 20;         y = 90;
        color = Color.BLUE;
        window.setVisible(true);
    }
    // paint(): display the rectangle in its window
    public void paint() {
        Graphics g = window.getGraphics();
        g.setColor(color);
        g.fillRect(x, y, width, height);
    }
}
```

85

Graphical context

- Graphics
  - Defined in java.awt.Graphics
  - Represents the information for a rendering request
    - Color
    - Component
    - Font
    - ...
  - Provides methods
  - Text drawing
    - Line drawing
    - Shape drawing
      - Rectangles
      - Ovals
      - Polygons

Java coordinate system

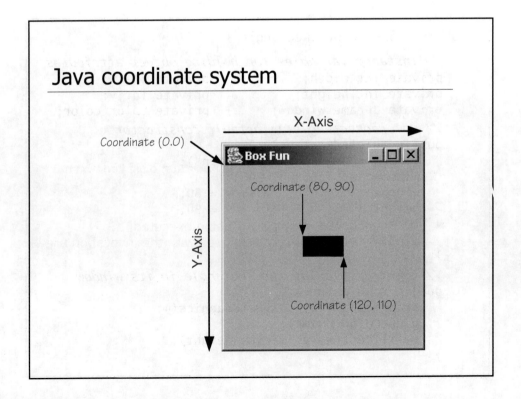

```
public class ColoredRectangle {

    // instance variables for holding object attributes
    private int width;              private int x;
    private int height;             private int y;
    private JFrame window;          private Color color;
    // ColoredRectangle(): default constructor
    public ColoredRectangle() {
        window = new JFrame("Box Fun");
        window.setSize(200, 200);
        width = 40;              x = 80;
        height = 20;             y = 90;
        color = Color.BLUE;
        window.setVisible(true);
    }
    // paint(): display the rectangle in its window
    public void paint() {
        Graphics g = window.getGraphics();
        g.setColor(color);
        g.fillRect(x, y, width, height);
    }
}
```

Method invocation

☐ Consider

```
r1.paint();  // display window associated with r1

r2.paint();  // display window associated with r2
```

☐ Observe
- When an instance method is being executed, the attributes of the object associated with the invocation are accessed and manipulated

- Important that you understand what object is being manipulated

Method invocation

```java
public class ColoredRectangle {
  // instance variables to describe object attributes
  ...

  // paint(): display the rectangle in its window
  public void paint() {
    window.setVisible(true);  ◄─────────────────────┐
    Graphics g = window.getGraphics();               │
    g.setColor(color);
    g.fillRect(x, y, width, height);
  }
  ...

}
```

The values of these instance variables are also from the ColoredRectangle object that invoked method paint().

Instance variable window references the JFrame attribute of the object that caused the invocation. That is, the invocation r1.paint() causes the window attribute of the Colored-Rectangle referenced by r1 to be accessed. Similarly, the invocation r2.paint() causes the window attribute of the ColoredRectangle referenced by r2 to be accessed.

Improving ColoredRectangle

☐ Analysis
  - A ColoredRectangle object should
    ☐ Be able to have any color
    ☐ Be positionable anywhere within its window
    ☐ Have no restrictions on its width and height
    ☐ Accessible attributes
    ☐ Updateable attributes

Improving ColoredRectangle

□ Additional constructions and behaviors
  ■ Specific construction
    □ Construct a rectangle representation using supplied values for its attributes
  ■ Accessors
    □ Supply the values of the attributes
    □ Individual methods for providing the width, height, x-coordinate position, y-coordinate position, color, or window of the associated rectangle
  ■ Mutators
    □ Manage requests for changing attributes
    □ Ensure objects always have sensible values
    □ Individual methods for setting the width, height, x-coordinate position, y-coordinate position, color, or window of the associated rectangle to a given value

A mutator method

□ Definition

// setWidth(): width mutator
public void setWidth(int w) {
    width = w;
}

□ Usage

```
ColoredRectangle s = new ColoredRectangle();
s.setWidth(80);
```

Object to be manipulated is the one referenced by s

Initial value of the formal parameter comes from the actual parameter

```
public void setWidth(int w) {
    ...
}
```

Changes to the formal parameter do not affect the actual parameter

89

Mutator setWidth() evaluation

```
ColoredRectangle s = new ColoredRectangle();
s.setWidth(80);
```

The invocation sends a message to the ColoredRectangle referenced by s to modify its width attribute. To do so, there is a temporary transfer of flow of control to setWidth(). The value of the actual parameter is 80

```
public class ColoredRectangle {
   ...
   // setWidth(): width mutator
   public void setWidth(int  w) {
      width = w;
   }
   ...
}
```

For this invocation of method setWidth(), w is initialized to 80. The object being referenced within the method body is the object referenced by s

Method setWidth() sets the instance variable width of its ColoredRectangle. For this invocation, width is set to 80 and the ColoredRectangle is the one referenced by s

Method setWidth() is completed. Control is transferred back to the statement that invoked setWidth()

Subtleties

☐ Consider

```
ColoredRectangle r = new ColoredRectangle();
r.paint();
r.setWidth(80);
r.paint();
```

☐ What is the width is the rectangle on the screen after the mutator executes?

Other mutators

```
public void setHeight(int h) {
    height = h;
}
public void setX(int ulx) {
    x = ulx;
}
public void setY(int uly) {
    y = uly;
}
public void setWindow(JFrame f) {
    window = f;
}
public void setColor(Color c) {
    color = c;
}
```

Mutator usage

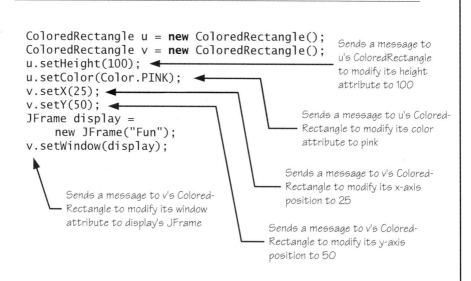

```
ColoredRectangle u = new ColoredRectangle();
ColoredRectangle v = new ColoredRectangle();
u.setHeight(100);
u.setColor(Color.PINK);
v.setX(25);
v.setY(50);
JFrame display =
    new JFrame("Fun");
v.setWindow(display);
```

Sends a message to u's ColoredRectangle to modify its height attribute to 100

Sends a message to u's Colored-Rectangle to modify its color attribute to pink

Sends a message to v's Colored-Rectangle to modify its x-axis position to 25

Sends a message to v's Colored-Rectangle to modify its window attribute to display's JFrame

Sends a message to v's Colored-Rectangle to modify its y-axis position to 50

91

Accessors

- ☐ Properties
  - ■ Do not require parameters
  - ■ Each accessor execution produces a return value
    - ☐ Return value is the value of the invocation

The method return type precedes the name of the method in the method definition

```
public int getWidth() {
  return width;
}
```

For method getWidth(), the return value is the value of the width attribute for the ColoredRectangle associated with the invocation. In invocation t.getWidth(), the return value is the value of the instance variable width for the ColoredRectangle referenced by t

Accessor usage

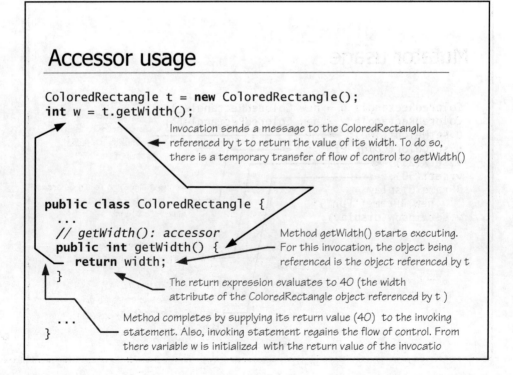

```
ColoredRectangle t = new ColoredRectangle();
int w = t.getWidth();
```

Invocation sends a message to the ColoredRectangle referenced by t to return the value of its width. To do so, there is a temporary transfer of flow of control to getWidth()

```
public class ColoredRectangle {
  ...
  // getWidth(): accessor
  public int getWidth() {
    return width;
  }

  ...
}
```

Method getWidth() starts executing. For this invocation, the object being referenced is the object referenced by t

The return expression evaluates to 40 (the width attribute of the ColoredRectangle object referenced by t)

Method completes by supplying its return value (40) to the invoking statement. Also, invoking statement regains the flow of control. From there variable w is initialized with the return value of the invocatio

Specific construction

```
public ColoredRectangle(int w, int h, int ulx, int uly,
                                JFrame f, Color c) {
    setWidth(w);
    setHeight(h);
    setX(ulx);
    setY(uly);
    setWindow(f);
    setColor(c);
}
```

☐ Requires values for each of the attributes
```
    JFrame display = new JFrame("Even more fun");
    display.setSize(400, 400);
    ColoredRectangle w = new ColoredRectangle(60, 80,
                20, 20, display, Color.YELLOW);
```

Specific construction

```
public ColoredRectangle(int w, int h, int ulx, int uly,
                                JFrame f, Color c) {
    setWidth(w);
    setHeight(h);
    setX(ulx);
    setY(uly);
    setWindow(f);
    setColor(c);
}
```

☐ Advantages to using mutators
- Readability
- Less error prone
- Facilitates enhancements through localization

Seeing double

```java
import java.io.*;
import java.awt.*;

public class SeeingDouble {

    public static void main(String[] args)
                        throws IOException {

        ColoredRectangle r = new ColoredRectangle();

        System.out.println("Enter when ready");
        System.in.read();

        r.paint();

        r.setY(50);
        r.setColor(Color.RED);
        r.paint();
    }
}
```

Seeing double

Decisions

Background

- ☐ Our problem-solving solutions so far have the straight-line property
    - ■ They execute the same statements for every run of the program

```java
public class DisplayForecast
    // main(): application entry point
    public static void main(String[] args) {
        System.out.print("I think there is a world");
        System.out.print(" market for maybe five ");
        System.out.println("computers. ");
        System.out.print(" Thomas Watson, IBM, ");
        System.out.println("1943.");
    }
}
```

95

Background

- ☐ For general problem solving we need more capabilities
  - ■ The ability to control which statements are executed
  - ■ The ability to control how often a statement is executed

- ☐ We will concentrate first on controlling which statements are executed

- ☐ Java provides the *if* and *switch* conditional constructs to control whether a statement list is executed
  - ■ The *if* constructs use logical expressions to determine their course of action

- ☐ Examination begins with logical expressions

Logical expressions

- ☐ The branch of mathematics dealing with logical expressions is Boolean algebra
  - ■ Developed by the British mathematician George Boole

Logical expressions

- A logical expression has either the value logical true or logical false
  - Some expressions whose values are logical true
    - The year 2004 is a leap year
    - A meter equals 100 centimeters
  - Some expressions whose values are logical false
    - A triangle has four sides
    - The area of square is always equal to twice its perimeter

Logical expressions

- There are three primary logical operators for manipulating logical values
  - Logical and
  - Logical or
  - Logical not

- The operators work as most of us would expect

97

Truth tables

- We use truth tables to give formal specifications of the operators
  - "It works as most of us would expect" allows for ambiguity of interpretation
    - Jim is smiling or Patty is smiling
      - Can both Jim and Patty both be smiling?
- Truth tables
  - Lists all combinations of operand values and the result of the operation for each combination

p	q	p and q
False	False	False
False	True	False
True	False	False
True	True	True

Or and not truth tables

p	q	p or q
False	False	False
False	True	True
True	False	True
True	True	True

p	not q
False	True
True	False

Boolean algebra

- ☐ Can create complex logical expressions by combining simple logical expressions

    - ■ not (p and q)

p	q	p and q	not (p and q)
False	False	False	True
False	True	False	True
True	False	False	True
True	True	True	False

DeMorgan's laws

- ☐ not (p and q) equals (not p) or (not q)

p	q	p and q	not (p and q)	(not p)	(not q)	(not p) or (not q)
False	False	False	True	True	True	True
False	True	False	True	True	False	True
True	False	False	True	False	True	True
True	True	True	False	False	False	False

DeMorgan's laws

☐ not (p or q) equals (not p) and (not q)

p	q	p or q	not (p or q)	(not p)	(not q)	(not p) and (not q)
False	False	False	True	True	True	True
False	True	False	False	True	False	False
True	False	False	False	False	True	False
True	True	True	False	False	False	False

A boolean type

☐ Java has the logical type `boolean`

☐ Type boolean has two literal constants
- `true`
- `false`

☐ Operators
- The and operator is **&&**
- The or operator is **||**
- The not operator is **!**

Defining boolean variables

☐ Local boolean variables are uninitialized by default

```
boolean isWhitespace;
boolean receivedAcknowledgement;
boolean haveFoundMissingLink;
```

isWhitespace	-
receivedAcknowledgement	-
haveFoundMissingLink	-

Defining boolean variables

☐ Local boolean variables with initialization

```
boolean canProceed = true;
boolean preferCyan = false;
boolean completedSecretMission = true;
```

canProceed	true
preferCyan	false
completedSecretMission	true

Other operators

- ☐ Equality operators == and !=
  - ■ Operator ==
    - ☐ Returns true if the operands have the same value; otherwise, returns false
  - ■ Operator !=
    - ☐ Returns true if the operands have different values; otherwise, returns false

  - ■ The operators work with all types of values

Evaluating boolean expressions

- ☐ Suppose

  boolean p = true;
  boolean q = false;
  boolean r = true;
  boolean s = false;

- ☐ What is the value of

p	p && s
!s	p == q
q	q != r
p && r	r == s
q || s	q != s

Evaluating boolean expressions

- Suppose
  ```
  int i = 1;
  int j = 2;
  int k = 2;
  char c = '#';
  char d = '%';
  char e = '#';
  ```

- What is the value of

j == k	i != k
i == j	j != k
c == e	d != e
c == d	c != e

Take care with floating-point values

- Consider
  ```
  double a = 1;
  double b = 0.1 + 0.1 + 0.1 + 0.1 + 0.1 + 0.1
                   + 0.1 + 0.1 + 0.1 + 0.1
  double c = .9999999999999999;
  ```

- Two true expressions!
  ```
  a == b      b != c
  ```

- Two false expressions!
  ```
  a != b      b == c
  ```

- Problem lies with the finite precision of the floating-point types
  - Instead with the ordering operators for closeness

103

Ordering operators

☐ Java provides ordering operators for the primitive types
  ■ Four ordering operators, <, >, <=, and >=
  ■ They correspond to mathematical operators of <. >, ≤, and

☐ Together the equality and ordering operators are known as the relational operators

☐ False is less than true

Evaluation boolean expressions

☐ Suppose
```
int i = 1;
int j = 2;
int k = 2;
```

☐ What is the value of
```
i < j
j < k
i <= k
j >= k
i >= k
```

Unicode values

- Character comparisons are based on their Unicode values

- Characters '0', '1', ... '9' have expected order
    - Character '0' has the encoding 48
    - Character '1' has the encoding 49, and so on.

- Upper case Latin letters 'A', 'B', ... 'Z' have expected order
    - Character 'A' has the encoding 65, character 'B' has the encoding 66, and so on.

- Lower case Latin letters 'a', 'b', ... 'z' have expected order
    - Character 'a' has the encoding 97
    - Character 'b' has the encoding 98, and so on.

Evaluation boolean expressions

- Suppose
    ```
    char c = '2';
    char d = '3';
    char e = '2';
    ```

- What is the value of
    ```
    c < d
    c < e
    c <= e
    d >= e
    c >= e
    ```

Operator precedence revisited

☐ Highest to lowest
- Parentheses
- Unary operators
- Multiplicative operators
- Additive operators
- Relational ordering
- Relational equality
- Logical and
- Logical or
- Assignment

Conditional constructs

☐ Provide
- Ability to control whether a statement list is executed

☐ Two constructs
- If statement
  - ☐ if
  - ☐ if-else
  - ☐ if-else-if
- Switch statement

Basic if statement

- Syntax

    ```
    if (Expression)
        Action
    ```

- If the *Expression* is true then execute *Action*

- *Action* is either a single statement or a group of statements within braces

- For us, it will always be a group of statements within braces

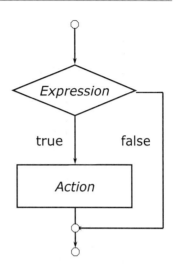

Example

```
if (value < 0) {
    value = -value;
}
```

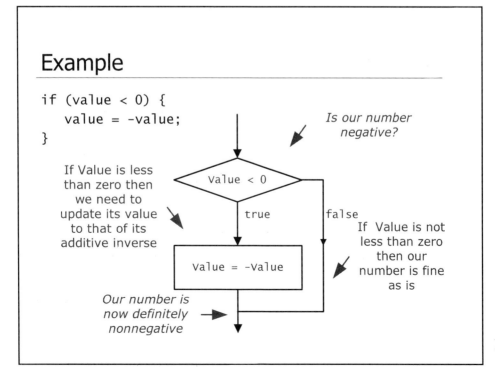

If Value is less than zero then we need to update its value to that of its additive inverse

Is our number negative?

If Value is not less than zero then our number is fine as is

Our number is now definitely nonnegative

107

Sorting two values

```
System.out.print("Enter an integer number: ");
int value1 = Integer.parseInt(stdin.readLine());
System.out.print("Enter another integer number: ");
int value2 = Integer.parseInt(stdin.readLine());

// rearrange numbers if necessary
if (value2 < value1) {
    // values are not in sorted order
    int rememberValue1 = value1;
    value1 = value2;
    value2 = rememberValue1;
}

// display values
System.out.println("The numbers in sorted order are "
    + value1 + " and then " + value2);
```

What happens if the user enters 11 and 28?

What happens if the user enters 11 and 4?

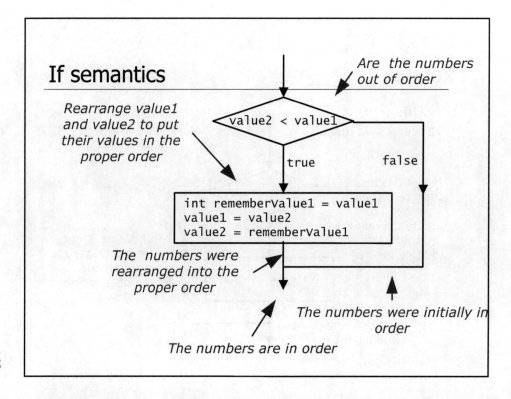

If semantics

Are the numbers out of order

Rearrange value1 and value2 to put their values in the proper order

value2 < value1

true   false

```
int rememberValue1 = value1
value1 = value2
value2 = rememberValue1
```

The numbers were rearranged into the proper order

The numbers were initially in order

The numbers are in order

108

Why we always use braces

□ What is the output?

```
int m = 5;
int n = 10;

if (m < n)
    ++m;
    ++n;

System.out.println(" m = " + m + " n = " n);
```

The if-else statement

□ Syntax

if (*Expression*)
    *Action*₁
  else
    *Action*₂

□ If *Expression* is true then execute
*Action*₁ otherwise execute *Action*₂

□ The actions are either a single statement or a list of statements within braces

109

Finding the maximum of two values

```
System.out.print("Enter an integer number: ");
int value1 = Integer.parseInt(stdin.readLine());
System.out.print("Enter another integer number: ");
int value2 = Integer.parseInt(stdin.readLine());

int maximum;
if (value1 < value2) {    // is value2 larger?
    maximum = value2;      // yes: value2 is larger
}
else { // (value1 >= value2)
    maximum = value1;      // no: value2 is not larger
}
System.out.println("The maximum of " + value1
        + " and " + value2 + " is " + maximum);
```

Finding the maximum of two values

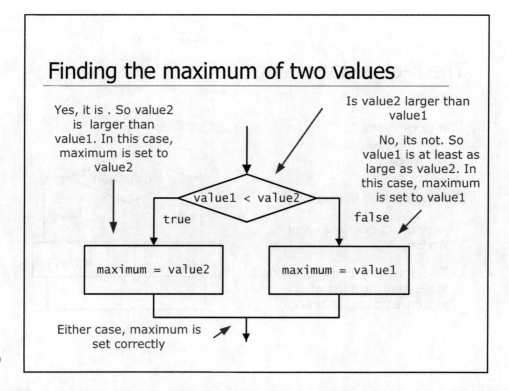

Yes, it is . So value2 is larger than value1. In this case, maximum is set to value2

Is value2 larger than value1

No, its not. So value1 is at least as large as value2. In this case, maximum is set to value1

value1 < value2

true

false

maximum = value2

maximum = value1

Either case, maximum is set correctly

Why we use whitespace

☐ What does the following do?

```
System.out.print("Enter an integer number: ");
int value1 = Integer.parseInt(stdin.readLine());
System.out.print("Enter another integer number: ");
int value2 = Integer.parseInt(stdin.readLine());
if (value2 < value1) {
int rememberValue1 = value1;
value1 = value2;
value2 = rememberValue1;
}
System.out.println("The numbers in sorted order are "
+ value1 + " and then " + value2);
```

Testing objects for equality

☐ Consider
```
System.out.print("Enter an integer number: ");
int n1 = Integer.parseInt(stdin.readLine());
System.out.print("Enter another integer number: ");
int n2 = Integer.parseInt(stdin.readLine());

if (n1 == n2) {
    System.out.println("Same");
}
else {
    System.out.println("Different");
}
```
What is the output if the user enters 88 both times?

What is the output if the user enters 88 and 3?

Testing objects for equality

☐ Consider
```
System.out.print("Enter a string: ");
String s1 = stdin.readLine();
System.out.print("Enter another string: ");
String s2 = stdin.readLine();

if (s1 == s2) {
    System.out.println("Same");
}
else {
    System.out.println("Different");
}
```
What is the output if the user enters "pastel" both times?

Testing objects for equality

☐ When it is executed
```
System.out.print("Enter a string: ");
String s1 = stdin.readLine();
System.out.print("Enter another string: ");
String s2 = stdin.readLine();
```

☐ Memory looks like

☐ As a result no matter what is entered s1 and s2 are not the same
- They refer to different objects

Testing operators for equality

☐ Consider

```
System.out.print("Enter a string: ");
String s1 = stdin.readLine();
System.out.print("Enter another string: ");
String s2 = stdin.readLine();

if (s1.equals(s2)) {
    System.out.println("Same");
}
else {
    System.out.println("Different");
}
```

Tests whether s1 and s2 represent the same object

All objects have a method equals(). Their implementation is class-specific. The String equals() method – like many others – tests for equivalence in representation

Some handy String class methods

☐ isDigit()
  ■ Tests whether character is numeric
☐ isLetter()
  ■ Tests whether character is alphabetic
☐ isLowerCase()
  ■ Tests whether character is lowercase alphabetic
☐ isWhiteSpace()
  ■ Tests whether character is one of the space, tab, formfeed, or newline characters

Some handy String class methods

- isUpperCase()
  - Tests whether character is uppercase alphabetic
- toLowerCase()
  - If the character is alphabetic then the lowercase equivalent of the character is returned; otherwise, the character is returned
- toUpperCase()
  - If the character is alphabetic then the uppercase equivalent of the character is returned; otherwise, the character is returned

If-else-if

- Consider

```
if (number == 0) {
    System.out.println("zero");
}
else {
    if (number > 0) {
        System.out.println("positive");
    }
    else {
        System.out.println("negative");
    }
}
```

If-else-if

☐ Better

```
if (number == 0) {
    System.out.println("zero");
}
else if (number > 0) {
    System.out.println("positive");
}
else {
    System.out.println("negative");
}
```

Same results as previous segment – but this segment better expresses the meaning of what is going on

Sorting three values

☐ For sorting values n1, n2, and n3 there are six possible orderings

- $n1 \le n2 \le n3$
- $n1 \le n3 \le n2$
- $n2 \le n1 \le n3$
- $n2 \le n3 \le n1$
- $n3 \le n1 \le n2$
- $n3 \le n2 \le n1$

☐ Suppose s1, s2, s3 are to made a sorted version of n1, n2, and n3

115

Sorting three values

```java
if ((n1 <= n2) && (n2 <= n3)) {          // n1 <= n2 <= n2
    s1 = n1;    s2 = n2;    s3 = n3;
}
else if ((n1 <= n3) && (n3 <= n2)) { // n1 <= n3 <= n2
    s1 = n1;    s2 = n3;    s3 = n2;
}
else if ((n2 <= n1) && (n1 <= n3)) { // n2 <= n1 <= n3
    s1 = n2;    s2 = n1;    s3 = n3;
}
else if ((n2 <= n3) && (n3 <= n1)) { // n2 <= n3 <= n1
    s1 = n2;    s2 = n3;    s3 = n1;
}
else if ((n3 <= n1) && (n1 <= n2)) { // n3 <= n1 <= n2
    s1 = n3;    s2 = n1;    s3 = n2;
}
else { // n3 <= n2 <= n1
    s1 = n3;    s2 = n2;    s3 = n1;
}
```

Switch statement

- ☐ Software engineers often confronted with programming tasks where required action depends on the values of integer expressions
  - ■ The if-else-if construct can be used
    - ☐ Separately compare the desired expression to a particular value
      - ■ If the expression and value are equal, then perform the appropriate action

- ☐ Because such programming tasks occur frequently
  - ■ Java includes a switch statement
    - ☐ The task is often more readable with the switch then with the if-else-if

Switch statement

Integral expression
to be matched with
a case expression

```
switch ( SwitchExpression )  {
        case CaseExpression₁ :
              Action₁ ;
        case CaseExpression₂ :
              Action₂ ;
        ...
        case CaseExpression_n :
              Action_n;
        default :
              Action_{n+1} ;
}
```

Java
statements

Constant
integral
expression

Testing for vowel-ness

```
switch (ch) {
   case 'a': case 'A':
   case 'e': case 'E':
   case 'i': case 'I':
   case 'o': case 'O':
   case 'u': case 'U':
       System.out.println("vowel");
       break;
   default:
       System.out.println("not a vowel");
}
```

The break causes an exiting of the switch

Handles all of the other cases

117

Processing a request

```
System.out.print("Enter a number: ");
int n1 = Integer.parseInt(stdin.readLine());

System.out.print("Enter another number: ");
int n2 = Integer.parseInt(stdin.readLine());

System.out.print("Enter desired operator: ");
char operator = stdin.readLine().charAt(0);

switch (operator) {
    case '+' : System.out.println(n1 + n2); break;
    case '-' : System.out.println(n1 - n2); break;
    case '*' : System.out.println(n1 * n2); break;
    case '/' : System.out.println(n1 / n2); break;
    default: System.out.println("Illegal request");
}
```

Short-circuit evaluation

- The value of a logical expression can be known before all the operands have been considered
  - If left operand of && is false, then the value must be false
  - If right operand of || is true, then the value must be true

- Java uses these properties to make logical operations efficient
  - Evaluates left operand before it evaluates right operand
  - If the operator value is determined from the left operand, then the right operand is not evaluated
    - The operation is short-circuited

Short-circuit evaluation

☐ Short-circuit evaluation is useful when some property must be true for some other expression to be evaluated

☐ Suppose you are interested in knowing whether scoreSum divided by nbrScores is greater than value
   - The condition can be evaluated only if nbrScores is nonzero

☐ The following expression correctly represents the condition
   (nbrScores != 0) && ((scoreSum / nbrScores) > value)

ColoredTriangle

☐ Background
   - Triangles are an important shape in the world of computer graphics
   - When computer animations are created, scenes are typically decomposed into a collection of colored triangles

☐ Informal specification
   - Represent a colored triangle in two-dimensional space
   - Provide the constructors and methods a reasonable user would expect

ColoredTriangle – see the cat

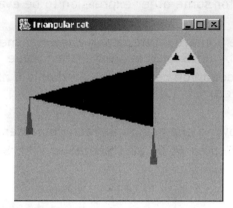

ColoredTriangle – expected constructors

☐ Default construction
- Construct a reasonable triangle representation even though no explicit attributes values are given

    public ColoredTriangle()

☐ Specific construction
- Construct a triangle representation from explicit attributes values

    public ColoredTriangle(Point v1, Point v2, Point v3, Color c)

ColoredTriangle – expected behaviors

☐ Provide the area
  - Return the area of the associated triangle

    public double getArea()

☐ Provide the perimeter
  - Return the perimeter of the associated triangle

    public double getPerimeter()

☐ Access an endpoint
  - Provide a requested endpoint of the associated triangle

    public Point getPoint(int i)

ColoredTriangle – expected behaviors

☐ Access the color
  - Provide the color of the associated triangle

    public Point getColor()

☐ Set an endpoint
  - Set a particular endpoint point of the associated triangle to a given value

    public void setPoint(int i, Point p)

☐ Set color of the triangle
  - Set the color of the associated triangle to a given value

    public void setColor(Color c)

121

ColoredTriangle – expected behaviors

☐ Render
  ■ Draw the associated triangle in a given graphical context

  public void paint(Graphics g)

☐ Test equality
  ■ Report whether the associated triangle is equivalent to a given triangle

  public boolean equals(Object v)

☐ String representation
  ■ Provide a textual representation of the attributes of the associated triangle

  public String toString()

ColoredTriangle – attributes

☐ To implement the behaviors
  ■ Knowledge of the triangle color and three endpoints suffices
  ■ Endpoint can be represented using two int values per location or as a Point
    ☐ Point seem more natural

private Color color
  ☐ Color of the associated triangle
private Point p1
  ☐ References the first point of the associated triangle
private Point p2
  ☐ References the second point of the associated triangle
private Point p3
  ☐ References the third point of the associated triangle

Default constructor – implementation

```
// ColoredTriangle(): default constructor
public ColoredTriangle() {
  Point a = new Point(1, 1);
  Point b = new Point(2, 2);      Create endpoint values
  Point c = new Point(3, 3);
  setPoint(1, a);
  setPoint(2, b);                 Copy desired endpoint values
  setPoint(3, c);                 to data fields
  setColor(Color.BLACK);          Copy desired color to data fields
}
```

Implementation – accessor getPoint()

```
// getPoint(): endpoint accessor
public Point getPoint(int i) {
    if (i == 1) {
        return p1;
    }
    else if (i == 2) {
        return p2;
    }
    else if (i == 3) {
        return p3;
    }
    else {
        System.output.println("Unexpected endpoint access: "
                                  + i);
        System.exit(i);
        return null;        Won't be executed but compiler
    }                        wants every execution path to end
}                            with a return
```

123

Implementation – facilitator toString()

```
// toString(): string facilitator
public String toString() {
    Point v1 = getPoint(1);
    Point v2 = getPoint(2);
    Point v3 = getPoint(3);
    Color c = getColor();

    return "ColoredRectangle[" + v1 + ", " + v2 + ", " + v3
                      + ", " + c + "]";
}
```

Standard to include class name
when expected use is for debugging

Implementation – facilitator toString()

```
Point a = new Point(2,1),
Point b = new Point(1,2)
Point c = new Point(3,2);
ColoredTriangle u = new ColoredTriangle(a, b, c, Color.RED);
System.out.println(u);  // displays string version of u

ColoredTriangle[java.awt.Point[x=2,y=1],
    java.awt.Point[x=1,y=2], java.awt.Point[x=3,y=2],
    java.awt.Color[r=255,g=0,b=0]]
```

Implementation – facilitator equals()

```java
// equals(): equals facilitator
public boolean equals(Object p) {
    if (p instanceof ColoredTriangle) {
        Point v1 = getPoint(1);
        Point v2 = getPoint(2);
        Point v3 = getPoint(3);
        Color c = getColor();
        ColoredTriangle t = (ColoredTriangle) p;

        return v1.equals(t.getPoint(1))
                && v2.equals(t.getPoint(2))
                && v3.equals(t.getPoint(3))
                && c.equals(t.getColor());
    }
    else {
        return false;
    }
}
```

Because its an override
the parameter type is
Object

instanceof tests whether
left operand is an instance
of right operand

Implementation – facilitator equals()

```java
ColoredTriangle e = new ColoredTriangle();
ColoredTriangle f = new ColoredTriangle(new Point(2,1),
      new Point(1,2), new Point(3,2), Color.YELLOW);
ColoredTriangle g = new ColoredTriangle(new Point(2,1),
      new Point(1,2), new Point(3,2), Color.YELLOW);

boolean flag1 = e.equals(f);
boolean flag2 = e.equals(g);
boolean flag2 = e.equals(g);

System.out.println(flag1 + " " + flag2 + " "  + flag3);
```

Implementation – facilitator equals()

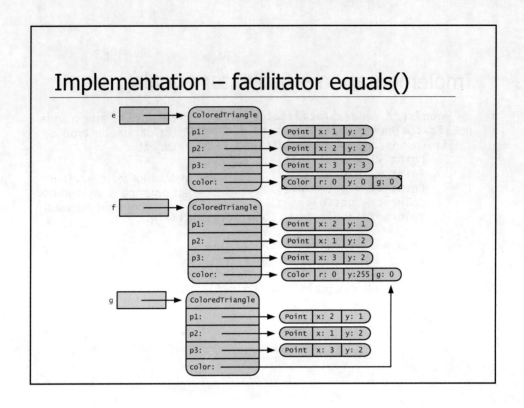

Implementation – facilitator paint()

```
// paint(): render facilitator
public void paint(Graphics g) {
    Point v1 = getPoint(1);
    Point v2 = getPoint(2);
    Point v3 = getPoint(3);
    Color c = getColor();

    g.setColor(c);                    Part of awt

    Polygon t = new Polygon();
    t.addPoint(v1.x, v1.y);
    t.addPoint(v2.x, v2.y);
    t.addPoint(v3.x, v3.y);
                                      Renders a polygon using the
                                      list of points in the polygon
    g.fillPolygon(t);                 referenced by t
}
```

Iteration

Java looping

- ☐ Options
  - ■ while
  - ■ do-while
  - ■ for

- ☐ Allow programs to control how many times a statement list is executed

Averaging

- □ Problem
  - ■ Extract a list of positive numbers from standard input and produce their average
    - □ Numbers are one per line
    - □ A negative number acts as a *sentinel* to indicate that there are no more numbers to process

- □ Observations
  - ■ Cannot supply sufficient code using just assignments and conditional constructs to solve the problem
    - □ Don't how big of a list to process
  - ■ Need ability to repeat code as needed

Averaging

- □ Problem
  - ■ Extract a list of positive numbers from standard input and produce their average
    - □ Numbers are one per line
    - □ A negative number acts as a *sentinel* to indicate that there are no more numbers to process

- □ Algorithm
  - ■ Prepare for processing
  - ■ Get first input
  - ■ While there is an input to process do {
    - □ Process current input
    - □ Get the next input
  - ■ }
  - ■ Perform final processing

Averaging

- ☐ Problem
  - ■ Extract a list of positive numbers from standard input and produce their average
    - ☐ Numbers are one per line
    - ☐ A negative number acts as a *sentinel* to indicate that there are no more numbers to process

- ☐ Sample run
  ```
  Enter positive numbers one per line.
  Indicate end of list with a negative number.
  4.5
  0.5
  1.3
  -1
  Average 2.1
  ```

```java
public class NumberAverage {
    // main(): application entry point
    public static void main(String[] args)
            throws IOException {
        // set up the list processing

        // prompt user for values

        // get first value

        // process values one-by-one
        while (value >= 0) {
            // add value to running total
            // processed another value
            // prepare next iteration - get next value
        }
        // display result
        if (valuesProcessed > 0)
            // compute and display average
        else
            // indicate no average to display
    }
}
```

```
System.out.println("Enter positive numbers 1 per line.\n"
    + "Indicate end of the list with a negative number.");
BufferedReader stdin = new BufferedReader(
        new InputStreamReader(System.in));

int valuesProcessed = 0;
double valueSum = 0;

double value = Double.parseDouble(stdin.readLine());
while (value >= 0) {
    valueSum += value;
    ++valuesProcessed;
    value = Double.parseDouble(stdin.readLine());
}

if (valuesProcessed > 0) {
    double average = valueSum / valuesProcessed;
    System.out.println("Average: " + average);
}
else {
    System.out.println("No list to average");
}
```

While syntax and semantics

```
while ( Expression ) Action
```

Logical expression that determines whether Action is to be executed — if Expression evaluates to true, then Action is executed; otherwise, the loop is terminated

Action is either a single statement or a statement list within braces. The action is also known as the body of the loop. After the body is executed, the test expression is reevaluated. If the expression evaluates to true, the body is executed again. The process repeats until the test expression evaluates to false

While semantics for averaging problem

Test expression is evaluated at the start of each iteration of the loop. Its value indicates whether there is a number to process

```
// process values one-by-one
while (value >= 0) {
    // add value to running total
    valueSum += value;
    // processed another value
    ++valuesProcessed;
    // prepare to iterate -- get the next input
    value = Double.parseDouble(stdin.readLine());
}
```

If test expression is true, these statements are executed. Afterward, the test expression is reevaluated and the process repeats

While Semantics

Expression is evaluated at the start of each iteration of the loop

If Expression is true, Action is executed

Expression

true   false

If Expression is false, program execution continues with next statement

Action

131

Execution Trace

```
int valuesProcessed = 0;
double valueSum = 0;

double value = Double.parseDouble(stdin.readLine());

while (value >= 0) {
   valueSum += value;
   ++valuesProcessed;
   value = Double.parseDouble(stdin.readLine());
}

if (valuesProcessed > 0) {
   double average = valueSum / valuesProcessed;
   System.out.println("Average: " + average);
}
else {
   System.out.println("No list to average");
}
```

Execution Trace

valuesProcessed | 0 |

```
int valuesProcessed = 0;
double valueSum = 0;

double value = Double.parseDouble(stdin.readLine());

while (value >= 0) {
   valueSum += value;
   ++valuesProcessed;
   value = Double.parseDouble(stdin.readLine());
}

if (valuesProcessed > 0) {
   double average = valueSum / valuesProcessed;
   System.out.println("Average: " + average);
}
else {
   System.out.println("No list to average");
}
```

Suppose input contains: 4.5 0.5 1.3 -1

Execution Trace

valuesProcessed	0
valueSum	0

```
int valuesProcessed = 0;
double valueSum = 0;

double value = Double.parseDouble(stdin.readLine());

while (value >= 0) {
   valueSum += value;
   ++valuesProcessed;
   value = Double.parseDouble(stdin.readLine());
}

if (valuesProcessed > 0) {
   double average = valueSum / valuesProcessed;
   System.out.println("Average: " + average);
}
else {
   System.out.println("No list to average");
}
```

Suppose input contains: 4.5 0.5 1.3 -1

Execution Trace

valuesProcessed	0
valueSum	0
value	4.5

```
int valuesProcessed = 0;
double valueSum = 0;

double value = Double.parseDouble(stdin.readLine());

while (value >= 0) {
   valueSum += value;
   ++valuesProcessed;
   value = Double.parseDouble(stdin.readLine());
}

if (valuesProcessed > 0) {
   double average = valueSum / valuesProcessed;
   System.out.println("Average: " + average);
}
else {
   System.out.println("No list to average");
}
```

133

Suppose input contains: 4.5 0.5 1.3 -1

Execution Trace

valuesProcessed	0
valueSum	0
value	4.5

```
int valuesProcessed = 0;
double valueSum = 0;

double value = Double.parseDouble(stdin.readLine());

while (value >= 0) {
   valueSum += value;
   ++valuesProcessed;
   value = Double.parseDouble(stdin.readLine());
}

if (valuesProcessed > 0) {
   double average = valueSum / valuesProcessed;
   System.out.println("Average: " + average);
}
else {
   System.out.println("No list to average");
}
```

Suppose input contains: 4.5 0.5 1.3 -1

Execution Trace

valuesProcessed	0
valueSum	4.5
value	4.5

```
int valuesProcessed = 0;
double valueSum = 0;

double value = Double.parseDouble(stdin.readLine());

while (value >= 0) {
   valueSum += value;
   ++valuesProcessed;
   value = Double.parseDouble(stdin.readLine());
}

if (valuesProcessed > 0) {
   double average = valueSum / valuesProcessed;
   System.out.println("Average: " + average);
}
else {
   System.out.println("No list to average");
}
```

Suppose input contains: 4.5 0.5 1.3 -1

Execution Trace

valuesProcessed	1
valueSum	4.5
value	4.5

```
int valuesProcessed = 0;
double valueSum = 0;

double value = Double.parseDouble(stdin.readLine());

while (value >= 0) {
   valueSum += value;
   ++valuesProcessed;
   value = Double.parseDouble(stdin.readLine());
}

if (valuesProcessed > 0) {
   double average = valueSum / valuesProcessed;
   System.out.println("Average: " + average);
}
else {
   System.out.println("No list to average");
}
```

Suppose input contains: 4.5 0.5 1.3 -1

Execution Trace

valuesProcessed	1
valueSum	4.5
value	0.5

```
int valuesProcessed = 0;
double valueSum = 0;

double value = Double.parseDouble(stdin.readLine());

while (value >= 0) {
   valueSum += value;
   ++valuesProcessed;
   value = Double.parseDouble(stdin.readLine());
}

if (valuesProcessed > 0) {
   double average = valueSum / valuesProcessed;
   System.out.println("Average: " + average);
}
else {
   System.out.println("No list to average");
}
```

135

Execution Trace

valuesProcessed	1
valueSum	4.5
value	0.5

```
int valuesProcessed = 0;
double valueSum = 0;

double value = Double.parseDouble(stdin.readLine());

while (value >= 0) {
   valueSum += value;
   ++valuesProcessed;
   value = Double.parseDouble(stdin.readLine());
}

if (valuesProcessed > 0) {
   double average = valueSum / valuesProcessed;
   System.out.println("Average: " + average);
}
else {
   System.out.println("No list to average");
}
```

Suppose input contains: 4.5 0.5 1.3 -1

Execution Trace

valuesProcessed	1
valueSum	5.0
value	0.5

```
int valuesProcessed = 0;
double valueSum = 0;

double value = Double.parseDouble(stdin.readLine());

while (value >= 0) {
   valueSum += value;
   ++valuesProcessed;
   value = Double.parseDouble(stdin.readLine());
}

if (valuesProcessed > 0) {
   double average = valueSum / valuesProcessed;
   System.out.println("Average: " + average);
}
else {
   System.out.println("No list to average");
}
```

136

Suppose input contains: 4.5 0.5 1.3 -1

Execution Trace

valuesProcessed	2
valueSum	5.0
value	0.5

```java
int valuesProcessed = 0;
double valueSum = 0;

double value = Double.parseDouble(stdin.readLine());

while (value >= 0) {
   valueSum += value;
   ++valuesProcessed;
   value = Double.parseDouble(stdin.readLine());
}

if (valuesProcessed > 0) {
   double average = valueSum / valuesProcessed;
   System.out.println("Average: " + average);
}
else {
   System.out.println("No list to average");
}
```

Suppose input contains: 4.5 0.5 1.3 -1

Execution Trace

valuesProcessed	2
valueSum	5.0
value	1.3

```java
int valuesProcessed = 0;
double valueSum = 0;

double value = Double.parseDouble(stdin.readLine());

while (value >= 0) {
   valueSum += value;
   ++valuesProcessed;
   value = Double.parseDouble(stdin.readLine());
}

if (valuesProcessed > 0) {
   double average = valueSum / valuesProcessed;
   System.out.println("Average: " + average);
}
else {
   System.out.println("No list to average");
}
```

137

Execution Trace — Slide 1

Execution Trace

valuesProcessed	2
valueSum	5.0
value	1.3

```java
int valuesProcessed = 0;
double valueSum = 0;

double value = Double.parseDouble(stdin.readLine());

while (value >= 0) {
   valueSum += value;
   ++valuesProcessed;
   value = Double.parseDouble(stdin.readLine());
}

if (valuesProcessed > 0) {
   double average = valueSum / valuesProcessed;
   System.out.println("Average: " + average);
}
else {
   System.out.println("No list to average");
}
```

Execution Trace — Slide 2

Suppose input contains: 4.5 0.5 1.3 -1

Execution Trace

valuesProcessed	2
valueSum	6.3
value	1.3

```java
int valuesProcessed = 0;
double valueSum = 0;

double value = Double.parseDouble(stdin.readLine());

while (value >= 0) {
   valueSum += value;
   ++valuesProcessed;
   value = Double.parseDouble(stdin.readLine());
}

if (valuesProcessed > 0) {
   double average = valueSum / valuesProcessed;
   System.out.println("Average: " + average);
}
else {
   System.out.println("No list to average");
}
```

Suppose input contains: 4.5 0.5 1.3 -1

Execution Trace

valuesProcessed	3
valueSum	6.3
value	1.3

```
int valuesProcessed = 0;
double valueSum = 0;

double value = Double.parseDouble(stdin.readLine());

while (value >= 0) {
   valueSum += value;
   ++valuesProcessed;
   value = Double.parseDouble(stdin.readLine());
}

if (valuesProcessed > 0) {
   double average = valueSum / valuesProcessed;
   System.out.println("Average: " + average);
}
else {
   System.out.println("No list to average");
}
```

Suppose input contains: 4.5 0.5 1.3 -1

Execution Trace

valuesProcessed	3
valueSum	6.3
value	-1

```
int valuesProcessed = 0;
double valueSum = 0;

double value = Double.parseDouble(stdin.readLine());

while (value >= 0) {
   valueSum += value;
   ++valuesProcessed;
   value = Double.parseDouble(stdin.readLine());
}

if (valuesProcessed > 0) {
   double average = valueSum / valuesProcessed;
   System.out.println("Average: " + average);
}
else {
   System.out.println("No list to average");
}
```

Suppose input contains: 4.5 0.5 1.3 -1

Execution Trace

valuesProcessed	3
valueSum	6.3
value	-1

```
int valuesProcessed = 0;
double valueSum = 0;

double value = Double.parseDouble(stdin.readLine());

while (value >= 0) {
   valueSum += value;
   ++valuesProcessed;
   value = Double.parseDouble(stdin.readLine());
}

if (valuesProcessed > 0) {
   double average = valueSum / valuesProcessed;
   System.out.println("Average: " + average);
}
else {
   System.out.println("No list to average");
}
```

Suppose input contains: 4.5 0.5 1.3 -1

Execution Trace

valuesProcessed	3
valueSum	6.3
value	-1

```
int valuesProcessed = 0;
double valueSum = 0;

double value = Double.parseDouble(stdin.readLine());

while (value >= 0) {
   valueSum += value;
   ++valuesProcessed;
   value = Double.parseDouble(stdin.readLine());
}

if (valuesProcessed > 0) {
   double average = valueSum / valuesProcessed;
   System.out.println("Average: " + average);
}
else {
   System.out.println("No list to average");
}
```

Slide 1

Execution Trace

valuesProcessed	3
valueSum	6.3
value	-1
average	2.1

```java
int valuesProcessed = 0;
double valueSum = 0;

double value = Double.parseDouble(stdin.readLine());

while (value >= 0) {
   valueSum += value;
   ++valuesProcessed;
   value = Double.parseDouble(stdin.readLine());
}

if (valuesProcessed > 0) {
   double average = valueSum / valuesProcessed;
   System.out.println("Average: " + average);
}
else {
   System.out.println("No list to average");
}
```

Slide 2

Execution Trace

valuesProcessed	3
valueSum	6.3
value	-1
average	2.1

```java
int valuesProcessed = 0;
double valueSum = 0;

double value = Double.parseDouble(stdin.readLine());

while (value >= 0) {
   valueSum += value;
   ++valuesProcessed;
   value = Double.parseDouble(stdin.readLine());
}

if (valuesProcessed > 0) {
   double average = valueSum / valuesProcessed;
   System.out.println("Average: " + average);
}
else {
   System.out.println("No list to average");
}
```

141

Converting text to strictly lowercase

```java
public static void main(String[] args) throws
        IOException {
    BufferedReader stdin = new BufferedReader(
        new InputStreamReader(System.in));

    System.out.println("Enter input to be converted:");

    String converted = "";

    String currentLine = stdin.readLine();

    while (currentLine != null) {
        String currentConversion =
                currentLine.toLowerCase();
        converted += (currentConversion + "\n");
        currentLine = stdin.readLine();
    }

    System.out.println("\nConversion is:\n" + converted);
}
```

Sample run

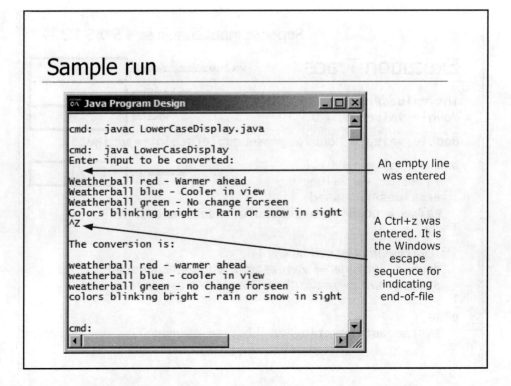

cmd: javac LowerCaseDisplay.java

cmd: java LowerCaseDisplay
Enter input to be converted:

Weatherball red - Warmer ahead
Weatherball blue - Cooler in view
Weatherball green - No change forseen
Colors blinking bright - Rain or snow in sight
^Z

The conversion is:

weatherball red - warmer ahead
weatherball blue - cooler in view
weatherball green - no change forseen
colors blinking bright - rain or snow in sight

cmd:

An empty line was entered

A Ctrl+z was entered. It is the Windows escape sequence for indicating end-of-file

Program trace

```
public static void main(String[] args) throws
     IOException {
   BufferedReader stdin = new BufferedReader(
     new InputStreamReader(System.in));

   System.out.println("Enter input to be converted:");

   String converted = "";

   String currentLine = stdin.readLine();

   while (currentLine != null) {
      String currentConversion =
            currentLine.toLowerCase();
      converted += (currentConversion + "\n");
      currentLine = stdin.readLine();
   }

   System.out.println("\nConversion is:\n" + converted);
}
```

Program trace

```
public static void main(String[] args) throws
     IOException {
   BufferedReader stdin = new BufferedReader(
     new InputStreamReader(System.in));

   System.out.println("Enter input to be converted:");

   String converted = "";

   String currentLine = stdin.readLine();

   while (currentLine != null) {
      String currentConversion =
            currentLine.toLowerCase();
      converted += (currentConversion + "\n");
      currentLine = stdin.readLine();
   }

   System.out.println("\nConversion is:\n" + converted);
}
```

Program trace

```java
public static void main(String[] args) throws
        IOException {
    BufferedReader stdin = new BufferedReader(
        new InputStreamReader(System.in));

    System.out.println("Enter input to be converted:");

    String converted = "";

    String currentLine = stdin.readLine();

    while (currentLine != null) {
        String currentConversion =
                currentLine.toLowerCase();
        converted += (currentConversion + "\n");
        currentLine = stdin.readLine();
    }

    System.out.println("\nConversion is:\n" + converted);
}
```

Program trace

```java
public static void main(String[] args) throws
        IOException {
    BufferedReader stdin = new BufferedReader(
        new InputStreamReader(System.in));

    System.out.println("Enter input to be converted:");

    String converted = "";

    String currentLine = stdin.readLine();

    while (currentLine != null) {
        String currentConversion =
                currentLine.toLowerCase();
        converted += (currentConversion + "\n");
        currentLine = stdin.readLine();
    }

    System.out.println("\nConversion is:\n" + converted);
}
```

Program trace

The append assignment operator updates the representation of converted to include the current input line

```
converted += (currentConversion + "\n");
```

Representation of lower case conversion of current input line

Newline character is needed because method readLine() "strips" them from the input

---

Converting text to strictly lowercase

```
public static void main(String[] args) throws
      IOException {
   BufferedReader stdin = new BufferedReader(
      new InputStreamReader(System.in));

   System.out.println("Enter input to be converted:");

   String converted = "";

   String currentLine = stdin.readLine();

   while (currentLine != null) {
      String currentConversion =
            currentLine.toLowerCase();
      converted += (currentConversion + "\n");
      currentLine = stdin.readLine();
   }

   System.out.println("\nConversion is:\n" + converted);
}
```

Loop design

☐ Questions to consider in loop design and analysis

  ■ What initialization is necessary for the loop's test expression?

  ■ What initialization is necessary for the loop's processing?

  ■ What causes the loop to terminate?

  ■ What actions should the loop perform?

  ■ What actions are necessary to prepare for the next iteration of the loop?

  ■ What conditions are true and what conditions are false when the loop is terminated?

  ■ When the loop completes what actions are need to prepare for subsequent program processing?

Reading a file

☐ Background

BufferedReader is an input stream that uses a buffer to store character inputs for efficiency purposes

System.in is an InputStream variable. InputStream is the superclass of Java's input streams

```
BufferedReader stdin
  = new BufferedReader(new InputStreamReader(System.in));
```

InputStreamReader provides a character view of the bytes that make up an input stream

Reading a file

- ☐ Class FileReader
  - ■ Subclass of InputStreamReader that provides an input view of a file

- ☐ Constructor FileReader(String s)
  - ■ Opens the file with name s so that values can be extracted
  - ■ Name can be either an absolute pathname or a pathname relative to the current working folder

Reading a file

```
BufferedReader stdin = new BufferedReader(
    new InputStreamReader(System.in));

System.out.print("Filename: ");
String filename = stdin.readLine();

BufferedReader fileIn = new BufferedReader(
    new FileReader( filename ) );

String currentLine = fileIn.readLine();

while (currentLine != null) {
    System.out.println(currentLine);

    currentLine = fileIn.readLine();
}

fileIn.close();
```

Reading a file

```
BufferedReader stdin = new BufferedReader(
    new InputStreamReader(System.in));

System.out.print("Filename: ");
String filename = stdin.readLine();

BufferedReader fileIn = new BufferedReader(
    new FileReader( filename ) );

String currentLine = fileIn.readLine();

while (currentLine != null) {
    System.out.println(currentLine);

    currentLine = fileIn.readLine();
}
fileIn.close();                  Set up standard input stream
```

Reading a file

```
BufferedReader stdin = new BufferedReader(
    new InputStreamReader(System.in));

System.out.print("Filename: ");
String filename = stdin.readLine();

BufferedReader fileIn = new BufferedReader(
    new FileReader( filename ) );

String currentLine = fileIn.readLine();

while (currentLine != null) {
    System.out.println(currentLine);

    currentLine = fileIn.readLine();
}
fileIn.close();                  Determine file name
```

Reading a file

```
BufferedReader stdin = new BufferedReader(
      new InputStreamReader(System.in));

System.out.print("Filename: ");
String filename = stdin.readLine();

BufferedReader fileIn = new BufferedReader(
      new FileReader( filename ) );

String currentLine = fileIn.readLine();

while (currentLine != null) {
    System.out.println(currentLine);

    currentLine = fileIn.readLine();
}
fileIn.close();                  Set up file stream
```

Reading a file

```
BufferedReader stdin = new BufferedReader(
      new InputStreamReader(System.in));

System.out.print("Filename: ");
String filename = stdin.readLine();

BufferedReader fileIn = new BufferedReader(
      new FileReader( filename ) );

String currentLine = fileIn.readLine();

while (currentLine != null) {
    System.out.println(currentLine);

    currentLine = fileIn.readLine();
}
fileIn.close();             Process lines one by one
```

149

Reading a file

```
BufferedReader stdin = new BufferedReader(
      new InputStreamReader(System.in));

System.out.print("Filename: ");
String filename = stdin.readLine();

BufferedReader fileIn = new BufferedReader(
      new FileReader( filename ) );

String currentLine = fileIn.readLine();

while (currentLine != null) {
   System.out.println(currentLine);

   currentLine = fileIn.readLine();
}

fileIn.close();                    Get first line
```

Reading a file

```
BufferedReader stdin = new BufferedReader(
      new InputStreamReader(System.in));

System.out.print("Filename: ");
String filename = stdin.readLine();

BufferedReader fileIn = new BufferedReader(
      new FileReader( filename ) );

String currentLine = fileIn.readLine();

while (currentLine != null) {
   System.out.println(currentLine);

   currentLine = fileIn.readLine();
}

fileIn.close();          Make sure got a line to process
```

Reading a file

```
BufferedReader stdin = new BufferedReader(
      new InputStreamReader(System.in));

System.out.print("Filename: ");
String filename = stdin.readLine();

BufferedReader fileIn = new BufferedReader(
      new FileReader( filename ) );

String currentLine = fileIn.readLine();

while (currentLine != null) {
   System.out.println(currentLine);

   currentLine = fileIn.readLine();
}
fileIn.close();
```
Display current line

Reading a file

```
BufferedReader stdin = new BufferedReader(
      new InputStreamReader(System.in));

System.out.print("Filename: ");
String filename = stdin.readLine();

BufferedReader fileIn = new BufferedReader(
      new FileReader( filename ) );

String currentLine = fileIn.readLine();

while (currentLine != null) {
   System.out.println(currentLine);

   currentLine = fileIn.readLine();
}
fileIn.close();
```
Get next line

151

Reading a file

```
BufferedReader stdin = new BufferedReader(
        new InputStreamReader(System.in));

System.out.print("Filename: ");
String filename = stdin.readLine();

BufferedReader fileIn = new BufferedReader(
        new FileReader( filename ) );

String currentLine = fileIn.readLine();

while (currentLine != null) {
    System.out.println(currentLine);

    currentLine = fileIn.readLine();
}

fileIn.close();
```

Make sure got a line to process
If not, loop is done

Reading a file

```
BufferedReader stdin = new BufferedReader(
        new InputStreamReader(System.in));

System.out.print("Filename: ");
String filename = stdin.readLine();

BufferedReader fileIn = new BufferedReader(
        new FileReader( filename ) );

String currentLine = fileIn.readLine();

while (currentLine != null) {
    System.out.println(currentLine);

    currentLine = fileIn.readLine();
}

fileIn.close();
```

Close the file stream

The For Statement

```
int currentTerm = 1;

for (int i = 0; i < 5; ++i) {
    System.out.println(currentTerm);
    currentTerm *= 2;
}
```

The For Statement

Initialization
step is
performed
only once --
just prior to
the first
evaluation of
the test
expression

```
int currentTerm = 1;

for (int i = 0; i < 5; ++i) {
    System.out.println(currentTerm);
    currentTerm *= 2;
}
```

153

The For Statement

Initialization step is performed only once -- just prior to the first evaluation of the test expression

The body of the loop iterates while the test expression is true

```java
int currentTerm = 1;

for (int i = 0; i < 5; ++i) {
    System.out.println(currentTerm);
    currentTerm *= 2;
}
```

The For Statement

Initialization step is performed only once -- just prior to the first evaluation of the test expression

The body of the loop iterates while the test expression is true

```java
int currentTerm = 1;

for (int i = 0; i < 5; ++i) {
    System.out.println(currentTerm);
    currentTerm *= 2;
}
```

The body of the loop displays the current term in the number series. It then determines what is to be the new current number in the series

The For Statement

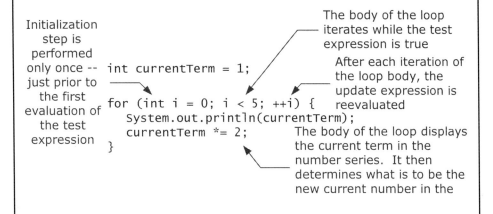

Initialization step is performed only once -- just prior to the first evaluation of the test expression

```
int currentTerm = 1;

for (int i = 0; i < 5; ++i) {
    System.out.println(currentTerm);
    currentTerm *= 2;
}
```

The body of the loop iterates while the test expression is true

After each iteration of the loop body, the update expression is reevaluated

The body of the loop displays the current term in the number series. It then determines what is to be the new current number in the

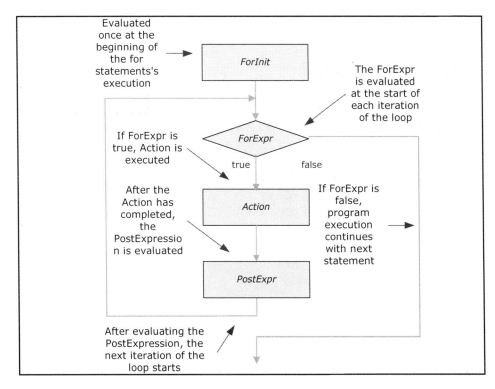

Evaluated once at the beginning of the for statements's execution

ForInit

The ForExpr is evaluated at the start of each iteration of the loop

If ForExpr is true, Action is executed

ForExpr

true   false

If ForExpr is false, program execution continues with next statement

After the Action has completed, the PostExpressio n is evaluated

Action

PostExpr

After evaluating the PostExpression, the next iteration of the loop starts

155

For statement syntax

Logical test expression that determines whether the action and update step are executed

Initialization step prepares for the first evaluation of the test expression

Update step is performed after the execution of the loop body

```
for ( ForInit ; ForExpression ; ForUpdate ) Action
```

The body of the loop iterates whenever the test expression evaluates to true

Execution Trace

```
for (int i = 0; i < 3; ++i) {
    System.out.println("i is " + i);
}

System.out.println("all done");
```

i | 0

Execution Trace

```
for (int i = 0; i < 3; ++i) {
    System.out.println("i is " + i);
}

System.out.println("all done");
```

i [0]

Execution Trace

```
for (int i = 0; i < 3; ++i) {
    System.out.println("i is " + i);
}

System.out.println("all done");

i is 0
```

i [0]

Execution Trace

```
for (int i = 0; i < 3; ++i) {
    System.out.println("i is " + i);
}

System.out.println("all done");
```

i	0

i is 0

Execution Trace

```
for (int i = 0; i < 3; ++i) {
    System.out.println("i is " + i);
}

System.out.println("all done");
```

i	1

i is 0

Execution Trace

```
for (int i = 0; i < 3; ++i) {
    System.out.println("i is " + i);
}

System.out.println("all done");
```

i | 1

i is 0

Execution Trace

```
for (int i = 0; i < 3; ++i) {
    System.out.println("i is " + i);
}

System.out.println("all done");
```

i | 1

i is 0
i is 1

Execution Trace

```
for (int i = 0; i < 3; ++i) {
    System.out.println("i is " + i);
}

System.out.println("all done");
```

i | 1 |

```
i is 0
i is 1
```

Execution Trace

```
for (int i = 0; i < 3; ++i) {
    System.out.println("i is " + i);
}

System.out.println("all done");
```

i | 2 |

```
i is 0
i is 1
```

Execution Trace

```
for (int i = 0; i < 3; ++i) {
    System.out.println("i is " + i);
}

System.out.println("all done");
```

i [2]

```
i is 0
i is 1
```

Execution Trace

```
for (int i = 0; i < 3; ++i) {
    System.out.println("i is " + i);
}

System.out.println("all done");
```

i [2]

```
i is 0
i is 1
i is 2
```

161

Execution Trace

```
for (int i = 0; i < 3; ++i) {
    System.out.println("i is " + i);
}

System.out.println("all done");
```

i [2]

```
i is 0
i is 1
i is 2
```

Execution Trace

```
for (int i = 0; i < 3; ++i) {
    System.out.println("i is " + i);
}

System.out.println("all done");
```

i [3]

```
i is 0
i is 1
i is 2
```

Execution Trace

```
for (int i = 0; i < 3; ++i) {
    System.out.println("i is " + i);
}

System.out.println("all done");
```

i | 3 |

```
i is 0
i is 1
i is 2
```

Execution Trace

```
for (int i = 0; i < 3; ++i) {
    System.out.println("i is " + i);
}

System.out.println("all done");
```

| 3 |

```
i is 0
i is 1
i is 2
all done
```

Variable i has gone
out of scope – it
is *local* to the loop

163

Nested loops

```java
int m = 2;
int n = 3;
for (int i = 0; i < n; ++i) {
    System.out.println("i is " + i);
    for (int j = 0; j < m; ++j) {
        System.out.println("   j is " + j);
    }
}
```

Nested loops

```java
int m = 2;
int n = 3;
for (int i = 0; i < n; ++i) {
    System.out.println("i is " + i);
    for (int j = 0; j < m; ++j) {
        System.out.println("   j is " + j);
    }
}
```

```
i is 0
    j is 0
    j is 1
i is 1
    j is 0
    j is 1
i is 2
    j is 0
    j is 1
```

164

The do-while statement

□ Syntax
> do *Action*
> while (*Expression*)

□ Semantics
- ■ Execute *Action*
- ■ If *Expression* is true then execute *Action* again
- ■ Repeat this process until *Expression* evaluates to false

□ *Action* is either a single statement or a group of statements within braces

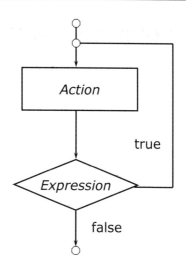

Picking off digits

□ Consider
```
System.out.print("Enter a positive number: ");
int number = Integer.parseInt(stdin.readLine());
do {
    int digit = number % 10;
    System.out.println(digit);
    number = number / 10;
} while (number != 0);
```

□ Sample behavior
```
Enter a positive number: 1129
9
2
1
1
```

165

Problem solving

Internet per 100 people for 189 entities

0.09	0.16	8.97	0.23	6.52	6.75	1.42	13.65	34.45
0.16	4.32	5.84	0.08	3.74	1.78	22.89	6.24	0.25
1.44	1.01	1.54	2.94	9.14	5.28	0.08	0.07	0.05
41.3	1.84	0.04	0.04	16.58	1.74	38.64	13.7	2.07
5.67	0.27	5.59	0.54	17.88	9.71	0.01	36.59	0.22
1.86	1.42	0.71	0.8	0.15	0.13	27.21	73.4	1.47
14.43	6.43	1.22	0.92	0.42	29.18	0.15	9.47	4.36
0.7	0.1	0.25	6.04	0.25	0.62	7.15	59.79	0.54
0.39	20.7	20.26	23.04	3.11	29.31	2.53	0.62	0.65
40.25	7.84	1.06	0.11	6.19	8.58	0.19	0.02	0.18
22.66	0.19	0.15	15.9	2.23	0.17	13.08	1.17	0.19
2.74	39.71	1.26	0.71	0.06	0.01	1.71	0.22	24.39
21.67	0.99	0.04	0.18	49.05	25.05	3.55	0.09	1.1
2.81	0.73	9.74	2.01	7.25	24.94	10.22	5.01	1.2
3.57	0.06	4.79	3.09	0.56	48.7	4.36	0.93	0.42
0.1	29.87	12.03	15.08	0.46	0.01	5.49	13.43	0.64
2.7	0.99	45.58	29.62	0.19	28.1	0.05	3.79	2.47
7.73	2.61	3.06	0.13	0.18	0.69	28.2	30.12	0.33
11.09	0.49	2.03	3.93	0.25	0.08	3.76	0.19	0.37
25.86	0.22	0.27	7.78	37.23	1.75	0.94	1.8	6.09
3.17	18.6	7.4	0.1	0.86	45.07	11.15	7.29	

Data set manipulation

☐ Often five values of particular interest
- Minimum
- Maximum
- Mean
- Standard deviation
- Size of data set

☐ Let's design a data set representation

What facilitators are needed?

Implication on facilitators

- □ public double getMinimum()
  - ■ Returns the minimum value in the data set. If the data set is empty, then Double.NaN is returned, where Double.NaN is the Java double value representing the status not-a-number

- □ public double getMaximum()
  - ■ Returns the maximum value in the data set. If the data set is empty, then Double.NaN is returned

Implication on facilitators

- □ public double getAverage()
  - ■ Returns the average value in the data set. If the data set is empty, then Double.NaN is returned

- □ public double getStandardDeviation()
  - ■ Returns the standard deviation value of the data set. If the data set is empty, then Double.NaN is returned

    - □ Left to the interested student

- □ public int getSize()
  - ■ Returns the number of values in the data set being represented

What constructors are needed?

Constructors

- □ public DataSet()
  - ■ Initializes a representation of an empty data set

- □ public DataSet(String s)
  - ■ Initializes the data set using the values from the file with name s

- □ public DataSet(FileReader filein)
  - ■ Initializes the data set using the values from the file represented by filein
    - □ Left to interested student

169

Other methods

- [ ] public void addValue(double x)
    - Adds the value x to the data set being represented

- [ ] public void clear()
    - Sets the representation to that of an empty data set

- [ ] public void load(String s)
    - Adds the vales from the file with name s to the data set being represented

- [ ] public void load(FileReader filein)
    - Adds the vales from the file represented by filein to the data set being represented
        - [ ] Left to interested student

What instance variables are needed?

Instance variables

- private int n
  - Number of values in the data set being represented

- private double minimumValue
  - Minimum value in the data set being represented

- private double maximumValue
  - Maximum value in the data set being represented

- private double xSum
  - The sum of values in the data set being represented

Example usage

```
DataSet dataset = new DataSet("age.txt");
System.out.println();
System.out.println("Minimum: " + dataset.getMinimum());
System.out.println("Maximum: " + dataset.getMaximum());
System.out.println("Mean: " + dataset.getAverage());
System.out.println("Size: " + dataset.getSize());
System.out.println();
dataset.clear();

dataset.load("stature.txt");
System.out.println("Minimum: " + dataset.getMinimum());
System.out.println("Maximum: " + dataset.getMaximum());
System.out.println("Mean: " + dataset.getAverage());
System.out.println("Size: " + dataset.getSize());
System.out.println();
dataset.clear();
```

171

Example usage

```
dataset.load("foot-length.txt");
System.out.println("Minimum: " + dataset.getMinimum());
System.out.println("Maximum: " + dataset.getMaximum());
System.out.println("Mean: " + dataset.getAverage());
System.out.println("Size: " + dataset.getSize());
System.out.println();
dataset.clear();

System.out.println("Minimum: " + dataset.getMinimum());
System.out.println("Maximum: " + dataset.getMaximum());
System.out.println("Mean: " + dataset.getAverage());
System.out.println("Size: " + dataset.getSize());
System.out.println();
```

Example usage

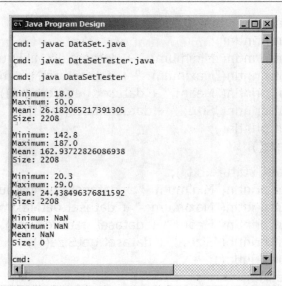

172

Methods getMinimum() and getMaximum()

☐ Straightforward implementations given correct setting of
instance variables

```
public double getMinimum() {
        return minimumValue;
}

public double getMaximum() {
        return maximumValue;
}
```

Method getSize()

☐ Straightforward implementations given correct setting of
instance variables

```
public int getSize() {
        return n;
}
```

Method getAverage()

☐ Need to take into account that data set might be empty

```
public double getAverage() {
        if (n == 0) {
                return Double.NaN;
        }
        else {
                return xSum / n;
        }
}
```

DataSet constructors

☐ Straightforward using clear() and load()

```
public DataSet() {
        clear();
}

public DataSet(String s) throws IOException {
        clear();
        load(s);
}
```

Facilitator clear()

```java
public void clear() {
    n = 0;
    xSum = 0;
    minimumValue = Double.NaN;
    maximumValue = Double.NaN;
}
```

Facilitator add()

```java
public void addValue(double x) {
    xSum += x;
    ++n;
    if (n == 1) {
            minimumValue = maximumValue = x;
    }
    else if (x < minimumValue) {
            minimumValue = x;
    }
    else if (x > maximumValue) {
            maximumValue = x;
    }
}
```

175

Facilitator load()

```java
public void load(String s) throws IOException {
    // get a reader for the file
    BufferedReader fileIn = new BufferedReader(
            new FileReader(s));

    // add values one by one
    String currentLine = fileIn.readLine();
    while (currentLine != null) {
            double x = Double.parseDouble(currentLine);
            addValue(x);
            currentLine = fileIn.readLine();
    }

    // close up file
    fileIn.close();
}
```

Programming with methods and classes

Methods

- □ Instance method
    - ■ Operates on a object (i.e., and *instance* of the class)

    ```
    String s = new String("Help every cow reach its "
        + "potential!");
    int n = s.length();  ← Instance method
    ```

- □ Class method
    - ■ Service provided by a class and it is not associated with a particular object

    ```
    String t = String.valueOf(n);  ← Class method
    ```

Data fields

- ☐ Instance variable and instance constants
  - ■ Attribute of a particular object
  - ■ Usually a variable

  ```
  Point p = new Point(5, 5);
  int px = p.x;    ← Instance variable
  ```

- ☐ Class variable and constants
  - ■ Collective information that is not specific to individual objects of the class
  - ■ Usually a constant

  ```
  Color favoriteColor = Color.MAGENTA;
  double favoriteNumber = MATH.PI - MATH.E;
                              ← Class constants
  ```

Task – Conversion.java

- ☐ Support conversion between English and metric values
  - ■ d degrees Fahrenheit = (d – 32)/1.8 degrees Celsius
  - ■ 1 mile = 1.609344 kilometers
  - ■ 1 gallon = 3.785411784 liters
  - ■ 1 ounce (avdp) = 28.349523125 grams
  - ■ 1 acre = 0.0015625 square miles = 0.40468564 hectares

Conversion Implementation

```
public class Conversion {

    // conversion equivalencies
    private static final double
        KILOMETERS_PER_MILE = 1.609344;
    private static final double
        LITERS_PER_GALLON = 3.785411784;
    private static final double
        GRAMS_PER_OUNCE = 28.349523125;
    private static final double
        HECTARES_PER_ACRE = 0.40468564;
```

Conversion Implementation

```
    // temperature conversions methods
    public static double fahrenheitToCelsius(double f) {
        return (f - 32) / 1.8;
    }

    public static double celsiusToFahrenheit(double c) {
        return 1.8 * c + 32;
    }

    // length conversions methods
    public static double kilometersToMiles(double km) {
        return km / KILOMETERS_PER_MILE;
    }
```

Conversion implementation

Modifier public indicates other classes can use the method

Modifier static indicates the method is a class method

```
public static double fahrenheitToCelsius(double f) {
    return (f - 32) / 1.8;
}
```

Observe there is no reference in the method to an attribute of an implicit Conversion object (i.e., a "this" object). This absence is a class method requirement. Class methods are invoked without respect to any particular object

Conversion Implementation

```
// mass conversions methods
public static double litersToGallons(double liters) {
    return liters / LITERS_PER_GALLON;
}

public static double gallonsToLiters(double gallons) {
    return gallons * LITERS_PER_GALLON;
}

public static double gramsToOunces(double grams) {
    return grams / GRAMS_PER_OUNCE;
}

public static double ouncesToGrams(double ounces) {
    return ounces * GRAMS_PER_OUNCE;
}
```

Conversion Implementation

```java
// area conversions methods
public static double hectaresToAcres(double hectares) {
    return hectares / HECTARES_PER_ACRE;
}

public static double acresToHectares(double acres) {
    return acres * HECTARES_PER_ACRE;
}
}
```

Conversion use

Consider

```java
BufferedReader stdin = new BufferedReader(
    new InputStreamReader(System.in));

System.out.print("Enter a mass in liters: ");
double liters = Double.parseDouble(stdin.readLine());

System.out.print("Enter a mass in grams: ");
double grams = Double.parseDouble(stdin.readLine());

double gallons = Conversion.litersToGallons(liters);
double ounces = Conversion.gramsToOunces(grams);
```

Produces

```
3.0 liters = 0.7925161570744452 gallons
4.0 grams = 0.14109584779832166 ounces
```

181

A preferred Conversion use

Part of java.text

```
NumberFormat style = NumberFormat.getNumberInstance();

style.setMaximumFractionDigits(2);
style.setMinimumFractionDigits(2);

System.out.println(liters + " liters = "
      + style.format(gallons) + " gallons");
System.out.println(grams + " grams = "
      + style.format(ounces) + " ounces");
```

```
3.0 liters = 0.79 gallons
4.0 grams = 0.14 ounces
```

Method invocations

- ☐ Actual parameters provide information that is otherwise unavailable to a method

- ☐ When a method is invoked
  - ■ Java sets aside memory for that particular invocation
    - ☐ Called the *activation record*
      - ■ Activation record stores, among other things, the values of the formal parameters

  - ■ Formal parameters initialized with values of the actual parameters
    - ☐ After initialization, the actual parameters and formal parameters are independent of each other

  - ■ Flow of control is transferred temporarily to that method

182

Value parameter passing demonstration

```java
public class Demo {
    public static double add(double x, double y) {
        double result = x + y;
        return result;
    }

    public static double multiply(double x, double y) {
        x = x * y;
        return x;
    }

    public static void main(String[] args) {
        double a = 8;
        double b = 11;

        double sum = add(a, b);
        System.out.println(a + " + " + b + " = " + sum);

        double product = multiply(a, b);
        System.out.println(a + " * " + b + " = " + product);
    }
}
```

Value parameter passing demonstration

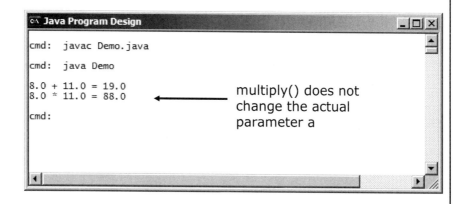

183

Demo.java walkthrough

```
                            double sum = add(a, b);
    Initial values of formal
parameters come from the    ──►
    actual parameters
public static double add(double x, double y) {
    double result = x + y
    return result;
}
```

main()	
a	8.0
b	11.0
sum	19.0
product	-

add()	
x	8.0
y	11.0
result	19.0

Demo.java walkthrough

```
                    double multiply = multiply(a, b);
Initial values of formal parameters
 come from the actual parameters    ──►

public static double multiply(double x, double y) {
    x = x + y
    return x;
}
```

main()	
a	8.0
b	11.0
sum	19.0
product	88.0

multiply()	
x	88.0
y	11.0

PassingReferences.java run

```
C:\  Java Program Design                          _ □ ✕

cmd:   javac PassingReferences.java

cmd:   java PassingReferences

java.awt.Point[x=10, y=10]
java.awt.Point[x=10, y=10]
java.awt.Point[x=0, y=0]  ←

cmd:
```

g() can change the attributes of the object to which p refers

---

PassingReferences.java

```java
public static void main(String[] args) {
    Point p = new Point(10, 10);
    System.out.println(p);

    f(p);
```

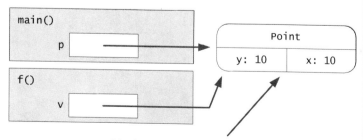

java.awt.Point[x=10, y=10]

Method main()'s variable p and method f()'s formal parameter v have the same value, which is a reference to an object representing location (10, 10)

185

PassingReferences.java

```java
public class PassingReferences {
    public static void f(Point v) {
        v = new Point(0, 0);
    }

    public static void g(Point v) {
        v.setLocation(0, 0);
    }

    public static void main(String[] args) {
        Point p = new Point(10, 10);
        System.out.println(p);

        f(p);
        System.out.println(p);

        g(p);
        System.out.println(p);
    }
}
```

PassingReferences.java

```java
public static void f(Point v) {
    v = new Point(0, 0);
}
```

186

PassingReferences.java

```
public static void main(String[] args) {
    Point p = new Point(10, 10);
    System.out.println(p);

    f(p);
```

```
    System.out
    g(p);
```

Method main()'s variable p and method g()'s formal parameter v have the same value, which is a reference to an object representing location (10, 10)

```
java.awt.Point[x=10,y=10]
java.awt.Point[x=10,y=10]
```

What's wrong?

```
class Scope {
    public static void f(int a) {
        int b = 1;                  // local definition
        System.out.println(a);  // print 10
        a = b;                      // update a
        System.out.println(a);  // print 1
    }

    public static void main(String[] args) {
        int i = 10;             // local definition
        f(i);                       // invoking f() with i as parameter
        System.out.println(a);
        System.out.println(b);
    }
}
```

Variables a and b do not exist in the *scope* of method main()

187

PassingReferences.java

```
public static void g(Point v) {
    v.setLocation(0, 0);
}
```

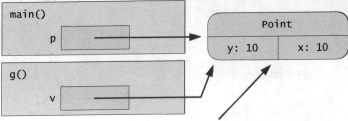

Method main()'s variable p and method
g()'s formal parameter v have the same
value, which is a reference to an object
representing location (10, 10)

PassingReferences.java

```
public static void main(String[] args) {
    Point p = new Point(10, 10);
    System.out.println(p);

    f(p);
```

```
System.out.println(p);

    g(p);
    System.out.println(p);
```

```
java.awt.Point[x=10,y=10]
java.awt.Point[x=10,y=10]
java.awt.Point[x=0,y=0]
```

Blocks and scope rules

- ☐ A block is a list of statements nested within braces
  - ■ A method body is a block
  - ■ A block can be placed anywhere a statement would be legal
    - ☐ A block contained within another block is a nested block

- ☐ A formal parameter is considered to be defined at the beginning of the method body

- ☐ A local variable can be used only in a statement or nested blocks that occurs after its definition

- ☐ An identifier name can be reused as long as the blocks containing the duplicate declarations are not nested one within the other

- ☐ Name reuse within a method is permitted as long as the reuse occurs in distinct blocks

Legal

```
class Scope2 {
    public static void main(String[] args) {
        int a = 10;
        f(a);
        System.out.println(a);
    }

    public static void f(int a) {
        System.out.println(a);
        a = 1;
        System.out.println(a);
    }
}
```

Legal but not recommended

```
public void g() {
    {
        int j = 1;                    // define j
        System.out.println(j);        // print 1
    }
    {
        int j = 10;                   // define a different j
        System.out.println(j);        // print 10
    }
    {
        char j = '@';                 // define a different j
        System.out.println(j);        // print '@'
    }
}
```

What's the output?

```
for (int i = 0; i < 3; ++i) {
    int j = 0;
    ++j;
    System.out.println(j);
}
```

☐ The scope of variable j is the body of the for loop
  ■ j is not in scope when ++i
  ■ j is not in scope when i < 3 are evaluated
  ■ j is redefined and re-initialized with each loop iteration

Task – Triple.java

☐ Represent objects with three integer attributes

☐ What constructors should we have?

☐ What accessors and mutators should we have?

☐ What facilitators should we have?

Task – Triple.java

☐ `public Triple()`   , three zeros
  - Constructs a default Triple value repre′

☐ public Triple(int a, int b, int c)   ɘs a, b, and c
  - Constructs a representation of th

Task – Triple.java

☐ public int getValue(int i)
- Returns the i-th element of the associated Triple

☐ public void setValue(int i, int value)
- Sets the i-th element of the associated Triple to value

☐ ⋯k – Triple.java

- String toString()
- ⋯s a textual representation of the associated Triple
☐ public ⋯

- Return⋯lone()
  the asso⋯w Triple whose representation is the same as ⋯Triple
☐ public boolean ⋯

- Returns wheth⋯Object v)
  ⋯equivalent to the associated Triple

These three met⋯
inherited methods ⋯re overrides of

192

Triple.java implementation

```java
// Triple(): specific constructor
public Triple(int a, int b, int c) {
    setValue(1, a);
    setValue(2, b);
    setValue(3, c);
}
```

Triple.java implementation

```java
// Triple(): specific constructor - alternative definition
public Triple(int a, int b, int c) {
    this.setValue(1, a);
    this.setValue(2, b);
    this.setValue(3, c);
}
```

Triple.java implementation

```
// Triple(): default constructor
public Triple() {
    this(0, 0, 0);
}
```
The new Triple object (the this object) is constructed by invoking the Triple constructor expecting three int values as actual parameters

```
public Triple() {
    int a = 0;
    int b = 0;
    int c = 0;
    this(a, b, c);
}
```
Illegal this() invocation. A this() invocation must begin its statement body

Triple.java implementation

- ☐ Class Triple like every other Java class
  - ■ Automatically an extension of the standard class Object
  - ■ Class Object specifies some basic behaviors common to all objects
    - ☐ These behaviors are said to be inherited

  - ■ Three of the inherited Object methods
    - ☐ toString()
    - ☐ clone()
    - ☐ equals()

194

Recommendation

- Classes should override (i.e., provide a class-specific implementation)
    - toString()
    - clone()
    - equals()

- By doing so, the programmer-expected behavior can be provided

```
System.out.println(p); // displays string version of
                       // object referenced by p
System.out.println(q); // displays string version of
                       // object referenced by q
```

Triple.java toString() implementation

```java
public String toString() {
    int a = getValue(1);
    int b = getValue(2);
    int c = getValue(3);

    return "Triple[" + a + ", " + b + ", " + c + "]");
}
```

- Consider

```java
Triple t1 = new Triple(10, 20, 30);
System.out.println(t1);

Triple t2 = new Triple(8, 88, 888);
System.out.println(t2);
```

- Produces

```
Triple[10, 20, 30]
Triple[8, 88, 888]
```

Triple.java clone() implementation

```
public object clone() {  ← Return type is Object
    int a = getValue(1);    (Every class is a specialized Object)
    int b = getValue(2);
    int c = getValue(3);

    return new Triple(a, b, c);
}
```

☐ Consider

```
    Triple t1 = new Triple(9, 28, 29);
    Triple t2 = (Triple) t1.clone();   ← Must cast!

    System.out.println("t1 = " + t1);
    System.out.println("t2 = " + t2);
```

☐ Produces

```
Triple[9, 28, 29]
Triple[9, 28, 29]
```

Triple.java equals() implementation

```
public boolean equals(Object v) {   Can't be equal
    if (v instanceof Triple) {  ← unless it's a Triple
        int a1 = getValue(1);
        int b1 = getValue(2);
        int c1 = getValue(3);

        Triple t = (Triple) v;
        int a2 = t.getValue(1);
        int b2 = t.getValue(2);
        int c2 = t.getValue(3);

        return (a1 == a2) && (b1 == b2) && (c1 == c2);
    }
    else {                         ↖ Compare corresponding
        return false;                  attributes
    }
}
```

Triple.java equals()

```
Triple e = new Triple(4, 6, 10);
Triple f = new Triple(4, 6, 11);,
Triple g = new Triple(4, 6, 10);
Triple h = new Triple(4, 5, 11);
boolean flag1 = e.equals(f);
```

Triple.java equals()

```
Triple e = new Triple(4, 6, 10);
Triple f = new Triple(4, 6, 11);,
Triple g = new Triple(4, 6, 10);
Triple h = new Triple(4, 5, 11);
boolean flag2 = e.equals(g);
```

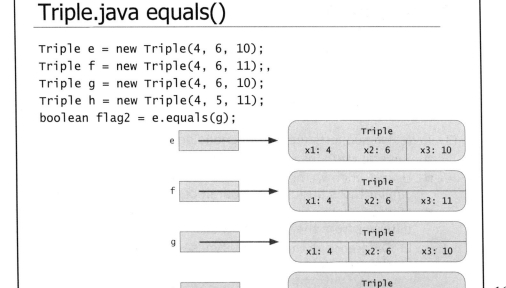

197

Triple.java equals()

```
Triple e = new Triple(4, 6, 10);
Triple f = new Triple(4, 6, 11);,
Triple g = new Triple(4, 6, 10);
Triple h = new Triple(4, 5, 11);
boolean flag3 = g.equals(h);
```

		Triple		
e	→	x1: 4	x2: 6	x3: 10

		Triple		
f	→	x1: 4	x2: 6	x3: 11

		Triple		
g	→	x1: 4	x2: 6	x3: 10

		Triple		
h	→	x1: 4	x2: 5	x3: 11

Overloading

- Have seen it often before with operators
  ```
  int i = 11 + 28;
  double x = 6.9 + 11.29;
  String s = "April " + "June";
  ```

- Java also supports method overloading
  - Several methods can have the same name
  - Useful when we need to write methods that perform similar tasks but different parameter lists
  - Method name can be overloaded as long as its signature is different from the other methods of its class
    - Difference in the names, types, number, or order of the parameters

198

Legal

```
public static int min(int a, int b, int c) {
    return Math.min(a, Math.min(b, c));
}

public static int min(int a, int b, int c, int d) {
    return Math.min(a, min(b, c, d));
}
```

Legal

```
public static int power(int x, int n) {
    int result = 1;
    for (int i = 1; i <= n; ++i) {
        result *= x;
    }
    return result;
}

public static double power(double x, int n) {
    double result = 1;
    for (int i = 1; i <= n; ++i) {
        result *= x;
    }
    return result;
}
```

199

What's the output?

```
public static void f(int a, int b) {
    System.out.println(a + b);
}

public static void f(double a, double b) {
    System.out.println(a - b);
}

public static void main(String[] args) {
    int i = 19;
    double x = 54;

    f(i, x);
}
```

Arrays

Background

☐ Programmer often need the ability to represent a group of values as a list
  - List may be one-dimensional or multidimensional

☐ Java provides arrays and the collection classes

☐ Consider arrays first

Basic terminology

☐ List is composed of *elements*

☐ Elements in a list have a *common name*

☐ The list as a whole is referenced through the common name

☐ List elements are of the same type — the base type

☐ Elements of a list are referenced by *subscripting* (indexing) the common name

Java array features

☐ Subscripts are denoted as expressions within brackets: [ ]

☐ Base (element) type can be any type

☐ Size of array can be specified at run time

☐ Index type is integer and the index range must be 0 ... n-1
   ■ Where n is the number of elements

☐ Automatic bounds checking
   ■ Ensures any reference to an array element is valid

☐ Data field length specifies the number of elements in the list

☐ Array is an object
   ■ Has features common to all other objects

Array variable definition styles

☐ Without initialization

$$ElementType[] \quad id \quad ;$$

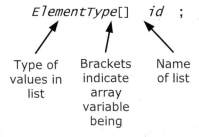

| Type of values in list | Brackets indicate array variable being | Name of list |

Array variable definition styles

☐ With initialization

Nonnegative integer expression specifying
number of elements in the array

↓

$$ElementType[] \quad id \quad = \text{new} \quad ElementType[n];$$

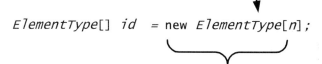

Reference to a new array of n
elements

203

Example

☐ Definitions
```
char[] c;
int[] value = new int[10];
```

☐ Causes
- Array object variable c is un-initialized
- Array object variable v references a new ten element list of integers
  - ☐ Each of the integers is default initialized to 0

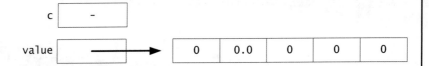

Consider

```
int[] v = new int[10];
int i = 7;
int j = 2;
int k = 4;
v[0] = 1;
v[i] = 5;
v[j] = v[i] + 3;
v[j+1] = v[i] + v[0];
v[v[j]] = 12;
System.out.println(v[2]);
v[k] = Integer.parseInt(stdin.readLine());
```

v	0	0	0	0	0	0	0	0	0	0
	v[0]	v[1]	v[2]	v[3]	v[4]	v[5]	v[6]	v[7]	v[8]	v[9]

Consider

```
int[] v = new int[10];
int i = 7;
int j = 2;
int k = 4;
v[0] = 1;
v[i] = 5;
v[j] = v[i] + 3;
v[j+1] = v[i] + v[0];
v[v[j]] = 12;
System.out.println(v[2]);
v[k] = Integer.parseInt(stdin.readLine());
```

v	1	0	0	0	0	0	0	0	0	0
	v[0]	v[1]	v[2]	v[3]	v[4]	v[5]	v[6]	v[7]	v[8]	v[9]

Consider

```
int[] v = new int[10];
int i = 7;
int j = 2;
int k = 4;
v[0] = 1;
v[i] = 5;
v[j] = v[i] + 3;
v[j+1] = v[i] + v[0];
v[v[j]] = 12;
System.out.println(v[2]);
v[k] = Integer.parseInt(stdin.readLine());
```

v	1	0	0	0	0	0	0	5	0	0
	v[0]	v[1]	v[2]	v[3]	v[4]	v[5]	v[6]	v[7]	v[8]	v[9]

Consider

```
int[] v = new int[10];
int i = 7;
int j = 2;
int k = 4;
v[0] = 1;
v[i] = 5;
v[j] = v[i] + 3;
v[j+1] = v[i] + v[0];
v[v[j]] = 12;
System.out.println(v[2]);
v[k] = Integer.parseInt(stdin.readLine());
```

v	1	0	8	0	0	0	0	5	0	0
	v[0]	v[1]	v[2]	v[3]	v[4]	v[5]	v[6]	v[7]	v[8]	v[9]

Consider

```
int[] v = new int[10];
int i = 7;
int j = 2;
int k = 4;
v[0] = 1;
v[i] = 5;
v[j] = v[i] + 3;
v[j+1] = v[i] + v[0];
v[v[j]] = 12;
System.out.println(v[2]);
v[k] = Integer.parseInt(stdin.readLine());
```

v	1	0	8	6	0	0	0	5	0	0
	v[0]	v[1]	v[2]	v[3]	v[4]	v[5]	v[6]	v[7]	v[8]	v[9]

Consider

```
int[] v = new int[10];
int i = 7;
int j = 2;
int k = 4;
v[0] = 1;
v[i] = 5;
v[j] = v[i] + 3;
v[j+1] = v[i] + v[0];
v[v[j]] = 12;
System.out.println(v[2]);
v[k] = Integer.parseInt(stdin.readLine());
```

v	1	0	8	6	0	0	0	5	12	0
	v[0]	v[1]	v[2]	v[3]	v[4]	v[5]	v[6]	v[7]	v[8]	v[9]

Consider

```
int[] v = new int[10];
int i = 7;
int j = 2;
int k = 4;
v[0] = 1;
v[i] = 5;
v[j] = v[i] + 3;
v[j+1] = v[i] + v[0];
v[v[j]] = 12;
System.out.println(v[2]);
v[k] = Integer.parseInt(stdin.readLine());
```

8 is displayed

v	1	0	8	6	0	0	0	5	12	0
	v[0]	v[1]	v[2]	v[3]	v[4]	v[5]	v[6]	v[7]	v[8]	v[9]

207

Consider

```
int[] v = new int[10];
int i = 7;
int j = 2;
int k = 4;
v[0] = 1;
v[i] = 5;
v[j] = v[i] + 3;
v[j+1] = v[i] + v[0];
v[v[j]] = 12;
System.out.println(v[2]);
v[k] = Integer.parseInt(stdin.readLine());
```

Suppose 3 is extracted

v	1	0	8	6	3	0	0	5	12	0
	v[0]	v[1]	v[2]	v[3]	v[4]	v[5]	v[6]	v[7]	v[8]	v[9]

Consider

□ Segment
```
int[] b = new int[100];
b[-1] = 0;
b[100] = 0;
```

□ Causes
- Array variable to reference a new list of 100 integers
  - □ Each element is initialized to 0
- Two exceptions to be thrown
  - □ -1 is not a valid index – too small
  - □ 100 is not a valid index – too large

- IndexOutOfBoundsException

Consider

```
Point[] p = new Point[3];
p[0] = new Point(0, 0);
p[1] = new Point(1, 1);
p[2] = new Point(2, 2);
p[0].setX(1);
p[1].setY(p[2].getY());
Point vertex = new Point(4,4);
p[1] = p[0];
p[2] = vertex;
```

Consider

```
Point[] p = new Point[3];
p[0] = new Point(0, 0);
p[1] = new Point(1, 1);
p[2] = new Point(2, 2);
p[0].setX(1);
p[1].setY(p[2].getY());
Point vertex = new Point(4,4);
p[1] = p[0];
p[2] = vertex;
```

209

Consider

```
Point[] p = new Point[3];
p[0] = new Point(0, 0);
p[1] = new Point(1, 1);
p[2] = new Point(2, 2);
p[0].setX(1);
p[1].setY(p[2].getY());
Point vertex = new Point(4,4);
p[1] = p[0];
p[2] = vertex;
```

Consider

```
Point[] p = new Point[3];
p[0] = new Point(0, 0);
p[1] = new Point(1, 1);
p[2] = new Point(2, 2);
p[0].setX(1);
p[1].setY(p[2].getY());
Point vertex = new Point(4,4);
p[1] = p[0];
p[2] = vertex;
```

Consider

```
Point[] p = new Point[3];
p[0] = new Point(0, 0);
p[1] = new Point(1, 1);
p[2] = new Point(2, 2);
p[0].setX(1);
p[1].setY(p[2].getY());
Point vertex = new Point(4,4);
p[1] = p[0];
p[2] = vertex;
```

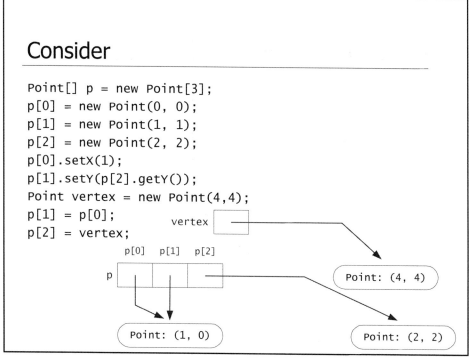

Consider

```
Point[] p = new Point[3];
p[0] = new Point(0, 0);
p[1] = new Point(1, 1);
p[2] = new Point(2, 2);
p[0].setX(1);
p[1].setY(p[2].getY());
Point vertex = new Point(4,4);
p[1] = p[0];
p[2] = vertex;
```

211

Consider

```
Point[] p = new Point[3];
p[0] = new Point(0, 0);
p[1] = new Point(1, 1);
p[2] = new Point(2, 2);
p[0].setX(1);
p[1].setY(p[2].getY());
Point vertex = new Point(4,4);
p[1] = p[0];
p[2] = vertex;
```

Explicit initialization

□ Syntax

id references an array of n elements. id[0] has
value exp_0, id[1] has value exp_1, and so on.

$$ElementType[] \quad id = \{ \ exp_0 \ , \ exp_1 \ , \ \ldots \ exp_{n-1} \ \};$$

Each exp_i is an expression that
evaluates to type ElementType

212

Explicit initialization

☐ Example
```
String[] puppy = { "nilla", "darby", "galen",
    "panther" };
int[] unit = { 1 };
```

☐ Equivalent to
```
String[] puppy = new String[4];
puppy[0] = "nilla";    puppy[1] = "darby";
puppy[2] = "galen";    puppy[4] = "panther";

int[] unit = new int[1];
unit[0] = 1;
```

Array members

☐ Member length
- Size of the array
```
for (int i = 0; i < puppy.length; ++i) {
    System.out.println(puppy[i]);
}
```

Array members

□ Member clone()
- ■ Produces a shallow copy
```
Point[] u = { new Point(0, 0), new Point(1, 1)};
Point[] v = u.clone();
                    v[1] = new Point(4, 30);
```

Array members

□ Member clone()
- ■ Produces a shallow copy
```
Point[] u = { new Point(0, 0), new Point(1, 1)};
Point[] v = u.clone();
                    v[1] = new Point(4, 30);
```

214

Array members

☐ Member clone()
- Produces a shallow copy
```
Point[] u = { new Point(0, 0), new Point(1, 1)};
Point[] v = u.clone();
                            v[1] = new Point(4, 30);
```

Making a deep copy

☐ Example
```
Point[] w = new Point[u.length];
for (int i = 0; i < u.length; ++i) {
    w[i] = u[i].clone();
}
```

Making a deep copy

Searching for a value

```
System.out.println("Enter search value (number): ");
int key = Integer.parseInt(stdin.readLine());

int index = -1; // assume its not there

for (int i = 0; i < data.length; ++i) {
    if (key == data[i]) {
        index = i; // its there
        break;
    }
}
if (index != -1) {
    System.out.println(key + " is the " + i + "-th element");
}
else {
    System.out.println(key + " is not in the list");
}
```

216

Searching for a value

```
System.out.println("Enter search value (number): ");
int key = Integer.parseInt(stdin.readLine());

int index = -1; // assume its not there

for (int i = 0; i < data.length; ++i) {
    if (key == data[i]) {
        index = i; // its there
        break;
    }
}

if (index != -1) {
    System.out.println(key + " is the " + i + "-th element");
}
else {
    System.out.println(key + " is not in the list");
}
```

Searching for a value

```
System.out.println("Enter search value (number): ");
int key = Integer.parseInt(stdin.readLine());

int index = -1; // assume its not there

for (int i = 0; i < data.length; ++i) {
    if (key == data[i]) {
        index = i; // its there
        break;
    }
}

if (index != -1) {
    System.out.println(key + " is the " + i + "-th element");
}
else {
    System.out.println(key + " is not in the list");
}
```

217

Searching for a value

```
System.out.println("Enter search value (number): ");
int key = Integer.parseInt(stdin.readLine());

int index = -1; // assume its not there

for (int i = 0; i < data.length; ++i) {
    if (key == data[i]) {
        index = i; // its there
        break;
    }
}

if (index != -1) {
    System.out.println(key + " is the " + i + "-th element");
}
else {
    System.out.println(key + " is not in the list");
}
```

	0	1	2
data	4	9	5

key	5	i	0

index	-1

Searching for a value

```
System.out.println("Enter search value (number): ");
int key = Integer.parseInt(stdin.readLine());

int index = -1; // assume its not there

for (int i = 0; i <data.length; ++i) {
    if (key == data[i]) {
        index = i; // its there
        break;
    }
}

if (index != -1) {
    System.out.println(key + " is the " + i + "-th element");
}
else {
    System.out.println(key + " is not in the list");
}
```

	0	1	2
data	4	9	5

key	5	i	0

index	-1

Searching for a value

```
System.out.println("Enter search value (number): ");
int key = Integer.parseInt(stdin.readLine());

int index = -1; // assume its not there

for (int i = 0; i < data.length; ++i) {
    if (key == data[i]) {
        index = i; // its there
        break;
    }
}

if (index != -1) {
    System.out.println(key + " is the " + i + "-th element");
}
else {
    System.out.println(key + " is not in the list");
}
```

	0	1	2
data	4	9	5

key: 5   i: 0

index: -1

Searching for a value

```
System.out.println("Enter search value (number): ");
int key = Integer.parseInt(stdin.readLine());

int index = -1; // assume its not there

for (int i = 0; i < data.length; ++i) {
    if (key == data[i]) {
        index = i; // its there
        break;
    }
}

if (index != -1) {
    System.out.println(key + " is the " + i + "-th element");
}
else {
    System.out.println(key + " is not in the list");
}
```

	0	1	2
data	4	9	5

key: 5   i: 1

index: -1

Searching for a value

```
System.out.println("Enter search value (number): ");
int key = Integer.parseInt(stdin.readLine());

int index = -1; // assume its not there

for (int i = 0; i < data.length; ++i) {
    if (key == data[i]) {
        index = i; // its there
        break;
    }
}

if (index != -1) {
    System.out.println(key + " is the " + i + "-th element");
}
else {
    System.out.println(key + " is not in the list");
}
```

	0	1	2
data	4	9	5

key	5	i	1

index	-1

Searching for a value

```
System.out.println("Enter search value (number): ");
int key = Integer.parseInt(stdin.readLine());

int index = -1; // assume its not there

for (int i = 0; i < data.length; ++i) {
    if (key == data[i]) {
        index = i; // its there
        break;
    }
}

if (index != -1) {
    System.out.println(key + " is the " + i + "-th element");
}
else {
    System.out.println(key + " is not in the list");
}
```

	0	1	2
data	4	9	5

key	5	i	1

index	-1

Searching for a value

```
System.out.println("Enter search value (number): ");
int key = Integer.parseInt(stdin.readLine());

int index = -1; // assume its not there

for (int i = 0; i < data.length; ++i) {
    if (key == data[i]) {
        index = i; // its there
        break;
    }
}

if (index != -1) {
    System.out.println(key + " is the " + i + "-th element");
}
else {
    System.out.println(key + " is not in the list");
}
```

	0	1	2
data	4	9	5

key 5   i 2

index -1

Searching for a value

```
System.out.println("Enter search value (number): ");
int key = Integer.parseInt(stdin.readLine());

int index = -1; // assume its not there

for (int i = 0; i < data.length; ++i) {
    if (key == data[i]) {
        index = i; // its there
        break;
    }
}

if (index != -1) {
    System.out.println(key + " is the " + i + "-th element");
}
else {
    System.out.println(key + " is not in the list");
}
```

	0	1	2
data	4	9	5

key 5   i 2

index -1

221

Searching for a value

```
System.out.println("Enter search value (number): ");
int key = Integer.parseInt(stdin.readLine());

int index = -1; // assume its not there

for (int i = 0; i < data.length; ++i) {
    if (key == data[i]) {
        index = i; // its there
        break;
    }
}

if (index != -1) {
    System.out.println(key + " is the " + i + "-th element");
}
else {
    System.out.println(key + " is not in the list");
}
```

```
          0   1   2
data      4   9   5
key       5     i  2
index    -1
```

Searching for a value

```
System.out.println("Enter search value (number): ");
int key = Integer.parseInt(stdin.readLine());

int index = -1; // assume its not there

for (int i = 0; i < data.length; ++i) {
    if (key == data[i]) {
        index = i; // its there
        break;
    }
}

if (index != -1) {
    System.out.println(key + " is the " + i + "-th element");
}
else {
    System.out.println(key + " is not in the list");
}
```

```
          0   1   2
data      4   9   5
key       5     i  2
index     2
```

222

Searching for a value

```
System.out.println("Enter search value (number): ");
int key = Integer.parseInt(stdin.readLine());

int index = -1; // assume its not there

for (int i = 0; i < data.length; ++i) {
    if (key == data[i]) {
        index = i; // its there
        break;
    }
}

if (index != -1) {
    System.out.println(key + " is the " + i + "-th element");
}
else {
    System.out.println(key + " is not in the list");
}
```

	0	1	2
data	4	9	5

key `5`   i `2`

index `2`

Searching for a value

```
System.out.println("Enter search value (number): ");
int key = Integer.parseInt(stdin.readLine());

int index = -1; // assume its not there

for (int i = 0; i < data.length; ++i) {
    if (key == data[i]) {
        index = i; // its there
        break;
    }
}

if (index != -1) {
    System.out.println(key + " is the " + i + "-th element");
}
else {
    System.out.println(key + " is not in the list");
}
```

	0	1	2
data	4	9	5

key `5`

index `2`

Searching for the minimum value

- Segment

```
int minimumSoFar = sample[0];
for (int i = 1; i < sample.length; ++i) {
    if (sample[i] < minimumSoFar) {
        minimumSoFar = sample[i];
    }
}
```

ArrayTools.java method sequentialSearch()

```
public static int sequentialSearch(int[] data, int key) {
    for (int i = 0; i < data.length; ++i) {
        if (data[i] == key) {
            return i;
        }
    }

    return -1;
}
```

- Consider

```
int[] score = { 6, 9, 82, 11, 29, 85, 11, 28, 91 };
int i1 = sequentialSearch(score, 11);
int i2 = sequentialSearch(score, 30);
```

ArrayTools.java method sequentialSearch()

```
public static int sequentialSearch(int[] data, int key) {
    for (int i = 0; i < data.length; ++i) {
        if (data[i] == key) {
            return i;
        }
    }
    return -1;
}
```

key | 11 |

	0	1	2	3	4	5	6	7	8
data	6	9	82	11	29	85	11	29	91

☐ Consider
```
        int[] score = { 6, 9, 82, 11, 29, 85, 11, 28, 91 };
        int i1 = sequentialSearch(score, 11);
        int i2 = sequentialSearch(score, 30);
```

ArrayTools.java method putList()

```
public static void putList(int[] data) {
    for (int i = 0; i < data.length; ++i) {
        System.out.println(data[i]);
    }
}
```

☐ Consider
```
        int[] score = { 6, 9, 82, 11, 29, 85, 11, 28, 91 };
        putList(score);
```

```
public static int[] getList() throws IOException {
    BufferedReader stdin = new BufferedReader(
            new InputStreamReader(System.in));
    int[] buffer = new int[MAX_LIST_SIZE];
    int listSize = 0;
    for (int i = 0; i < MAX_LIST_SIZE; ++i) {
        String v = stdin.readLine();
        if (v != null) {
                int number = Integer.parseInt(v);
                buffer[i] = number;
                ++listSize;
        }
        else {
                break;                      ArrayTools.java
        }                                   method getList()
    }
    int[] data = new int[listSize];
    for (int i = 0; i < listSize; ++i) {
        data[i] = buffer[i];
    }
    return data;
}
```

ArrayTools.java – outline

```
public class ArrayTools {

    // class constant
    private static final int MAX_LIST_SIZE = 1000;

    // sequentialSearch(): examine unsorted list for key
    public static int binarySearch(int[] data, int key) { ...

    // putList(): produces a string representation
    public static void putList(int[] data) { ...

    // getList(): extract and return up to MAX_LIST_SIZE values
    public static int[] getList() throws IOException { ...

    // reverse(): reverses the order of the element values
    public static void reverse(int[] list) { ...

    // binarySearch(): examine sorted list for a key
    public static int binarySearch(char[] data, char key) { ...
}
```

Demo.java

```java
import java.io.*;

public class Demo {
    // main(): application entry point
    public static void main(String[] args) throws IOException {
        System.out.println("");
        System.out.println("Enter list of integers:");
        int[] number = ArrayTools.getList();

        System.out.println("");
        System.out.println("Your list");
        ArrayTools.putList(number);

        ArrayTools.reverse(number);
        System.out.println("");
        System.out.println("Your list in reverse");
        ArrayTools.putList(number);
        System.out.println();
    }
}
```

```
 c:\ Java Program Design                                    _ □ ✕

cmd: javac ArrayTools.java

cmd: javac Demo.java

cmd: java Demo

Enter list of integers, one per line:
12
11
10
^Z

Your list
12
11
10

Your list in reverse
10
11
12

cmd:
```

Sorting

- ☐ Problem
  - ■ Arranging elements so that they are ordered according to some desired scheme
    - ☐ Standard is non-decreasing order
      - ■ Why don't we say increasing order?

- ☐ Major tasks
  - ■ Comparisons of elements
  - ■ Updates or element movement

Selection sorting

- ☐ Algorithm basis
  - ■ On iteration i, a selection sorting method
    - ☐ Finds the element containing the ith smallest value of its list v and exchanges that element with v[i]

- ☐ Example – iteration 0
  - ■ Swaps smallest element with v[0]
  - ■ This results in smallest element being in the correct place for a sorted result

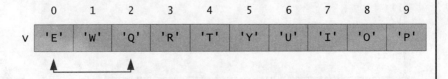

Selection sorting

☐ Algorithm basis
- On iteration i, a selection sorting method
  ☐ Finds the element containing the ith smallest value of its list v and exchanges that element with v[i]

☐ Example – iteration 0
- Swaps smallest element with v[0]
- This results in smallest element being in the correct place for a sorted result

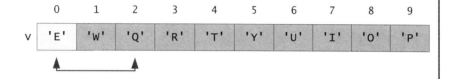

Selection sorting

☐ Algorithm basis
- On iteration i, a selection sorting method
  ☐ Finds the element containing the ith smallest value of its list v and exchanges that element with v[i]

☐ Example – iteration 1
- Swaps second smallest element with v[1]
- This results in second smallest element being in the correct place for a sorted result

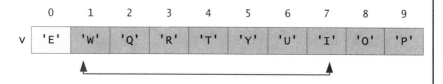

229

Selection sorting

□ Algorithm basis
- On iteration i, a selection sorting method
  □ Finds the element containing the ith smallest value of its list v and exchanges that element with v[i]

□ Example – iteration 1
- Swaps second smallest element with v[1]
- This results in second smallest element being in the correct place for a sorted result

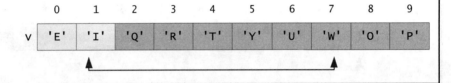

	0	1	2	3	4	5	6	7	8	9
v	'E'	'I'	'Q'	'R'	'T'	'Y'	'U'	'W'	'O'	'P'

ArrayTools.java selection sorting

```java
public static void selectionSort(char[] v) {
    for (int i = 0; i < v.length-1; ++i) {
        // guess the location of the ith smallest element
        int guess = i;
        for (int j = i+1; j < v.length; ++j) {
            if (v[j] < v[guess]) { // is guess ok?
                // update guess to index of smaller element
                guess = j;
            }
        }
        // guess is now correct, so swap elements
        char rmbr = v[i];
        v[i] = v[guess];
        v[guess] = rmbr;
    }
}
```

Iteration i

```
// guess the location of the ith smallest element
int guess = i;
for (int j = i+1; j < v.length; ++j) {
    if (v[j] < v[guess]) // is guess ok?
        // update guess with index of smaller element
        guess = j;
}

// guess is now correct, swap elements v[guess] and v[0]
```

Multidimensional arrays

☐ Many problems require information be organized as a two-dimensional or multidimensional list

☐ Examples
  ■ Matrices
  ■ Graphical animation
  ■ Economic forecast models
  ■ Map representation
  ■ Time studies of population change
  ■ Microprocessor design

Example

☐ Segment
```
int[][] m = new int[3][];
m[0] = new int[4];
m[1] = new int[4];
m[2] = new int[4];
```
☐ Produces

Example

☐ Segment
```
for (int r = 0; r < m.length; ++r) {
    for (int c = 0; c < m[r].length; ++c) {
    System.out.print("Enter a value: ");
    m[r][c] = Integer.parseInt(stdin.readLine());
    }
}
```

Example

□ Segment
```
String[][] s = new String[4][];
s[0] = new String[2];
s[1] = new String[2];
s[2] = new String[4];
s[3] = new String[3];
```
□ Produces

s   s[0] s[1] s[2] s[3]

null null null
s[3][0] s[3][1] s[3][2]

null null null null
s[2][0] s[2][1] s[2][2] s[2][3]

null null
s[0][0] s[0][1]

null null
s[1][0] s[1][1]

Example

□ Segment
```
int c[][] = {{1, 2}, {3, 4}, {5, 6}, {7, 8, 9}};
```

□ Produces

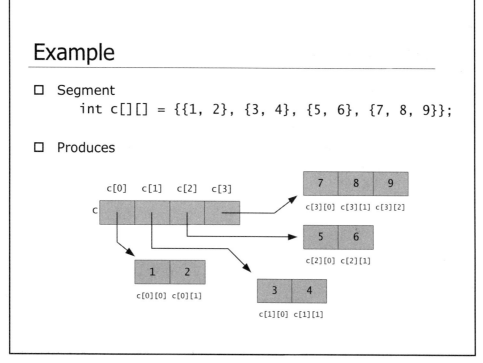

c   c[0] c[1] c[2] c[3]

7 8 9
c[3][0] c[3][1] c[3][2]

5 6
c[2][0] c[2][1]

1 2
c[0][0] c[0][1]

3 4
c[1][0] c[1][1]

233

Matrices

☐ A two-dimensional array is sometimes known as a matrix because it resembles that mathematical concept

☐ A matrix a with m rows and n columns is represented mathematically in the following manner

$$\begin{bmatrix} a_{1,1} & a_{1,2} & \cdots & a_{1,n} \\ a_{2,1} & a_{2,2} & \cdots & a_{2,n} \\ \cdots & & & \cdots \\ a_{m,1} & a_{m,2} & \cdots & a_{m,n} \end{bmatrix}$$

Matrix addition

☐ Definition C = A + B

  ■ $c_{ij} = a_{1i}b_{1j} + a_{i2}b_{2j} + \ldots + a_{in}b_{nj}$

  ■ c_{ij} is sum of terms produced by multipling the elements of a's row i with b's column c

Matrix addition

```
public static double[][] add(double[][] a, double[][]
           b) {
    // determine number of rows in solution
    int m = a.length;

    // determine number of columns in solution
    int n = a[0].length;

    // create the array to hold the sum
    double[][] c = new double[m][n];

    // compute the matrix sum row by row
    for (int i = 0; i < m; ++i) {
        // produce the current row
        for (int j = 0; j < n; ++j) {
            c[i][j] = a[i][j] + b[i][j];
        }
    }

    return c;
}
```

Inheritance and Polymorphism

Inheritance

- □ Organizes objects in a top-down fashion from most general to least general
- □ Inheritance defines a "is-a" relationship
  - ■ A mountain bike "is a" kind of bicycle
  - ■ A SUV "is a" kind of automobile
  - ■ A border collie "is a" kind of dog
  - ■ A laptop "is a" kind of computer

Musical instrument hierarchy

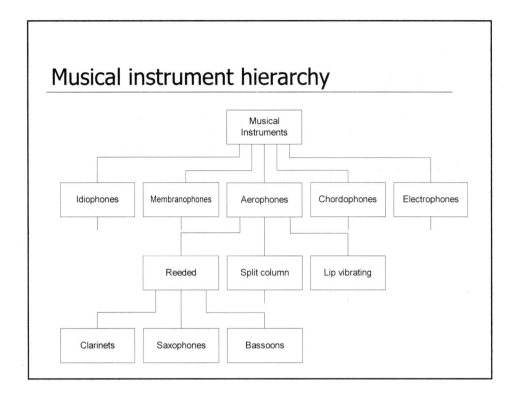

Musical instrument hierarchy

- ☐ The hierarchy helps us understand the relationships and similarities of musical instruments
  - ■ A clarinet "is a" kind of reeded instrument
  - ■ Reeded instruments "are a" kind of aerophone
- ☐ The "is-a" relationship is transitive
  - ■ A clarinet "is a" kind of reeded instrument
  - ■ A reeded instrument "is a" kind of aerophone
  - ■ A clarinet "is a" kind of aerophone

Object-oriented terminology

☐ In object-oriented programming languages, a class created by extending another class is called a *subclass*

☐ The class used for the basis is called the *superclass*

☐ Alternative terminology
  ■ The superclass is also referred to as the *base* class
  ■ The subclass is also referred to as the *derived* class

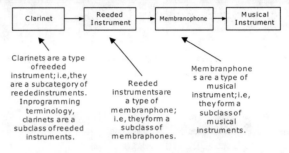

| Clarinet | → | Reeded Instrument | → | Membranophone | → | Musical Instrument |

Clarinets are a type of reeded instrument; i.e, they are a subcategory of reeded instruments. In programming terminology, clarinets are a subclass of reeded instruments.

Reeded instruments are a type of membranphone; i.e, they form a subclass of membraphones.

Membranphones are a type of musical instrument; i.e, they form a subclass of musical instruments.

ThreeDimensionalPoint

☐ Build a new class `ThreeDimensionalPoint` using inheritance
  ■ `ThreeDimensionalPoint` extends the awt class `Point`
    ☐ `Point` is the superclass (base class)
    ☐ `ThreeDimensionalPoint` is the subclass (derived class)
  ■ `ThreedimensionalPoint` extends `Point` by adding a new property to `Point`—a z-coordinate

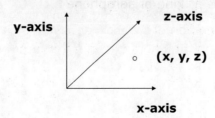

Class ThreeDimensionalPoint

```
package geometry;  ←——— See next slide

import java.awt.*;
```

Keyword extends indicates that `ThreeDimensionalPoint` **is a subclass of** `Point`

```
public class ThreeDimensionalPoint extends Point {
    // private class constant
    private final static int DEFAULT_Z = 0;

    // private instance variable
    public int z = DEFAULT_Z;  ←——— New instance variable
```

Packages

- ☐ Allow definitions to be collected together into a single entity— a package
- ☐ `ThreeDimensionalPoint` will be added to the `geometry` package
  - Classes and names in the same package are stored in the same folder
  - Classes in a package go into their own namespace and therefore the names in a particular package do not conflict with other names in other packages
  - For example, a package called `Graph` might have a different definition of `ThreeDimensionalPoint`
  - When defining members of a class or interface, Java does not require an explicit access specification. The implicit specification is known as *default access*. Members of a class with default access can be accessed only by members of the package.

Java's Mother-of-all-objects—Class Object

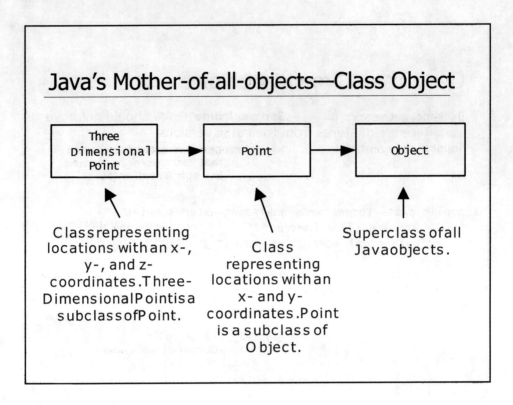

Three Dimensional Point → Point → Object

Class representing locations with an x-, y-, and z- coordinates. ThreeDimensionalPoint is a subclass of Point.

Class representing locations with an x- and y- coordinates. Point is a subclass of Object.

Superclass of all Java objects.

ThreeDimensionalPoint

```
ThreeDimensionalPoint a =
    new ThreeDimensionalPoint(6, 21, 54);
a.translate(1, 1);    // invocation of superclass translate()
a.translate(2, 2, 2); // invocation of subclass translate()
```

☐ Java determines which method to use based on the number of parameters in the invocation

☐ After the first call to translate, what is the value of a?

☐ After the second call to translate, what is the value of a?

ThreeDimensionalPoint

☐ Methods `toString()`, `equals()` , and `clone()` should not have different signatures from the `Point` versions

```
ThreeDimensionalPoint c = new ThreeDImensionalPoint(1, 4, 9);

ThreeDimensionalPoint d = (ThreeDimensionalPoint) c.clone();
```

Cast is necessary as return type of subclass method `clone()` **is Object**

```
String s = c.toString();
```

Invocation of subclass `toString()` **method**

```
boolean b = c.equals(d);
```

Invocation of subclass `equals()` **method**

ThreeDimensionalPoint

☐ Constructors

```
// ThreeDimensionalPoint(): default constructor
public ThreeDimensionalPoint() {
    super();
}

// ThreeDimensionalPoint(): specific constructor
public ThreeDimensionalPoint(int a, int b, int c) {
    super(a, b);
    setZ(c);
}
```

241

ThreeDimensionalPoint

☐ Accessors and mutators

```java
// getZ(): z-coordinate accessor
public double getZ() {
    return z;
}

// setZ(): y-coordinate mutator
public void setZ(int value) {
    z = value;
}
```

ThreeDimensionalPoint

☐ Facilitators

```java
// translate(): shifting facilitator
public void translate(int dx, int dy, int dz) {
    translate(dx, dy);

    int zValue = (int) getZ();

    setZ(zValue + dz);
}
```

ThreeDimensionalPoint

☐ Facilitators

```java
// toString(): conversion facilitator
public String toString() {
    int a = (int) getX();
    int b = (int) getY();
    int c = (int) getZ();
    return getClass() +
     "[" + a + ", " + b + ", " + c + "]";
}
```

ThreeDimensionalPoint

☐ Facilitators

```java
// equals(): equality facilitator
public boolean equals(Object v) {
    if (v instanceof ThreeDimensionalPoint) {
            ThreeDimensionalPoint p =
             (ThreeDimensionalPoint) v;
            int z1 = (int) getZ();
            int z2 = (int) p.getZ();

            return super.equals(p) && (z1 == z2);
    }
    else {
            return false;
    }
}
```

243

ThreeDimensionalPoint

☐ Facilitators

```
// clone(): clone facilitator
public Object clone() {
    int a = (int) getX();
    int b = (int) getY();
    int c = (int) getZ();

    return new ThreeDimensionalPoint(a, b, c);
}
```

ColoredPoint

☐ Suppose an application calls for the use of colored points.
☐ We can naturally extend class `Point` to create `ColoredPoint`
☐ Class `ColoredPoint` will be added to package geometry

```
package geometry;

import java.awt.*;

public class ColoredPoint extends Point {
    // instance variable
    Color color;
    ...
```

ColoredPoint

☐ Constructors

```java
// ColoredPoint(): default constructor
public ColoredPoint() {
    super();
    setColor(Color.blue);
}

// ColoredPoint(): specific constructor
public ColoredPoint(int x, int y, Color c) {
    super(x, y);
    setColor(c);
}
```

ColoredPoint

☐ Accessors and mutators

```java
// getColor(): color property accessor
public Color getColor() {
    return color;
}

// setColor(): color property mutator
public void setColor(Color c) {
    color = c;
}
```

ColoredPoint

☐ Facilitators

```java
// clone(): clone facilitator
public Object clone() {
    int a = (int) getX();
    int b = (int) getY();
    Color c = getColor();
    return new ColoredPoint(a, b, c);
}
```

ColoredPoint

☐ Facilitators

```java
// toString(): string representation facilitator
public String toString() {
    int a = (int) getX();
    int b = (int) getY();
    Color c = getColor();
    return getClass() +
      "[" + a + ", " + b + ", " + c + "]";
}
```

ColoredPoint

☐ Facilitators

```
// toString(): string representation facilitator
public String toString() {
    int a = (int) getX();
    int b = (int) getY();
    Color c = getColor();
    return getClass() +
     "[" + a + ", " + b + ", " + c + "]";
}
```

ColoredPoint

☐ Facilitators

```
// equals(): equal facilitator
public boolean equals(Object v) {
    if (v instanceof ColoredPoint) {
            Color c1 = getColor();
            Color c2 = ((ColoredPoint) v).getColor();
            return super.equals(v) && c1.equals(c2);
    }
    else {
            return false;
    }
```

Colored3DPoint

☐ Suppose an application needs a colored, three-dimensional point.
☐ Can we create such a class by extending both ThreeDimensionalPoint and ColoredPoint?
  - No. Java does not support multiple inheritance
  - Java only supports single inheritance

```
package Geometry;
import java.awt.*;

public class Colored3DPoint extends ThreeDimensionalPoint {
    // instance variable
    Color color;
```

Colored3DPoint

☐ Constructors
```
    // Colored3DPoint(): default constructor
    public Colored3DPoint() {
        setColor(Color.blue);
    }

    // Colored3DPoint(): specific constructor
    public Colored3DPoint(int a, int b, int c, Color d) {
        super(a, b, c);
        setColor(d);
    }
```

Colored3DPoint

☐ Accessors and mutators

```
// getColor(): color property accessor
public Color getColor() {
    return color;
}

// setColor(): color property mutator
public void setColor(Color c) {
    color = c;
}
```

Colored3DPoint

☐ Facilitators

```
// clone(): clone facilitator
public Object clone() {
    int a = (int) getX();
    int b = (int) getY();
    int c = (int) getZ();
    Color d = getColor();
    return new Colored3DPoint(a, b, c, d);
}
```

Colored3DPoint

□ Facilitators

```java
// toString(): string representation facilitator
public String toString() {
    int a = (int) getX();
    int b = (int) getY();
    int c = (int) getZ();
    Color d = getColor();
    return getClass() +
    "[" + a + ", " + b + ", " + c + ", " + d + "]";
}
```

Colored3DPoint

□ Facilitators

```java
// equals(): equal facilitator
public boolean equals(Object v) {
    if (v instanceof Colored3DPoint) {
        Color c1 = getColor();
        Color c2 = ((Colored3DPoint) v).getColor();
        return super.equals(v) && c1.equals(c2);
    }
    else {
        return false;
    }
```

Polymorphism

- ☐ A code expression can invoke different methods depending on the types of objects being manipulated
- ☐ Example: function overloading like method `min()` from `java.lang.Math`
  - ■ The method invoked depends on the types of the actual arguments

Example

```
int a, b, c;
double x, y, z;
...
c = min(a, b);    // invokes integer min()
z = min(x, y);    // invokes double min
```

Polymorphism

- ☐ Two types of polymorphism
  - ■ Syntactic polymorphism—Java can determine which method to invoke at compile time
    - ☐ Efficient
    - ☐ Easy to understand and analyze
    - ☐ Also known as primitive polymorphism
  - ■ Pure polymorphism—the method to invoke can only be determined at execution time

Polymorphism

□ Pure polymorphism example

```java
public class PolymorphismDemo {
    // main(): application entry point
    public static void main(String[] args) {
        Point[] p = new Point[4];

        p[0] = new Colored3DPoint(4, 4, 4, Color.BLACK);
        p[1] = new ThreeDimensionalPoint(2, 2, 2);
        p[2] = new ColoredPoint(3, 3, Color.RED);
        p[3] = new Point(4, 4);

        for (int i = 0; i < p.length; ++i) {
                String s = p[i].toString();
                System.out.println("p[" + i + "]: " + s);
        }

        return;
    }
}
```

Inheritance nuances

□ When a new object that is a subclass is constructed, the
  constructor for the superclass is always called.
  ■ Constructor invocation may be implicit or explicit
                          Example

```java
public class B {
    // B(): default constructor
    public B() {
        System.out.println("Using B's default constructor");
    }


    // B(): specific constructor
    public B(int i) {
        System.out.println("Using B's int constructor");
    }
}
```

Inheritance nuances

```java
public class C extends B {
    // C(): default constructor
    public C() {
        System.out.println("Using C's default constructor");
        System.out.println();
    }

    // C(int a): specific constructor
    public C(int a) {
        System.out.println("Using C's int constructor");
        System.out.println();
    }
```

Inheritance nuances

```java
    // C(int a, int b): specific constructor
    public C(int a, int b) {
        super(a + b);
        System.out.println("Using C's int-int constructor");
        System.out.println();
    }

    // main(): application entry point
    public static void main(String[] args) {
        C c1 = new C();
        C c2 = new C(2);
        C c3 = new C(2,4);
        return;
    }
```

Inheritance nuances

Output

```
Using B's default constructor
Using C's default constructor

Using B's default constructor
Using C's int constructor

Using B's int constructor
Using C's int-int constructor
```

Controlling access

☐ Class access rights

Member Restriction	this	Subclass	Package	General
public	✓	✓	✓	✓
protected	✓	✓	✓	—
default	✓	—	✓	—
private	✓	—	—	—

Controlling access

Example

```
package demo;

public class P {
    // instance variable
    private int data;

    // P(): default constructor
    public P() {
        setData(0);
    }

    // getData(): accessor
    public int getData() {
        return data;
    }
```

Controlling access

Example (continued)

```
    // setData(): mutator
    protected void setData(int v) {
        data = v;
    }

    // print(): facilitator
    void print() {
        System.out.println();
    }
}
```

Controlling access

Example

```
import demo.P;

public class Q extends P {
    // Q(): default constructor
    public Q() {
        super();           Q can access superclass's public
    }                      default constructor

    // Q(): specific constructor
    public Q(int v) {
        setData(v);        Q can access superclass's protected
    }                      mutator
```

Controlling access

Example

```
    // toString(): string facilitator
    public String toString() {        Q can access superclass's
        int v = getData();            public accessor
        return String.valueOf(v);
    }
    // invalid1(): illegal method
    public void invalid1() {
        data = 12;
    }                                 Q cannot access superclass's
                                      private data field
    // invalid2(): illegal method
    public void invalid2() {
        print();
    }
}                                     Q cannot directly access superclass's
                                      default access method print()
```

256

Controlling access

Example

```
package demo;

public class R {
    // instance variable
    private P p;

    // R(): default constructor
    public R() {
        p = new P();      ←
    }
    // set(): mutator
    public void set(int v) {
        p.setData(v);     ←
    }
```

R can access P's public default constructor

R can access P's protected mutator

Controlling access

Example

```
    // get(): accessor
    public int get() {
        return p.getData();   ←
    }
    // use(): facilitator
    public void use() {
        p.print();            ←
    }
    // invalid(): illegal method
    public void invalid() {
        p.data = 12;          ←
    }
```

R can access P's public accessor

R can access P's default access method

R cannot directly access P's private data

257

Controlling access

Example

```
import demo.P;

public class S {
    // instance variable
    private P p;

    // S(): default constructor
    public S() {
        p = new P();
    }
    // get(): inspector
    public int get() {
        return p.getData();
    }
}
```

S can access P's public default constructor

S can access P's public accessor

Controlling access

Example

```
// illegal1(): illegal method
public void illegal1(int v) {
    p.setData(v);
}
// illegal2(): illegal method
public void illegal2() {
    p.data = 12;
}
// illegal3(): illegal method
public void illegal3() {
    p.print();
}
}
```

S cannot access P's protected mutator

S cannot access directly P's private data field

S cannot access directly P's default access method print()

Data fields

☐ A superclass's instance variable can be hidden by a subclass's definition of an instance variable with the same name

Example

```
public class D {
    // D instance variable
    protected int d;

    // D(): default constructor
    public D() {
        d = 0;
    }
    // D(): specific constructor
    public D(int v) {
        d = v;
    }
```

Data fields

Class D (continued)

```
    // printD(): facilitator
    public void printD() {
        System.out.println("D's d: " + d);
        System.out.println();
    }
}
```

Data fields

☐ Class F extends D and introduces a new instance variable named d. F's definition of d hides D's definition.

```
public class F extends D {
    // F instance variable
    int d;

    // F(): specific constructor
    public F(int v) {                    Modification of this's d
        d = v;
        super.d = v*100;
    }                                    Modification of superclass's d
```

Data fields

                    Class F (continued)
```
    // printF(): facilitator
    public void printF() {
        System.out.println("D's d: " + super.d);
        System.out.println("F's d: " + this.d);
        System.out.println();
    }
```

Inheritance and types

```
public class X {
    // default constructor
    public X() {
        // no body needed
    }
    // isX(): class method
    public static boolean isX(Object v) {
        return (v instanceof X);
    }
    // isObject(): class method
    public static boolean isObject(X v) {
        return (v instanceof Object);
    }
}
```

Inheritance and types

Example

```
public class Y extends X {
    // Y(): default constructor
    public Y() {
        // no body needed
    }

    // isY(): class method
    public static boolean isY(Object v) {
        return (v instanceof Y);
    }
}
```

Inheritance and types

```java
public static void main(String[] args) {
    X x = new X();
    Y y = new Y();
    X z = y;

    System.out.println("x is an Object: " +
     X.isObject(x));
    System.out.println("x is an X: " + X.isX(x));
    System.out.println("x is a Y: " + Y.isY(x));
    System.out.println();
```

Inheritance and types

Example (continued)

```java
    System.out.println("y is an Object: " +
     X.isObject(y));
    System.out.println("y is an X: " + X.isX(y));
    System.out.println("y is a Y: " + Y.isY(y));
    System.out.println();

    System.out.println("z is an Object: " +
     X.isObject(z));
    System.out.println("z is an X: " + X.isX(z));
    System.out.println("z is a Y: " + Y.isY(z));
    return;
    }
}
```

Inheritance and types

☐ The program outputs the following:

```
x is an Object: true
x is an X: true
x is a Y: false

y is an Object: true
y is an X: true
y is a Y: true

z is an Object: true
z is an X: true
z is a Y: true
```

Polymorphism and late binding

Example

```
public class L {
    // L(): default constructor
    public L() {
    }
    // f(): facilitator
    public void f() {
        System.out.println("Using L's f()");
        g();
    }
    // g(): facilitator
    public void g() {
        System.out.println("using L's g()");
    }
}
```

Polymorphism and late binding

Example

```java
public class M extends L {
    // M(): default constructor
    public M() {
        // no body needed
    }
    // g(): facilitator
    public void g() {
        System.out.println("Using M's g()");
    }
```

Polymorphism and late binding

Example

```java
    // main(): application entry point
    public static void main(String[] args) {
        L l = new L();
        M m = new M();
        l.f();
        m.f();
        return;
    }
}
```
Outputs
```
    Using L's f()
    using L's g()
    Using L's f()
    Using M's g()
```

Finality

- ☐ A final class is a class that cannot be extended.
  - ■ Developers may not want users extending certain classes
  - ■ Makes tampering via overriding more difficult

Example

```
final public class U {
    // U(): default constructor
    public U() {
    }

    // f(): facilitator
    public void f() {
        System.out.println("f() can't be overridden:"
     + "U is final");
    }
}
```

Finality

- ☐ A final method is a method that cannot be overridden.

Example

```
public class V {
    // V(): default constructor
    public V() {
    }

    // f(): facilitator
    final public void f() {
        System.out.println("Final method f() can't be " +
         " overridden");
    }
}
```

Abstract base classes

☐ Allows creation of classes with methods that correspond to an abstract concept (i.e., there is not an implementation)

☐ Suppose we wanted to create a class `GeometricObject`
  - Reasonable concrete methods include
    - ☐ `getPosition()`
    - ☐ `setPosition()`
    - ☐ `getColor()`
    - ☐ `setColor()`
    - ☐ `paint()`
  - For all but `paint()`, we can create implementations.
  - For `paint()`, we must know what kind of object is to be painted. Is it a square, a triangle, etc.
  - Method `paint()` should be an abstract method

Abstract base classes

Example → **Makes** `GeometricObject` **an abstract class**

```java
import java.awt.*;

abstract public class GeometricObject {
    // instance variables
    Point position;
    Color color;

    // getPosition(): return object position
    public Point getPosition() {
        return position;
    }
    // setPosition(): update object position
    public void setPosition(Point p) {
        position = p;
    }
```

Abstract base classes

Example (continued)

```
// getColor(): return object color
public Color getColor() {
    return color;
}
// setColor(): update object color
public void setColor(Color c) {
    color = c;
}
// paint(): render the shape to graphics context g
abstract public void paint(Graphics g);
}
```

Indicates that an implementation of method paint() will not be supplied

Interfaces

☐ An interface is a template that specifies what must be in a class that imlements the interface

- An interface cannot specify any method implementations
- All the methods of an interface are public
- All the variables defined in an interface are `public`, `final`, and `static`

Interfaces

☐ An interface for a colorable object

```java
public interface Colorable {
    // getColor(): return the color of the object
    public Color getColor();
    // setColor(): set the color of the object
    public void setColor(Color c);
}
```

☐ Now the interface can be used to create classes that implement the interface

Interfaces

☐ ColorablePoint

```java
import java.awt.*;

public class ColorablePoint extends Point implements
    Colorable {
    // instance variable
    Color color;

    // ColorablePoint(): default constructor
    public ColorablePoint() {
        super();
        setColor(Color.blue);
    }
...
```

Class ColorablePoint must provide implementations of getColor() and setColor()

Exceptions

Exception

☐ Abnormal event occurring during program execution

☐ Examples
- Manipulate nonexistent files
  ```
  FileReader in = new FileReader("mumbers.txt");
  ```

- Improper array subscripting
  ```
  int[] a = new int[3];
  a[4] = 1000;
  ```

- Improper arithmetic operations
  ```
  a[2] = 1000 / 0;
  ```

Java treatment of an exception

- ☐ If exception occurs and a *handler* is in effect
  - ■ Flow of control is transferred to the handler
  - ■ After handler completes flow of control continues with the statement following the handler

- ☐ If exception occurs and there is no handler for it
  - ■ The program terminates

Task

- ☐ Prompt and extract the name of a file

- ☐ From that file, two integer values are to be extracted

- ☐ Compute and display the quotient of the values

Implementation

Necessary because main() does not handle its possible IOExceptions

```java
public static void main(String[] args) throws IOException {

    BufferedReader stdin = new BufferedReader(
        new InputStreamReader(System.in));
    System.out.print("Filename: ");
    String s = stdin.readLine();

    BufferedReader filein = new BufferedReader(
        new FileReader(s));

    int a = Integer.parseInt(filein.readLine());
    int b = Integer.parseInt(filein.readLine());

    System.out.println( a / b );
}
```

What can go wrong?

```java
public static void main(String[] args) throws IOException {

    BufferedReader stdin = new BufferedReader(
        new InputStreamReader(System.in));
    System.out.print("Filename: ");
    String s = stdin.readLine();

    BufferedReader filein = new BufferedReader(
        new FileReader(s));

    int a = Integer.parseInt(filein.readLine());
    int b = Integer.parseInt(filein.readLine());

    System.out.println( a / b );
}
```

271

How can we deal with the problems?

```java
public static void main(String[] args) throws IOException {

    BufferedReader stdin = new BufferedReader(
        new InputStreamReader(System.in));
    System.out.print("Filename: ");
    String s = stdin.readLine();

    BufferedReader filein = new BufferedReader(
        new FileReader(s));

    int a = Integer.parseInt(filein.readLine());
    int b = Integer.parseInt(filein.readLine());

    System.out.println( a / b );
}
```

Exception handlers

- ☐ Code that might generate an exception is put in a try block
  - ■ If there is no exception, then the handlers are ignored
- ☐ For each potential exception type there is a catch handler
  - ■ When handler finishes the program continues with statement after the handlers

```java
try {
    Code that might throw exceptions of types E or F
}
catch (E e) {
    Handle exception e
}
catch (F f) {
    Handle exception f
}
More code
```

Introduce try-catch blocks

```
public static void main(String[] args) throws IOException {

    BufferedReader stdin = new BufferedReader(
        new InputStreamReader(System.in));
    System.out.print("Filename: ");
    String s = stdin.readLine();

    BufferedReader filein = new BufferedReader(
        new FileReader(s));

    int a = Integer.parseInt(filein.readLine());
    int b = Integer.parseInt(filein.readLine());

    System.out.println( a / b );
}
```

Getting the filename

```
BufferedReader stdin = new BufferedReader(
    new InputStreamReader(System.in));
System.out.print("Filename: ");
String s = null;
try {
    s = stdin.readLine();
}
catch (IOException e) {
    System.err.println("Cannot read input");
    System.exit(0);
}
```

273

Set up the file stream processing

```
BufferedReader filein = null;
try {
    filein = new BufferedReader(new FileReader(s));
}
catch (FileNotFoundException e) {
    System.err.println(s + ": cannot be opened");
    System.exit(0);
}
```

How come the main() throws expression did not indicate
it could throw a FileNotFoundException?

Getting the inputs

```
try {
    int a = Integer.parseInt(filein.readLine());
    int b = Integer.parseInt(filein.readLine());
    System.out.println( a / b );
}
catch (IOException e) {
    System.err.println(s + ": unable to read values");
}
```

Converting the inputs

```
try {
    int a = Integer.parseInt(filein.readLine());
    int b = Integer.parseInt(filein.readLine());
    System.out.println( a / b );
}
catch (IOException e) {
    System.err.println(s + ": unable to read values");
}
catch (NumberFormatException e) {
    if (e.getMessage().equals("null")) {
        System.err.println(s + ": need two inputs");
    }
    else {
        System.err.println(s + ": invalid inputs");
    }
}
```

How come the main() throws expression did not indicate it could throw a NumberFormatException

Run time exceptions

☐ Java designers realized
  ■ Runtime exceptions can occur throughout a program
  ■ Cost of implementing handlers for runtime exceptions typically exceeds the expected benefit

☐ Java makes it optional for a method to catch them or to specify that it throws them

☐ However, if a program does not handle its runtime exceptions it is terminated when one occurs

Computing the quotient

```java
try {
    int a = Integer.parseInt(filein.readLine());
    int b = Integer.parseInt(filein.readLine());
    System.out.println( a / b );
}
catch (IOException e) {
    System.err.println(s + ": unable to read values");
}
catch (NumberFormatException e) {
    if (e.getMessage().equals("null")) {
        System.err.println(s + ": need two inputs");
    }
    else {
        System.err.println(s + ": invalid inputs");
    }
}
catch (ArithmeticException e) {
    System.err.println(s + ": unexpected 0 input value");
}
```

Commands type and cat

□ Most operating systems supply a command for listing the contents of files
- Windows: type
- Unix, Linux, and OS X: cat

  type filename$_1$ filename$_2$ ... filename$_n$

  □ Displays the contents of filename$_1$ filename$_2$ ... and filename$_n$ to the console window

Possible method main() for Type.java

```java
public static void main(String[] args) {
    for (int i = 0; i < args.length; ++i) {
        BufferedReader filein = new BufferedReader(
            new FileReader(args[i]));
        String s = filein.readLine();
        while (s != null) {
            System.out.println(s);
            s = filein.readLine();
        }
        filein.close();
    }
}
```

What can go wrong?

Use a finally block

```java
public static void main(String[] args) {
    for (int i = 0; i < args.length; ++i) {
        BufferedReader filein = new BufferedReader(
            new FileReader(args[i]));
        String s = filein.readLine();
        while (s != null) {
            System.out.println(s);
            s = filein.readLine();
        }
        filein.close();
    }
}
```

File should be closed once its processing
stops, regardless why it stopped

277

Use a finally block

```
try {
    String s = filein.readLine();
    while (s != null) {
        System.out.println(s);
        s = filein.readLine();
    }
}
catch (IOException e) {
    System.err.println(args[i] + ": processing error");
}
finally {       ⟵ Always executed after its try-catch blocks complete
    try {
        filein.close();
    }
    catch (IOException e) {
        System.err.println(args[i] + ": system error");
    }
}
```

Exceptions

☐ Can create your exception types

☐ Can throw exceptions as warranted

Task

☐ Represent the depositing and withdrawing of money from a
  bank account

☐ What behaviors are needed
  - Construct a new empty bank account
    ```
    BankAccount()
    ```
  - Construct a new bank account with initial funds
    ```
    BankAccount(int n)
    ```
  - Deposit funds
    ```
    addFunds(int n)
    ```
  - Withdraw funds
    ```
    removeFunds(int n)
    ```
  - Get balance
    ```
    Int getBalance()
    ```

Sample usage

```
public static void main(String[] args)
      throws IOException {

    BufferedReader stdin = new BufferedReader(
      new InputStreamReader(System.in));

    BankAccount savings = new BankAccount();

    System.out.print("Enter deposit: ");
    int deposit = Integer.parseInt(stdin.readLine());
    savings.addFunds(deposit);

    System.out.print("Enter widthdrawal: ");
    int withdrawal = Integer.parseInt(stdin.readLine());
    savings.removeFunds(withdrawl);

    System.out.println("Closing balance: "
      + savings.getBalance());
}
```

279

Task

☐ Represent the depositing and withdrawing of money from a bank account

☐ What behaviors are needed
- Construct a new empty bank account
  `BankAccount()`
- Construct a new bank account with initial funds
  `BankAccount(int n)`
- Deposit funds
  `addFunds(int n)`   What can go wrong?
- Withdraw funds
  `removeFunds(int n)`
- Get balance
  `int getBalance()`

Create a NegativeAmountException

```
// Represents an abnormal bank account event

public class NegativeAmountException extends Exception {
    // NegativeAmountException(): creates exception with
    // message s
    public NegativeAmountException(String s) {
                super(s);
    }
}
```

☐ Class Exception provides the exceptions behavior that might be needed
☐ Class NegativeAmountException gives the specialization of exception type that is needed

Sample usage

```
public static void main(String[] args)
      throws IOException, NegativeAmountException {

    BufferedReader stdin = new BufferedReader(
        new InputStreamReader(System.in));

    BankAccount savings = new BankAccount();

    System.out.print("Enter deposit: ");
    int deposit = Integer.parseInt(stdin.readLine());
    savings.addFunds(deposit);

    System.out.print("Enter widthdrawal: ");
    int withdrawal = Integer.parseInt(stdin.readLine());
    savings.removeFunds(withdrawl);

    System.out.println("Closing balance: "
        + savings.getBalance());
}
```

Class BankAccount

- ☐ Instance variable
    - balance
- ☐ Construct a new empty bank account
    - BankAccount()
- ☐ Construct a new bank account with initial funds
    - BankAccount(int n) throws NegativeAmountException
- ☐ Deposit funds
    - addFunds(int n) throws NegativeAmountException
- ☐ Withdraw funds
    - removeFunds(int n) throws NegativeAmountException
- ☐ Get balance
    - Int getBalance()

Class BankAccount

```java
// BankAccount(): default constructor for empty balance
public BankAccount() {
    balance = 0;
}


// BankAccount(): specific constructor for a new balance n
public BankAccount(int n) throws NegativeAmountException {
    if (n >= 0) {
                    balance = n;
    }
    else {
                    throw new NegativeAmountException("Bad
    balance");
    }
}
```

Class BankAccount

```java
// getBalance(): return the current balance
public int getBalance() {
    return balance;
}


// addFunds(): deposit amount n
public void addFunds(int n) throws NegativeAmountException {
    if (n >= 0) {
                    balance += n;
    }
    else {
                    throw new NegativeAmountException("Bad
    deposit");
    }
}
```

282

Class BankAccount

```java
// removeFunds(): withdraw amount n
public void removeFunds(int n) throws NegativeAmountException
    {
    if (n < 0) {
        throw new NegativeAmountException("Bad withdrawal");
    }
    else if (balance < n) {
        throw new NegativeAmountException("Bad balance");
    }
    else {
        balance -= n;
    }
}
```

Using NegativeAmountException

```java
System.out.print("Enter deposit: ");
try {
    int deposit = Integer.parseInt(stdin.readLine());
    savings.addFunds(deposit);
}
catch (NegativeAmountException e) {
    System.err.println("Cannot deposit negative funds");
    System.exit(0);
}
```

Using NegativeAmountException

```
System.out.print("Enter withdrawal: ");
try {
    int withdrawal = integer.parseInt(stdin.readLine());
    savings.removeFunds(withdrawl);
}
catch (NegativeAmountException e) {
    if (e.message().equals("Bad withdrawal"))
        System.err.println("Cannot withdraw negative funds");
    else {
        System.err.println("Withdrawal cannot leave "
            "negative balance");
    }
    System.exit(0);
}
```

Recursion

Recursive definitions

- A definition that defines something in terms of itself is called a recursive definition
  - The *descendants* of a person are the person's children and all of the *descendants* of the person's children
  - A *list of numbers* is a number or a number followed by a comma and a *list of numbers*
- A recursive algorithm is an algorithm that invokes itself to solve smaller or simpler instances of a problem instances
  - The factorial of a number n is n times the factorial of n-1

Factorial

☐ An imprecise definition

$$n! = \begin{matrix} 1 & n = 0 \\ n \cdot (n-1) \cdot \ldots \cdot 1 & n \geq 1 \end{matrix}$$

Ellipsis tells the reader to use intuition to recognize the pattern

☐ A precise definition

$$n! = \begin{matrix} 1 & n = 0 \\ n \cdot (n-1)! & n \geq 1 \end{matrix}$$

Recursive methods

☐ A recursive method generally has two parts.
- A termination part that stops the recursion.
  - ☐ This is called the base case.
  - ☐ The base case should have a simple or trivial solution.
- One or more recursive calls.
  - ☐ This is called the recursive case.
  - ☐ The recursive case calls the same method but with simpler or smaller arguments.

Method factorial()

```java
public static int factorial(int n) {
    if (n == 0) {                          Base case
        return 1;
    }
    else {
        return n * factorial(n-1);
    }
}
```

Recursive case deals with a simpler
(smaller) version of the task

Method factorial()

```java
public static int factorial(int n) {
    if (n == 0) {
        return 1;
    }
    else {
        return n * factorial(n-1);
    }
}

public static void main(String[] args) {
    BufferedReader stdin = new BufferedReader(
        new InputStreamReader(System.in));
    int n = Integer.parseInt(stdin.readLine());
    int nfactorial = factorial(n);
    System.out.println(n + "! = " + nfactorial;
}
```

287

Recursive invocation

☐ A new activation record is created for *every* method invocation
  - Including recursive invocations

main() [   ]   int nfactorial = factorial(n);

Recursive invocation

☐ A new activation record is created for *every* method invocation
  - Including recursive invocations

main() [   ]   int nfactorial = factorial(n);

factorial() [n = 3]   return n * factorial(n-1);

Recursive invocation

□ A new activation record is created for *every* method invocation
- Including recursive invocations

main()		int nfactorial = factorial(n);
factorial()	n = 3	return n * factorial(n-1);
factorial()	n = 2	return n * factorial(n-1);

Recursive invocation

□ A new activation record is created for *every* method invocation
- Including recursive invocations

main()		int nfactorial = factorial(n);
factorial()	n = 3	return n * factorial(n-1);
factorial()	n = 2	return n * factorial(n-1);
factorial()	n = 1	return n * factorial(n-1);

Recursive invocation

☐ A new activation record is created for *every* method invocation
- ■ Including recursive invocations

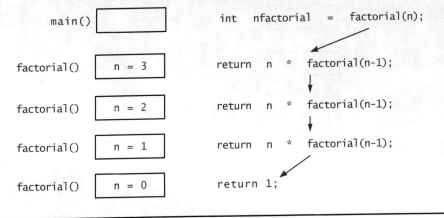

```
            main()  ┌──────────┐        int  nfactorial  =  factorial(n);
                    └──────────┘

  factorial()   ┌──────────┐           return  n  *  factorial(n-1);
                │  n = 3   │
                └──────────┘

  factorial()   ┌──────────┐           return  n  *  factorial(n-1);
                │  n = 2   │
                └──────────┘

  factorial()   ┌──────────┐           return  n  *  factorial(n-1);
                │  n = 1   │
                └──────────┘

  factorial()   ┌──────────┐           return  1;
                │  n = 0   │
                └──────────┘
```

Recursive invocation

☐ A new activation record is created for *every* method invocation
- ■ Including recursive invocations

```
            main()  ┌──────────┐        int  nfactorial  =  factorial(n);
                    └──────────┘

  factorial()   ┌──────────┐           return  n  *  factorial(n-1);
                │  n = 3   │
                └──────────┘

  factorial()   ┌──────────┐           return  n  *  factorial(n-1);
                │  n = 2   │
                └──────────┘

  factorial()   ┌──────────┐           return  n  *  factorial(n-1);
                │  n = 1   │
                └──────────┘

  factorial()   ┌──────────┐           return  1;
                │  n = 0   │
                └──────────┘
```

Recursive invocation

☐ A new activation record is created for *every* method invocation
  - ■ Including recursive invocations

```
main()    [          ]        int  nfactorial  =  factorial(n);

factorial()  [  n = 3  ]      return  n  *  factorial(n-1);

factorial()  [  n = 2  ]      return  n  *  factorial(n-1);

factorial()  [  n = 1  ]              return  n  *  1;

factorial()  [  n = 0  ]          return 1;
```

Recursive invocation

☐ A new activation record is created for *every* method invocation
  - ■ Including recursive invocations

```
main()    [          ]        int  nfactorial  =  factorial(n);

factorial()  [  n = 3  ]      return  n  *  factorial(n-1);

factorial()  [  n = 2  ]      return  n  *  factorial(n-1);

factorial()  [  n = 1  ]              return  1  *  1;
```

291

Recursive invocation

- ☐ A new activation record is created for *every* method invocation
  - ■ Including recursive invocations

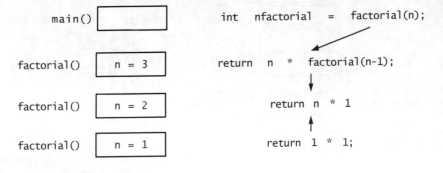

```
                                 int   nfactorial  =  factorial(n);
main()   [          ]

factorial()  [ n = 3 ]           return  n  *  factorial(n-1);

factorial()  [ n = 2 ]                  return  n  *  1

factorial()  [ n = 1 ]                  return  1  *  1;
```

Recursive invocation

- ☐ A new activation record is created for *every* method invocation
  - ■ Including recursive invocations

```
                                 int   nfactorial  =  factorial(n);
main()   [          ]

factorial()  [ n = 3 ]           return  n  *  factorial(n-1);

factorial()  [ n = 2 ]                  return  2  *  1
```

Recursive invocation

☐ A new activation record is created for *every* method
  invocation

  ■ Including recursive invocations

  ```
  main()     [          ]        int  nfactorial  =  factorial(n);


  factorial()   [  n = 3  ]              return  n  *  2;


  factorial()   [  n = 2  ]              return  2  *  1;
  ```

Recursive invocation

☐ A new activation record is created for *every* method
  invocation

  ■ Including recursive invocations

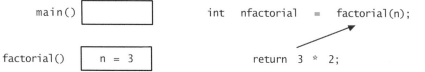

  ```
  main()     [          ]        int  nfactorial  =  factorial(n);


  factorial()   [  n = 3  ]              return  3  *  2;
  ```

Recursive invocation

☐ A new activation record is created for *every* method invocation
  ■ Including recursive invocations

```
main()      [          ]              int  nfactorial  =  6;

factorial() [  n = 3   ]              return  3  *  2;
```

Recursive invocation

☐ A new activation record is created for *every* method invocation
  ■ Including recursive invocations

```
main()      [          ]              int  nfactorial  =  6;
```

Fibonacci numbers

- ☐ Developed by Leonardo Pisano in 1202.
  - ■ Investigating how fast rabbits could breed under idealized circumstances
  - ■ Assumptions
    - ☐ A pair of male and female rabbits always breed and produce another pair of male and female rabbits
    - ☐ A rabbit becomes sexually mature after one month, and that the gestation period is also one month
  - ■ Pisano wanted to know the answer to the question how many rabbits would there be after one year?

Fibonacci numbers

- ☐ The sequence generated is: 1, 1, 2, 3, 5, 8, 13, 21, 34, ...
- ☐ The number of pairs for a month is the sum of the number of pairs in the two previous months.
- ☐ Fibonacci equation

$$f_n = \begin{cases} f_n = 1 & \text{if } n = 1 \\ f_n = 1 & \text{if } n = 2 \\ f_{n-1} + f_{n-2} & \text{if } n > 2 \end{cases}$$

Fibonacci numbers

☐ Recursive method pattern

```
if ( termination code satisfied ) {
    return value;
}
else {
    make simpler recursive call;
}

public static int fibonacci(int n) {
    if (n <= 2) {
        return 1;
    }
    else {
        return fibonacci(n-1) + fibonacci(n-2);
    }
}
```

Fibonacci numbers

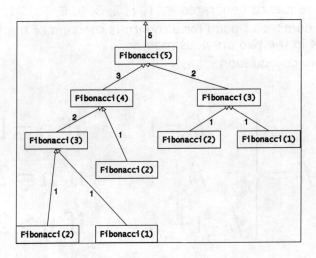

Infinite recursion

- ☐ A common programming error when using recursion is to not stop making recursive calls.
  - ■ The program will continue to recurse until it runs out of memory.
  - ■ Be sure that your recursive calls are made with simpler or smaller subproblems, and that your algorithm has a base case that terminates the recursion.

Binary search

- ☐ Compare the entry to the middle element of the list. If the entry matches the middle element, the desired entry has been located and the search is over
- ☐ If the entry doesn't match, then if the entry is in the list it must be either to the left or right of the middle element
- ☐ The correct sublist can be searched using the same strategy

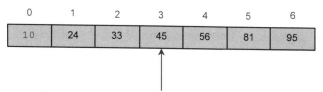

0	1	2	3	4	5	6
10	24	33	45	56	81	95

Compare entry to this element. If the entry matches, the search is successful. If the entry is less than 45, then the entry, if it is in the list, must be to the left in elements 0-2. If the entry is greater than 45, then the entry, if it is in the list, must be to the right in elements 4-6.

Develop search for an address book

```
public class AddressEntry {
    private String personName;
    private String telephoneNumber;

    public AddressEntry(String name, String number) {
        personName = name;
        telephoneNumber = number;
    }
    public String getName() {
        return personName;
    }
    public String getNumber() {
        return telephoneNumber;
    }
    public void setName(String Name) {
        personName = Name;
    }
    public void setTelephoneNumber(String number) {
        telephoneNumber = number;
    }
}
```

Binary search

- ☐ Public interface
  - ■ Should be as simple as possible
  - ■ No extraneous parameters

```
public static AddressEntry recSearch(AddressEntry[]
 addressBook, String name)
```

- ☐ Private interface
  - ■ Invoked by implementation of public interface
  - ■ Should support recursive invocation by implementation of private interface

```
private static AddressEntry recSearch(AddressEntry[]
 addressBook, String name, int first, int last)
```

Binary search

☐ Public interface implementation

```
public static AddressEntry recSearch(AddressEntry[]
    addressBook, String name) {
  return recSearch(addressBook, name, 0,
  addressBook.length-1);
}
```

Private interface implementation

```
static AddressEntry recSearch(AddressEntry[] addressBook,
 String name, int first, int last) {
   // base case: if the array section is empty, not found
   if (first > last)
      return null;
   else {
      int mid = (first + last) / 2;
      // if we found the value, we're done
      if (name.equalsIgnoreCase(addressBook[mid].getName()))
         return addressBook[mid];
      else if (name.compareToIgnoreCase(
       addressBook[mid].getName()) < 0) {
          // if value is there at all, it's in the left half
          return recSearch(addressBook, name, first, mid-1);
      }
       else { // array[mid] < value
          // if value is there at all, it's in the right half
          return recSearch(addressBook, name, mid+1, last);
      }
   }
}
```

Testing

□ Develop tests cases to exercise every possible
   unique situation

```java
public static void main(String[] args) {
    // list must be in sorted order
    AddressEntry addressBook[] = {
        new AddressEntry("Audrey", "434-555-1215"),
        new AddressEntry("Emily" , "434-555-1216"),
        new AddressEntry("Jack"  , "434-555-1217"),
        new AddressEntry("Jim"   , "434-555-2566"),
        new AddressEntry("John"  , "434-555-2222"),
        new AddressEntry("Lisa"  , "434-555-3415"),
        new AddressEntry("Tom"   , "630-555-2121"),
        new AddressEntry("Zach"  , "434-555-1218")
    };
```

Testing

□ Search for first element

```java
AddressEntry p;
// first element
p = recSearch(addressBook, "Audrey");
if (p != null) {
    System.out.println("Audrey's telephone number is " +
      p.getNumber());
}
else {
    System.out.println("No entry for Audrey");
}
```

Testing

☐ Search for middle element

```
p = recSearch(addressBook, "Jim");
if (p != null) {
   System.out.println("Jim's telephone number is " +
     p.getNumber());
}
else {
   System.out.println("No entry for Jim");
}
```

Testing

☐ Search for last element

```
p = recSearch(addressBook, "Zach");
if (p != null) {
   System.out.println("Zach's telephone number is " +
     p.getNumber());
}
else {
   System.out.println("No entry for Zach");
}
```

Testing

☐ Search for non-existent element

```
p = recSearch(addressBook, "Frank");
if (p != null) {
    System.out.println("Frank's telephone number is " +
      p.getNumber());
}
else {
    System.out.println("No entry for Frank");
}
```

Efficiency of binary search

☐ Height of a binary tree is the worst case number of comparisons needed to search a list

☐ Tree containing 31 nodes has a height of 5

☐ In general, a tree with n nodes has a height of $\log_2(n+1)$

☐ Searching a list with a billion nodes only requires 31 comparisons

☐ Binary search is efficient!

Mergesort

- Mergesort is a recursive sort that conceptually divides its list of *n* elements to be sorted into two sublists of size *n*/2.
  - If a sublist contains more than one element, the sublist is sorted by a recursive call to mergeSort().
  - After the two sublists of size *n*/2 are sorted, they are merged together to produce a single sorted list of size *n*.
- This type of strategy is known as a divide-and-conquer strategy—the problem is divided into subproblems of lesser complexity and the solutions of the subproblems are used to produced the overall solution.
- The running time of method mergeSort() is proportional to *n* log *n*.
- This performance is sometimes known as *linearithmic* performance.

Mergesort

- Suppose we are sorting the array shown below.

- After sorting the two sublists, the array would look like

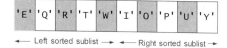

  ← Left sorted sublist →   ← Right sorted sublist →

  - Now we can do the simple task of merging the two arrays to get

Mergesort

- ☐ Public interface
  - ■ Should be as simple as possible
  - ■ No extraneous parameters

```
public static void mergeSort(char[] a)
```

- ☐ Private interface
  - ■ Invoked by implementation of public interface
  - ■ Should support recursive invocation by implementation of private interface

```
private static void mergeSort(char[] a, int left, int right)
```

Mergesort

```
private static void
    mergeSort(char[] a, int left, int right) {
    if (left < right) {
        // there are multiple elements to sort.

        // first, recursively sort the left and right sublists
        int mid = (left + right) / 2;
        mergeSort(a, left, mid);
        mergeSort(a, mid+1, right);
```

Mergesort

```
// next, merge the sorted sublists into
// array temp
char[] temp = new char[right - left + 1];

int j = left; // index of left sublist smallest ele.
int k = mid + 1; // index of right sublist smallest ele.
```

Mergesort

```
for (int i = 0; i < temp.length; ++i) {
    // store the next smallest element into temp
    if ((j <= mid) && (k <= right)) {
        // need to grab the smaller of a[j]
        // and a[k]
        if (a[j] <= a[k]) { // left has the smaller element
            temp[i] = a[j];
            ++j;
        }
        else { // right has the smaller element
            temp[i] = a[k];
            ++k;
        }
    }
```

Mergesort

```
else if (j <= mid) { // can only grab from left half
    temp[i] = a[j];
    ++j;
}
else { // can only grab from right half
    temp[i] = a[k];
    ++k;
}
}
```

Mergesort

```
// lastly, copy temp into a
for (int i = 0; i < temp.length; ++i) {
    a[left + i] = temp[i];
    }
}
}
```

Mergesort

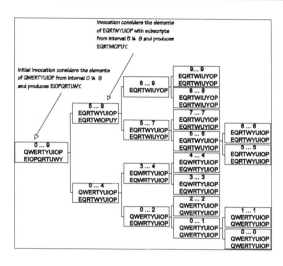

Recursion versus iteration

- Iteration can be more efficient
  - Replaces method calls with looping
  - Less memory is used (no activation record for each call)
- Many problems are more naturally solved with recursion
  - Towers of Hanoi
  - Mergesort
- Choice depends on problem and the solution context

Daily Jumble

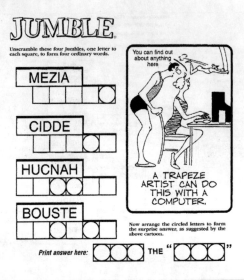

Daily Jumble

- ☐ Task
  - ■ Generate all possible permutation of letters
  - ☐ For n letters there are n! possibilities
    - ■ n choices for first letter
    - ■ n-1 choices for second letter
    - ■ n-2 choices for third letter
    - ■ ...

- ☐ Iterator
  - ■ Object that produces successive values in a sequence

- ☐ Design
  - ■ Iterator class `PermuteString` that supports the enumeration of permutations

Class PermuteString

- ☐ Constructor
    - `public PermuteString(String s)`
        - ☐ Constructs a permutation generator for string s

- ☐ Methods
    - `public String nextPermutation()`
        - ☐ Returns the next permutation of the associated string

    - **public** boolean morePermutations()
        - ☐ Returns whether there is unenumerated permutation of the associated string

Class PermuteString

- ☐ Instance variables
    - `private String word`
        - ☐ Represents the word to be permuted

    - `private int index`
        - ☐ Position within the word being operated on

    - `public PermuteString substringGenerator`
        - ☐ Generator of substrings

Constructor

```
public PermuteString(String s) {
    word = s;
    index = 0;
    if (s.length() > 1) {
        String substring = s.substring(1);
        substringGenerator = new PermuteString(substring);
    }
    else {
        substringGenerator = null;
    }
}
```

Consider

☐ What happens?
```
PermuteString p = new PermuteString("ath");
```

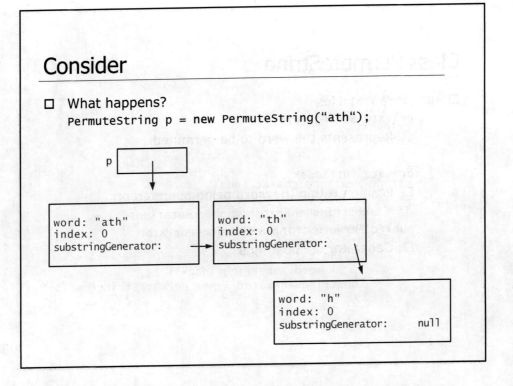

Method

```
public boolean morePermuations() {
    return index < word.length;
}
```

Method

```
public boolean nextPermutation() {
    if (word.length() == 1) {
        ++index;
        return word;
    }
    else {
        String r = word.charAt(index)
                + substringGenerator.nextPermutation();
        if (!substringGenerator.morePermutations()) {
            ++index;
            if (index < word.length()) {
                String tail = word.substring(0, index)
                    + word.substring(index + 1);
                substringGenerator = new permuteString(tail);
            }
        }
        return r;
    }
}
```

311

Daily Jumble

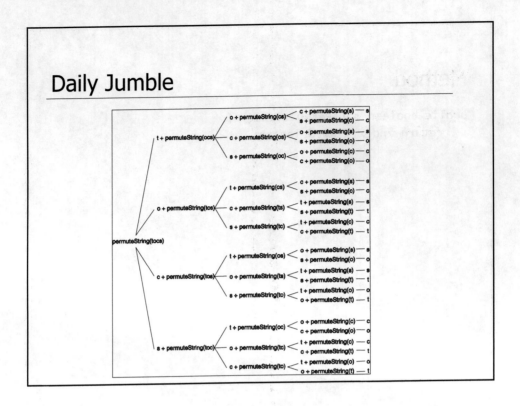

Threads

Story so far

☐ Our programs have consisted of single flows of control
  - Flow of control started in the first statement of method main() and worked its way statement by statement to the last statement of method main()
  - Flow of control could be passed temporarily to other methods through invocations, but the control returned to main() after their completion

☐ Programs with single flows of control are known as sequential processes

```
Single-threaded Program {        Although the statements within a
    Statement 1;                 single flow of control may invoke
    Statement 2;    ←────────        other methods, the next
    ...                          statement is not executed until
    Statement k;                 the current statement completes
}
```

313

Processes

- ☐ The ability to run more than one process at the same time is an important characteristic of modern operating systems
  - ■ A user desktop may be running a browser, programming IDE, music player, and document preparation system

- ☐ Java supports the creation of programs with concurrent flows of control – threads
  - ■ Threads run within a program and make use of its resources in their execution
    - ☐ Lightweight processes

Processes

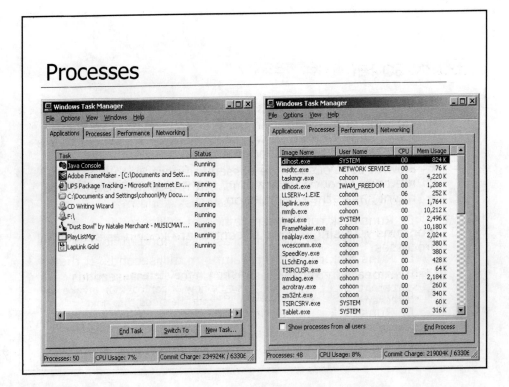

Multithread processing

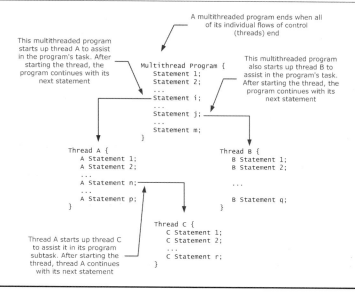

Timer and TimerTask

- ☐ Among others, Java classes java.util.Timer and java.util.TimerTask support the creation and scheduling of threads

- ☐ Abstract class Timer has methods for creating threads after either some specified delay or at some specific time
  - ■ public void schedule(TimerTask task, long m)
    - ☐ Runs task.run() after waiting m milliseconds.
  - ■ public void schedule(TimerTask task, long m, long n)
    - ☐ Runs task.run() after waiting m milliseconds. It then repeatedly reruns task.run() every n milliseconds.
  - ■ public void schedule(TimerTask task, Date y)
    - ☐ Runs task.run() at time t.
- ☐ A thread can be created By extending TimerTask and specifying a definition for abstract method run()

315

Running after a delay

□ Class DisplayCharSequence extends TimerTask to support the creation of a thread that displays 20 copies of some desired character (e.g., "H", "A", or "N")

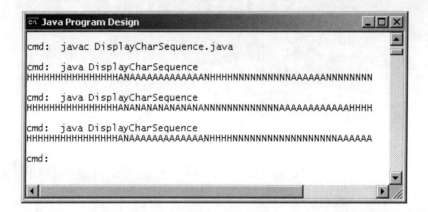

Using DisplayCharSequence

```
public static void main(String[] args) {
    DisplayCharSequence s1 =
        new DisplayCharSequence('H');

    DisplayCharSequence s2 =
        new DisplayCharSequence('A');

    DisplayCharSequence s3 =
        new DisplayCharSequence('N');
}
```

Defining DisplayCharSequence

```java
import java.util.*;
public class DisplayCharSequence extends TimerTask {
    private char displayChar;
    Timer timer;
    public DisplayCharSequence(char c) {
        displayChar = c;
        timer = new Timer();
        timer.schedule(this, 0);
    }
    public void run() {
        for (int i = 0; i < 20; ++i) {
            System.out.print(displayChar);
        }
        timer.cancel();
    }
}
```

Implementing a run() method

- ☐ A subclass implementation of TimerTask's abstract method run() has typically two parts
  - ■ First part defines the application-specific action the thread is to perform
  - ■ Second part ends the thread
    - ☐ The thread is ended when the application-specific action has completed

```java
// run(): display the occurences of the character of interest
public void run() {
    for (int i = 0; i < 20; ++i) {          ⎫ Desired action
        System.out.print(displayChar);      ⎬ to be performed
    }                                        ⎭ by thread

    timer.cancel();      ⎫ Desired action is
}                        ⎬ completed so
                         ⎭ thread is
                           canceled
```

317

Running repeatedly

□ Example
- Having a clock face update every second

```
public static void main(String[] args) {
    SimpleClock clock = new SimpleClock();
}
```

```
public class SimpleClock extends TimerTask {
    final static long MILLISECONDS_PER_SECOND = 1000;
    private JFrame window = new JFrame("Clock");
    private Timer timer = new Timer();
    private String clockFace = "";
    public SimpleClock() {
        window.setDefaultCloseOperation(JFrame.EXIT_ON_CLOSE);
        window.setSize(200, 60);
        Container c = window.getContentPane();
        c.setBackground(Color.white);
        window.setVisible(true);

        timer.schedule(this, 0, 1*MILLISECONDS_PER_SECOND);
    }
    public void run() {
        Date time = new Date();
        Graphics g = window.getContentPane().getGraphics();
        g.setColor(Color.WHITE);
        g.drawString(clockFace, 10, 20);

        clockFace = time.toString();
        g.setColor(Color.BLUE);
        g.drawString(clockFace, 10, 20);
    }
}
```

SimpleClock scheduling

```
timer.schedule(this, 0, 1*MILLISECONDS_PER_SECOND);
```

The millisecond delay
before the thread is
first scheduled

The number of
milliseconds between
runs of the thread

Running at a chosen time

- □ Example
  - ■ Scheduling calendar pop-ups using class DisplayAlert

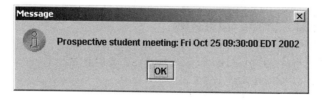

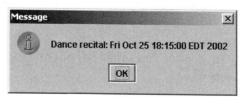

Using DisplayAlert

```java
public static void main(String[] args) {
    Calendar c = Calendar.getInstance();

    c.set(Calendar.HOUR_OF_DAY, 9);
    c.set(Calendar.MINUTE, 30);
    c.set(Calendar.SECOND, 0);

    Date studentTime = c.getTime();

    c.set(Calendar.HOUR_OF_DAY, 18);
    c.set(Calendar.MINUTE, 15);
    c.set(Calendar.SECOND, 0);

    Date danceTime = c.getTime();

    DisplayAlert alert1 = new DisplayAlert(
        "Prospective student meeting", studentTime);

    DisplayAlert alert2 = new DisplayAlert(
        "Dance recital", danceTime);
}
```

Defining DisplayAlert

```java
import javax.swing.JOptionPane;
import java.awt.*;
import java.util.*;

public class DisplayAlert extends TimerTask {
    private String message;
    private Timer timer;

    public DisplayAlert(String s, Date t) {
        message = s + ": " + t;
        timer = new Timer();
        timer.schedule(this, t);
    }

    public void run() {
        JOptionPane.showMessageDialog(null, message);
        timer.cancel();
    }
}
```

Sleeping

☐ Threads can be used to pause a program for a time
☐ Standard class java.lang.Thread has a class method sleep() for pausing a flow of control

public static void sleep(long n) throws InterruptedException
   ■ Pauses the current thread for n milliseconds. It then throws an InterruptedException.

Sleeping example

☐ Code
```
Date t1 = new Date();
System.out.println(t1);
try {
   Thread.sleep(10000);
}
catch (InterruptedException e) {
}
Date t2 = new Date();
System.out.println(t2);
```

☐ Output
```
Fri Jan 31 19:29:45 EST 2003
Fri Jan 31 19:29:55 EST 2003
```

Testing and Debugging

Testing Fundamentals

☐ Test as you develop
  - Easier to find bugs early rather than later
  - Prototyping helps identify problems early
☐ Categories of bugs
  - software crashes or data corruption
  - failure to meet or satisfy the specification
  - poor or unacceptable performance
  - hard or difficult to use

Testing fundamentals

☐ Impossible to test a program
completely

☐ Three distinct paths through
the program

☐ If the loop executes 20 times,
there are 3^{20} different
sequences of executions

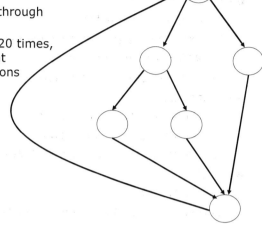

Reviews and inspections

☐ Inspections
  - Formal process of reviewing code
  - First employed by IBM in 1976
  - Early work showed that design and review inspections
    remove 60 percent of the bugs in a product

Reviews and inspections

☐ Roles of participants
  - Moderator
    - ☐ Runs the inspection
    - ☐ Ensure that the process moves along
    - ☐ Referees the discussion
    - ☐ Ensures action items done
  - Inspector
    - ☐ Someone other than author
    - ☐ Some interest in the code
    - ☐ Carefully review code before inspection meeting
  - Author
    - ☐ Minor role
    - ☐ May answer questions about code

Reviews and inspections

☐ Roles of participants
  - Scribe
    - ☐ Record all errors detected
    - ☐ Keep list of action items

Reviews and inspections

- ☐ Inspection process
  - ■ Planning
    - ☐ Code to review chosen
    - ☐ Moderator assigns task
    - ☐ Checklists created
    - ☐ Moderator assigns a presenter (usually one of the inspectors)
  - ■ Overview
    - ☐ Author describes high-level aspects of project that affected the design or code
    - ☐ Sometimes skipped (if all participants are knowledgeable)

Reviews and inspections

- ☐ Inspection process
  - ■ Preparation
    - ☐ Working alone, each inspector reviews code noting problems or questions
    - ☐ Shouldn't take more than a couple of hours
  - ■ Inspection meeting
    - ☐ Presenter walks through the code
    - ☐ Problems are discussed
    - ☐ Scribe records all errors and action items
    - ☐ Errors are not fixed at this time
  - ■ Inspection report
    - ☐ Moderator prepares a written report

Black-box and white-box testing

- White-box testing indicates that we can "see" or examine the code as we develop test cases
- Block-box testing indicates that we cannot examine the code as we devise test cases
  - Seeing the code can bias the test cases we create
  - Forces testers to use specification rather than the code
- Complementary techniques

Black-box and white-box testing

Test boundary conditions

```
public static int binarySearch(char[] data, char key) {
    int left = 0;
    int right = data.length - 1;
    while (left <= right) {
        int mid = (left + right)/2;
        if (data[mid] == key) {
            return mid;
        }
        else if (data[mid] < key) {
            left = mid + 1;
        }
        else {
            right = mid - 1;
        }
    }
    return data.length;
}
```

326

Black-box and white-box testing

Boundary conditions

```java
// validate input
if ((year < CALENDAR_START) || (month < 1) || (month > 12)) {
    System.output.println("Bad request: " + year + " "
        + month);
    return;
}
```

Black-box and white-box testing

☐ Suggests the following boundary tests

Input Year	Input Month
1582	2
1583	0
1583	13
1583	1
1583	12

Black-box and white-box testing

☐ Path coverage or path testing—create test cases that causes each edge of the program's controlflow graph to be executed

Example

```
if (x != y) {
    y = 5;
}
else {
    z = z - z;
}
if (x > 1) {
    z = z / x;
}
else {
    z = 0;
}
```

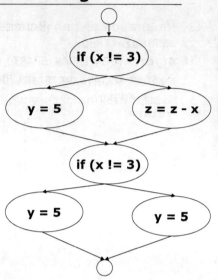

Black-box and white-box testing

☐ Testing tips
  - Test early
  - Use inspections
  - Test boundaries
  - Test exceptional conditions
  - Make testing easily repeatable

Integration and system testing

□ Integration testing is done as modules or components are assembled.
- Attempts to ensure that pieces work together correctly
- Test interfaces between modules

□ System testing occurs when the whole system is put together

Debugging

□ Use the scientific method
- Gather data
- Develop a hypothesis
- Perform experiments
- Predict new facts
- Perform experiments
- Prove or disprove hypothesis

Debugging

- ☐ Tips and techniques
  - ■ Simplify the problem
  - ■ Stabilize the error
  - ■ Locate the error
  - ■ Explain the bug to someone else
  - ■ Recognize common bugs
    - ☐ Oversubscripting
    - ☐ Dereferencing null
  - ■ Recompile everything
  - ■ Gather more information
  - ■ Pay attention to compiler warnings
  - ■ Fix bugs as you find them
  - ■ Take a break

LABORATORY 1
Background

Objective

As we all know, computers are vital tools in business, industry, and research. Understanding the computer's capabilities better enables us to pursue many different endeavors. This laboratory manual is a tool that allows us to experiment with computers to increase our understanding. As we progress through each laboratory, you may wonder how or why something works. The best way to discover the answer is to *try things out*.

Some of the activities in this lab might be familiar to you already. However, they are not familiar to everyone and our goal is to help everyone have a meaningful and rewarding experience. Several resources are available to help us achieve this goal. These resources include the laboratory instructor and any laboratory assistants, and the course text. Participants in the laboratory can assist in helping each other understand the material. Forming groups to complete this lab and subsequent labs can be beneficial, too. The goal is to permit each participant to complete each laboratory successfully and to experience the growth and satisfaction that comes with doing so.

Key Concepts

- Editing a Java program
- Compiling a Java program
- Executing a Java program
- Accessing the API specification

1.1 GETTING STARTED

Create the working directory `\javalab` on the appropriate disk drive and obtain a copy of self-extracting archive `lab01.exe`. Place the copy in the `javalab` directory. Execute the copy to extract the files necessary for this laboratory. If you are unfamiliar with creating a directory, obtaining a copy of the self-extracting archive, placing a copy of the archive in the directory, or executing the copy to extract the needed files, ask the laboratory instructor, a laboratory assistant, or another lab participant for guidance.

1.2 COMPILING AND RUNNING A JAVA PROGRAM

The most basic way to create and compile a Java program is to write the code using a text editor, and to compile and run the code in a shell window (on a Windows-based system, the shell is the MS-DOS prompt or Command Window). Integrated Development Environments (IDEs) allow us to create and edit programs, to compile and run the programs, and to perform debugging activities. Many IDEs also allow us to create graphical user interfaces (GUIs) and to generate automatically the Java code to display a custom interface. However, most of the commercial IDEs can be complex and difficult to learn for the beginning programmer. In between a complex IDE and a basic text editor is a specialized text editor that integrates with the Java SDK and allows us to compile and run applications or applets from the editor. Whether you are using an IDE or text editor, follow the steps below using the commands appropriate to your environment. Your lab instructor will give you instructions specific to your environment.

- In the *Open a File* window, select your `javalab` directory. You should see a list of `java` files that were created when you executed `lab01.exe`. The file you want is `MyQuote.java`.

- If your editor or IDE is integrated with the SDK, choose the *Compile* option to compile your program. If you are using a shell, open the shell window and compile the program using the following command:

  `javac MyQuote.java`

- If any error messages are displayed that you do not understand, you should consult the laboratory instructor. In a shell window, if the program is compiled correctly, the command prompt will appear again, usually with no message displayed. IDEs and integrated text editors usually display a message such as:

  `Tool completed successfully`

- If your editor or IDE is integrated with the SDK, choose the appropriate command to run the application (the command may be *Run Application*, *Execute* or a similar command). If you are using a shell, open the shell window and run the program using the following command:

  `java MyQuote`

- View the output in your console window (or output window if appropriate for your IDE).

```
Be dauntless in your pursuit of truth
and resist all demands for unthinking
conformity.
    - Hugh B. Brown
```

- Show the output to the lab instructor and have the lab instructor initial this step in the check-off sheet found at the back of this lab manual.

1.3 MAKING PROGRAM MODIFICATIONS

- If the file MyQuote.java is no longer open from the previous exercise, open it again, following the same procedure you used in the previous exercise.

```
// Author:
// Purpose: display a quotation in a console window
// Date:
// Lab Section:

public class MyQuote {

    // method main(): application entry point
    public static void main(String[] args) {
        System.out.println("Be dauntless in your pursuit of
truth");
        System.out.println("and resist all demands for
unthinking");
        System.out.println("conformity.");
        System.out.println("    - Hugh B. Brown");

    }
}
```

- Comments in the heading at the top of the file provide information about the program. Modify the heading to add your name as author, today's date, and your lab section. Comment lines begin with two forward slashes //. If you click somewhere in this window, you should see a blinking horizontal line called the insertion point. When you start typing, whatever you type will be inserted there. You can move the insertion point with the mouse or with the arrow keys. Your lab instructor will give you editing instructions specific to your editor.

- Don't worry if you don't fully understand the `System.out.println` statement. You will learn more about this statement in class lectures and in succeeding labs. For now, you just need to understand that this is the statement used to output text to the console.

- Change the quote in the program to a quote of your own choosing. Make sure that you change only the text in between the double-quotes. Do not type over or delete the double-quotes. If you choose to use a shorter quote, you may delete one or more entire `System.out.println(. . .` lines. You may add one or more `System.out.println(. . .` lines, if you choose a longer quote.

- Save your program by selecting the *Save* option from the *File* menu. If you do not save the program, you can lose everything you typed.

- Compile your program as you did in the preceding exercise.

- If you encounter problems as you attempt to compile, compare the program above with the source line in your program at which the compiler is signaling the error. Be sure that the lines are identical, including the punctuation! Sometimes it is necessary to check the preceding line for errant typing. After correcting the errors, if any, recompile the program. If you cannot determine the error, consult the laboratory instructor.

- Execute your program as you did in the preceding exercise.

- View the output in your console window (or output window if appropriate for your IDE).

- Show the output to the lab instructor and have the lab instructor initial this step in the check-off sheet found at the back of the lab manual.

1.4   ACCESSING THE API SPECIFICATION

Many IDEs provide a utility called context-sensitive help. By choosing from a menu while typing a keyword, or often by right-clicking on part of a Java statement, we can open a help window that will provide information on the syntax of the statement or more information about a method. There is no standard for context-sensitive help, so if you are using an IDE that provides this service, your lab instructor will explain how to use it.

Part of the SDK includes the API specification. There are many standard libraries with hundreds of classes provided with the Java SDK. This makes it almost impossible to remember the syntax of all the methods. Instead, we can access the API specification for all the classes and methods in the standard libraries to learn the correct use and syntax of the fields and methods of the classes. While you are just beginning to learn about Java, some of the words like "class" and "package" may be confusing to you. Don't worry. You will become familiar with these topics in later labs and in class. But, it is helpful to learn how to use the API Specification early so that you are able to access it easily in succeeding labs.

- Using your web browser, open the file `index.html` located in your Java root directory in the subdirectory `/docs/api/`. Your lab instructor will direct you to the correct location of the Java root directory on your computer.

- The browser window is divided into three subwindows. The top left subwindow contains a list of all the packages (groups of classes with similar function) in the standard library. The bottom left subwindow contains a list of all the classes in the specification. Scroll through the bottom left window. You will see that there are many classes in the standard library! The main subwindow lists the packages in the standard library together with a short description of the package.

- In the main subwindow, click on the link to the `java.lang` library. In the *Class Summary*, find and click on the class `System`.

- In the *Field Summary*, find and click on `out` (the "standard" output stream).

- Now you can read how to use the `System.out.println()` method.

- Scroll to the top of the document and click on the *Overview* link. Now you should be back to the starting point, `index.html`.

- The `java.lang` package contains a class `Math`. The `Math` class has a field `PI`. Find the description of the field `PI` and write it here:

  _____

  _____

- Show this description to the lab instructor and have the lab instructor initial this step in the check-off sheet found at the back of the lab manual.

1.7 FINISHING UP

- Using the Windows Explorer, copy to your own drive any files you wish to save.

- If you are instructed to do so, use the Windows Explorer to delete the `javalab` directory.

- Hand in your check-off sheet.

Congratulations! You have finished the first laboratory and you are on your way to becoming a Java programmer.

CHECK-OFF SHEET: LABORATORY 1

1.1   IDENTIFICATION

Name:	
Email:	
Section:	
Date:	

1.2   CHECK-OFFS

As you complete each laboratory activity, obtain a laboratory instructor's initials. Hand in the sheet at the end of the laboratory session so that your participation in the laboratory activities can be recorded.

✓	Activity	Lab Instructor's Initials
☐	**Ran "MyQuote.java"**	_____
☐	**Modified "MyQuote.java"**	_____
☐	**API description of PI**	_____

LABORATORY 2
Solving Our First Problem

Objective

This laboratory provides us with our first opportunity to decompose a problem into manageable pieces and to solve it. It also introduces the process of compiling a program that uses a library called an Application Programmer Interface or API. We will learn more about how to identify and use class methods. We will be doing a few things that probably are new to you. If you have any questions or problems, just ask your laboratory instructor for help.

Key Concepts

- Expression evaluation
- Hand-checking code
- Simple input and output
- Expressing mathematical equations in Java
- Class methods
- Deprecated methods

2.1 GETTING STARTED

Using the procedures in the introductory laboratory handout, create the working directory \javalab on the appropriate disk drive and obtain a copy of self-extracting archive lab02.exe. The copy should be placed in the javalab directory. Execute the copy to extract the files necessary for this laboratory.

2.1 SOLVING YOUR A, B, C'S

- Examine the program below. In the space provided below, write what you expect the program output to be.

```
public class SolvingABC {

    public static void main(String[] args)  {
       //Object definitions and initializations
       int a = 3;
       int b = 12;
       int c = 6;
       int d = 1;
```

```
//Now calculate the results
d = d * a;
c = c + 2 * a;
d = d - b / c;
c = c * b % c;
b = b / 2;

//Finally display the results
System.out.println("a : " + a);
System.out.println("b : " + b);
System.out.println("c : " + c);
System.out.println("d : " + d);

    }
}
```
Enter the expected program output here:

- Start the java compiler as described in the opening laboratory. Open the file called `SolvingABC.java`. It should contain the preceding program.
- Compile and run the program, and observe the output.
- Did you get the same answers for your manual calculations as you did from the computer program? If there are differences, try to determine why. If you cannot determine the reason for the differences, ask a laboratory instructor for help.
- Allowing a user to supply input values is a better technique than hardcoding the values in program instructions because it makes the program more general. Now we will modify `SolvingABC.java` to extract user input from the standard input stream.
- Delete the hard-coded initialization of `a`, `b`, `c`, and `d`. Do not delete the variable declarations, just the initialization values.
- In order to obtain input from the user, we need to use classes found in the standard Java software library `java.io`. To access a software library, also referred to as an *application programming interface (API)* or *package*, we need to add an import statement to the `SolvingABC` code. The import statement needs to be the first line of code in a program. Scroll to the top of your `SolvingABC` program and add the following line of code:

```
import java.io.*;
```

- Now we need to create a `BufferedReader` object to allow us to receive input from the user. Just below the variable declarations for a, b, c, and d, add the following:

```
BufferedReader stdin = new BufferedReader(
        new InputStreamReader(System.in));
```

- Add a prompt that tells the user of the program what you want him to do. In this case, we want to prompt the user to supply a value for the variable a. Add a statement to do the extraction. Your code might look like the following:

```
System.out.print("Enter value for variable a: ");
a = Integer.parseInt(stdin.readLine());
```

- It is important to prompt the user for each object separately. Add lines of code to the program that prompt the user to enter values for variables b, c, and d. Be sure to store the user's keyboard input in the appropriate object. Save the program.
- Compile and run your improved program.
- You should receive four error messages similar to the following:

```
D:\javalab\SolvingABC.java:16: unreported exception
    java.io.IOException; must be caught or declared to be thrown
        a = Integer.parseInt(stdin.readLine());
```

- If the user does not supply valid values for variables a, b, c, and d, Java signals the program that an *exception* (something unexpected) has occurred. Ideally, our program should be able to take this possibility into account. However, until we learn additional language features, our program will ignore any exceptions that arise. To allow our program to ignore the exceptions we received, we need to modify the declaration of our main method:

```
public static void main(String[] args) throws IOException  {
```
Compile and run your program again. You should receive no error messages. If you get an error message that you do not understand, ask a laboratory instructor for help.

- After developing a program or modifying an existing one, a key question is, "Does the program run correctly?" One way is to hand-check the program. Hand-checking a program involves computing the results by hand for some inputs and making sure the results agree with what the computer outputs for the same inputs. You can hand-check your modified program by using as inputs the values that were used to initialize the integer variables a, b, c, and d in the original program. Run your program and enter the values that were used to initialize the variables a, b, c, and d in the original program. Did you get the same results?
- Once the program is working, demonstrate it to a laboratory instructor.

2.3   OPERATION ORDER IS IMPORTANT

Now let us consider a slightly more challenging problem—writing the general
solution to an algebraic problem. Suppose you have a problem that you wish to
solve. You should take the following steps to write a program to solve the problem:

 ➢ Determine the inputs and outputs.
 ➢ Define variables for the inputs and outputs.
 ➢ Compute the answer (in parts, if it is complicated).
 ➢ Output the answer.

This process seems straightforward, so let us give it a try. For the next part of the
lab, we are going to write a program that solves the following equations:

 ➢ $2a^2 + 4a - 29$

 ➢ $\dfrac{4c + ac}{3b}$

 ➢ $\dfrac{10b + 4a}{3c} + \left(\dfrac{\frac{cb}{a}}{4/d} \right)$

 ➢ $\dfrac{10b + 4a}{3c} + \left(\dfrac{\frac{cb}{a}}{4/d} \right) \times \dfrac{10b + 4a}{3c} + \left(\dfrac{\frac{cb}{a}}{4/d} \right)$

- Determine the types of the variables.
  - ○ For these equations, we can use the type `double` because three of the
    equations contain a division operation. If we used `int` variables, the
    result of the division operation will be truncated, which would produce
    erroneous results.
- Determine how many inputs and outputs there will be.
- Will we need any temporary space to store partial computations?
- Alternatively, do we want to try computing the larger problem with one huge
  equation?
- List the definitions of all the objects you will need for input, for output, and for
  temporary computations in the area provided below. We will do the first
  declaration for you:

  ```
  double result1;
  ```

- Write the expression for each equation as it will need to appear in Java code in order to be correct. Pay particular attention to the order of operations in each problem. Be sure to use parentheses ( ) as needed to enforce the correct evaluation of each expression. We will do the first one for you. Does your solution agree? If not, review your answers for it and for the other equations.

```
result1 = (2 * a * a) + (4 * a) - 29;
```

- Write the Java expression of equation #2 here:

- Write the Java expression of equation #3 here:

- Write the Java expression of equation #4 here:

- Open the file `compute.java`. Use this file as a basis for computing the above equations.
- Complete the program in that file.
- Save your work often. In particular, always save it before you do a compile and run.
- Once it is working, demonstrate it to a laboratory instructor.

2.4   EXPLORING CLASS METHODS

In the text, we explored how to convert lowercase characters to uppercase characters using character encoding and `char` arithmetic. Because converting characters from one case to another is a common programming activity, the standard Java class `java.lang.Character` provides class methods to do the conversion quickly. We now explore these methods and some of the other useful class methods in the `Character` class.

- Using the procedure you followed in Lab 1, open the Java API Specification and find the specification for the `Character` class. You can either select the `java.lang` package in the main window, and then select the `Character` class, or you can scroll down in the bottom left window, *All Classes*, until you find (and select) the `Character` class.
- Once you have loaded the specification for the `Character` class, scroll down the main window until you reach the *Method Summary* section.
- Scroll through the methods. Since we are interested in *class methods*, we are interested only in the methods that contain the keyword `static` in the left column. Most of the methods we are interested in begin with "`to-`" or "`is-`." Choose three class methods and click on them to read their method details. Write the full method definition for your three chosen methods in the space provided below. For example, if you chose the method `toLowerCase`, you would select `toLowercase` in the *Method Summary* section. The link will take you to the *Method Detail*, where you will find the method definition and a description of the method. You should write the full method definition below as:

`public static char toLowerCase(char ch)`
This method definition tells you the `toLowerCase` is a class method (`static`) that, when passed a `char` value, returns a `char` value.

Write your three chosen method definitions here:

- Notice that some of the class methods such as `isJavaLetter` are described as **Deprecated**. Deprecated methods are methods that are contained in previous versions of Java, but may not be included in later versions. You may still use deprecated methods in your code, but there is no guarantee that later versions of Java will support the method. In general, use of deprecated methods is discouraged. If you compile code that uses a deprecated method, the code will compile, but the compiler will issue a warning. If you want to see a list of deprecated methods that you have used in your code, you can run the compiler with the deprecation flag set, such as below:

```
javac -deprecation CharMethods.java
```

- Open the file CharMethods.java. You will be modifying this program to include the Character class methods you chose above. Following the conventions in the CharMethods program, add lines that output the results of your methods calls.

```java
import java.io.*;

public class CharMethods {
    public static void main(String[] args) throws IOException {

        BufferedReader stdin = new BufferedReader(
                new InputStreamReader(System.in));

        //get the char value from the user
        System.out.print("Enter a character: ");
        char c = (char)stdin.read();

        //echo the user's input
        System.out.println("You entered character " + c);

        //execute several Character class methods on input c
        System.out.println("Your character in lower case is " +
                Character.toLowerCase(c));
        System.out.println("Is your character whitespace? " +
                Character.isWhitespace(c));

        //add your methods here

    }
}
```

- Notice the line

```java
char c = (char)stdin.read();
```

The BufferedReader.read method returns a byte value in an int. We cast the int return value to a char and then assign it to char c.

- Complete the program in that file. Once it is working, demonstrate it to a laboratory instructor.

2.5 FINISHING UP

- Copy any files you wish to keep to your drive.
- Delete the directory \javalab.
- Hand in your check-off sheet.

Congratulations. You have now finished the second laboratory.

CHECK-OFF SHEET: LABORATORY 2

2.1   IDENTIFICATION

Name: Email:	
Section: 	
Date:	

2.2   CHECK-OFFS

As you complete each laboratory activity, obtain a laboratory instructor's initials. Hand in the sheet at the end of the laboratory session so that your participation in the laboratory activities can be recorded.

✓	Activity	Lab Instructor's Initials
☐	**"SolvingABC.java" runs**	_____
☐	**Converting equations**	_____
☐	**Character methods**	_____

LABORATORY 3
Investigating Objects

Objective

This is our first real exposure to objects, which form the basis of the Java language. We will use the `string` class to investigate how to create and work with objects. Object data types are different from primitive data types. An object has attributes and behaviors, whereas primitive types have only attributes. We can access the attributes and behaviors of objects by calling member methods. Because the memory location of an object variable stores a reference to a memory locations that holds the object, rather than holding the object itself, we will learn how to compare `string` references and how to compare the actual values of `string` objects.

Key Concepts

- String class
- Object variable references
- Null references and unassigned variables
- Using member methods

3.1. GETTING STARTED

Using the procedures in the introductory laboratory handout, create the working directory `\javalab` on the appropriate disk drive and obtain a copy of self-extracting archive `lab03.exe`. Place the copy in the `javalab` directory. Execute the copy to extract the files necessary for this laboratory.

3.2. COMPARING STRINGS

One of the important standard classes provided by Java is the `string` class. The `string` class is a part of the `java.lang` package. Whereas the fundamental type `char` stores a single character, the `string` class enables us to create objects that hold a character sequence. The literal character strings that we have worked with in previous labs (such as `"Enter value for variable a: "`) all were treated internally by Java as instances of the `string` class.

- Start up your compiler and open the file `CompareStrings.java`.

- Compile and run `CompareStrings.java`.

- Because all strings in Java are objects, we cannot compare strings the same way that we compare numbers. That is, we cannot use the equality operators `==` and `!=` to determine if two strings contain the same sequence of characters. The equality operators compare the memory location of the objects, not the values stored at those locations. To compare the values of the `string` objects, we use the method `String.compareTo()`.

- The method `compareTo()` returns the value 0 if the both strings are equal. The method returns a negative number if the string calling the method is lexicographically (similar to "alphabetically," but not limited to the alphabetic characters) less than the string argument. The method returns a positive number if the string calling the method is lexicographically greater than the string argument. For example, the `"cat".compareTo("dog")` returns a negative number because `cat` "comes before" `dog`.

- Modify `CompareStrings.java` so that it accepts two strings as input from the user.

- Once you have your program working, try entering the following strings as input and record the results. In the first two columns, place a star next to the string that is lexicographically less than the other. If the two strings are equal, place a star next to each one.

FirstString	SecondString	FirstString == SecondString	FirstString.compareTo (SecondString)
cat	dog		
fish	fish		
fish	squid		
squid	Squid		
fish	fISH		

- Show your results to your laboratory instructor. Explain when `FirstString == SecondString` will return true.

3.3. UNASSIGNED STRINGS AND NULL STRINGS

- Open the file `Null.java`.

```
public class Null {
```

```
public static void main(String[] args) {
    String a;
    String b = null;
    String c = null;
    String d = "a string";
    String e = d;

    System.out.println("d == e : " + (d == e));
    System.out.println("d.compareTo(e) =  " + d.compareTo(e));
  }
}
```

- Compile and run `Null.java`. Observe the output. Why does `d == e` return true?

- What happens when we compare two null strings? Add the following line:

  ```
  System.out.println("b == c :" + (b == c));
  ```

- Compile and run the program again. Observe the output. Did you expect this output? Explain why the program produced this result.

- Can we compare two null strings? Add the following line:

  ```
  System.out.println("b.compareTo(c) =  " + b.compareTo(c));
  ```

- Compile and run the program. The program will compile, but what happens when you run it? You should get an output similar to the below:

  ```
  d == e : true
  d.compareTo(e) =  0
  b == c : true
  java.lang.NullPointerException
          at Null_working.main(Null_working.java:14)
  Exception in thread "main"
  ```

- It looks like the program ran correctly until it encountered the statement you just added that called `b.compareTo(c)`. Let's check the Java API Specification for the `string.compareTo()` method. Open the API Specification and find the class summary for `string`. It is located in the `java.lang` package. In the method summary, find the method detail for the `compareTo()` method. At the bottom of the method detail, you will see a statement similar to this:

  ```
  public int compareTo(String anotherString)
  . . .
  Throws:
  NullPointerException - if anotherString is null.
  ```

This method will cause an exception (an error) to occur if we call it using a null string. We will learn how to handle the exception in a later chapter. For now, we need to know only that our program will "throw" an exception and halt if we call this method using a null string.

- Delete the line that caused the exception.

- Let's try comparing a string with an unassigned string. Add the following line to your program:

```
System.out.println("d.compareTo(a) = " + d.compareTo(a));
```

- Compile your program. Your program should not compile correctly. You should receive an error message similar to the following:

```
D:\javalab\Null.java:15: variable a might not have been
initialized
        System.out.println("d.compareTo(a) = " + d.compareTo(a));
                                                              ^

1 error
```

- An unassigned object is different from a null object. The Java compiler will detect if a program attempts to access an object variable that has not been assigned a value. Since `string b` was assigned the value `null`, the compiler did not issue an error when our program called the `b.compareTo(c)` method.

3.4. UTILITY METHODS

- Open the file `ReplaceChars.java`. Although the file will compile and run, it contains an error that will produce incorrect output.

```java
import java.io.*;

public class ReplaceChars {

    public static void main(String[] args) throws IOException
    {
        final char OLD_CHAR = 'a';
        final char NEW_CHAR = 'o';

        BufferedReader stdin =
            new BufferedReader(new InputStreamReader(System.in));

        System.out.print("Enter a string: ");
        String input = stdin.readLine();

        System.out.println("Your string \"" + input +
          "\" has been converted to");
```

```
            input.replace(OLD_CHAR,NEW_CHAR);

            System.out.println(input);
        }
}
```

- Before you compile and run the program, let's examine the code. In the first two lines, we declare two character constants, `OLD_CHAR` and `NEW_CHAR`. In the second to last line, we call the `replace` method in the `string` class to replace all instances of the character `OLD_CHAR` ('a') with the character `NEW_CHAR` ('o'). It is possible to call the replace method without using constants such as:

```
input.replace( 'a', 'o');
```

However, good programmers prefer the systematic use of symbolic names over literal values—so called "magic" numbers—because the names provide meaning.

- Compile and run the program. Provide input containing several instances of the character 'a' to check the program. Is the output what you expected?

- Carefully review the code and try to identify what line of code is causing the problem.

- Let's focus on the following line of code:

```
            input.replace(OLD_CHAR,NEW_CHAR);
```

- The first step we should take is to check the API specification to make sure that we are using this method correctly. Open the Java API specification and find the class summary for `string`. It is located in the `java.lang` package. In the method summary, find the method detail for the `replace` method.

- Read the method detail. Does it look like we are using the method correctly?

- We should note that the method returns a new string with the appropriate replacement of characters. In our next line of code,

```
            System.out.println(input);
```

we are printing the value of `input`, not the returned string. `string` objects are immutable. That is, once they are initialized, their value cannot change. We called the method correctly, but we did not print the correct output.

- Create a `string` object reference named `output` and use it to reference the string returned by our call to the `replace` method. Change the code so that it prints this `string` and runs correctly.

- Now, modify your program so that a user can specify what character he wants to replace when the program is run. Although the `BufferReader.read()` method will return a character value, most users will strike the "enter" key after typing a character, so this is not a good method to use in this case to read a character from the standard input. Look up the specification on the `String.charAt()` method and use that method to extract the first character entered in the String returned by the `BufferedReader.readLine()` method.

- Make sure that you add meaningful prompts.

- Show your completed program to the lab instructor.

3.5. FINISHING UP

- Copy any files you wish to keep to your own drive.

- Delete the directory `\javalab`.

- Hand in your check-off sheet.

Congratulations. You have now finished the third laboratory.

CHECK-OFF SHEET: LABORATORY 3

3.1   IDENTIFICATION

Name:	
Email:	
Section:	
Date:	

3.2   CHECK-OFFS

As you complete each laboratory activity, obtain a laboratory instructor's initials. Hand in the sheet at the end of the laboratory session so that your participation in the laboratory activities can be recorded.

✓	Activity	Lab Instructor's Initials
☐	**Comparing strings**	_____
☐	**"Null.java"**	_____
☐	**Replacing characters**	_____

LABORATORY 4
Being Classy

Objective

Objects are the basic units of programming in object-oriented languages like Java. We define new types of objects by designing our own classes. A class is the "blueprint" from which objects can be created. This lab introduces us to designing and working with our own classes. We will build a program by creating two custom classes. We will explore information hiding and data abstraction. We will learn about some of the kinds of methods that classes can have.

Key Concepts

- Class design

- Data abstraction

- Information hiding

- Instance variables

- Accessor methods

- Mutator methods

- Constructors

- Facilitator methods

- `Graphics.drawArc()` and `Graphics.fillArc()` methods

4.1   GETTING STARTED

- Using the procedures in the introductory laboratory handout, create the working directory `\javalab` on the appropriate disk drive and obtain a copy of self-extracting archive `lab04.exe`. The copy should be placed in the `javalab` directory. Execute the copy to extract the files needed for this laboratory.

4.2 DESIGN

For this lab, we are going to design and create a program that will display a "smiley face" in a window, as in the figure below.

The size of the smiley face is dynamic and dependent upon the size of the window. That is, our program will automatically scale the smiley face to fit properly in whatever size window is created.

- The first step in creating a program to satisfy the specified requirements is the design phase. We need to develop the overall framework for the program. First, how will the user see the program? The user should be able to enter the size of a window and have a window of that size appear with a smiley face in the window. The user is not expected to provide the features of the face or the positions of these features. These will be calculated by our program.

- What variables should the user be able to access? What variables should the user be able to modify?

  _____

  _____

  _____

  _____

- In order to preserve encapsulation, a user should be able to specify only the size of the window. The user does not need to have any understanding of how the smiley face is drawn or scaled to the window.

- However, what do we as programmers need to know to draw a smiley face? List below the variables that we will need in order to render a smiley face in accordance with the specifications of our program.

358

_____

_____

_____

_____

   .

_____

- How many classes should we create? We could create one class **SmileyWindow** that reads input from the user, creates a window, and draws a smiley face in the window. In object-oriented programming, it is best to break tasks into easily managed pieces. Let's begin by creating a class **SmileyFace** that will do the actual rendering of the face. If we create a separate class, we can reuse that class in another application. For example, perhaps we will want to draw a button with a smiley face on it in a later program. We can create a button and then access the **SmileyFace** class to draw the face, instead of creating a completely new class from scratch.

4.3   MORE DESIGN AND CODE PRODUCTION

- Now let's begin building the **SmileyFace** class. Our program will compute the location of the eyes and smile on the face automatically. Therefore, we need to know only the diameter of the face and the location of the face.

- Open the file **SmileyFace.java**.

```
import java.awt.*;

public class SmileyFace {
    private int diameter;
    private int x;
    private int y;

    // constructors


    // accessor methods


    // mutator methods
```

```
// facilitator methods
public void draw(Graphics g) {

}

    . . .

}
```

- Notice that our `SmileyFace` class contains three *instance variables*: `diameter`, `x`, and `y`. Why are the variables declared as `private`?

- It is good programming practice to create *accessor* and *mutator* methods for each of our instance variables. Accessor methods typically begin with `get` followed by the variable name. Their return type is the same as the variable type. Add accessor methods to your program for each instance variable. We create the first one for you:

```
public int getDiameter() {
        return diameter;
}
```

- Compile your program. Although there is nothing to run right now, compiling your program helps find syntax errors early. After every code revision, it is a good idea to compile the code to check for and to correct syntax errors, such as a missed semicolon or a misspelled variable name.

- Mutator methods are methods that change the value of the variable. Mutator methods typically begin with `set` followed by the variable name. Mutator methods are passed a parameter of the same type as the variable. Mutator methods do not return a value, so their return type is `void`. Add mutator methods to your program for each instance variable. We create the first one for you:

```
public void setDiameter(int d) {
        diameter = d;
}
```

- In general, it is best to name the parameters in mutators with a name different from the instance variable. However, Java will allow you to have parameters that have the same name as instance variables. How does Java tell which variable is which?

```
    public void setDiameter(int diameter) {
        diameter = diameter; // the instance variable diameter is
not set!!
    }
```

The parameter name has precedence over the instance variable name. In the code above, the *parameter* `diameter` is set to the value of the *parameter* `diameter`; hardly a useful activity! To set the *instance variable* `diameter`, we need to use the following code:

```
public void setDiameter(int diameter) {
    this.diameter = diameter;
}
```

We will learn more about `this` in later chapters. For now, `this` refers to the class and `this.diameter` refers to the instance variable `diameter`.

- Although providing these methods may seem to be unnecessary, the methods are important for achieving *information hiding,* an important software engineering principle. Properly hiding information gives the program, not the user, control over the circumstances under which variables can be accessed or modified. You can also choose to modify the internal representation of the smiley face, but the user will not know the difference because he will still call the same accessors and mutators to set the diameter and coordinates of the face. Separating the internal representation from the user interface, including the accessors and mutators, is another important software engineering principle.

- Now we will add constructors to the code. Add a constructor that initializes the `diameter`, `x` and `y` variables with user-supplied values. To preserve information hiding, make sure that your constructor calls the appropriate mutator methods rather than accessing the variables directly. We provide the header for the constructor:

```
public SmileyFace(int d, int xPos, int yPos) {
}
```

- Do we need any other constructors? We may need to create a `SmileyFace` object before we know the diameter and position of the object. In this case, we need a default constructor that has no parameters and simply initializes the object. We can add constants to our object that provide the default value of each instance variable, or we can simply allow the compiler to initialize each `int` variable to `0` automatically. For now, since we will be setting the diameter and coordinates, we will choose to allow the compiler perform a default initialization for each variable. Add the following default constructor to your code

```
public SmileyFace() {
}
```

- If you do not have any constructors in your class, the compiler automatically adds a constructor like the one that you just added to your code. However, if you have any constructors in your class, the complier will not add a default constructor and you will need to add it yourself if you want one for your class.

- Now that we have created our accessor, mutator and constructor methods, we can concentrate on the *facilitator* methods. Facilitator methods are methods that help the object perform its intended task. In this case, we need to provide a `SmileyFace` object, including its `diameter` and `x` and `y` positions so that it can calculate the coordinates of its features and draw itself. Because of time constraints in the lab, we've provided the calculations for you in the file.

- Let's learn how we draw circles and arcs. Open up the Java API specification and find the method detail for `Graphics.drawArc()`, located in the

  `g.drawArc(x, y, width, height, _____, _____);`

  `g.drawArc(x, y, width, height, _____, _____);`

  `g.drawArc(x, y, width, height, _____, _____);`

  `java.awt` package. Fill in the blanks below to produce Java code to draw the following arcs:

- The method `Graphics.fillArc()` works the same way as `Graphics.drawArc`, except that it fills the arc with the current Graphics color setting.

- Review the methods `drawFace`, `drawEyes` and `drawMouth`. Do you understand how the methods work? It may help to work through the code with pencil and paper.

- You will notice that instead of calculating the facial feature coordinates and drawing them in a single method, we distributed the tasks across multiple

362

methods. In programming, it is generally recommended that you break down a task into easily manageable pieces. We could have placed all the code to draw the face in the **draw** method. But, it is easier to read and debug code that is broken down into manageable pieces, each represented by a separate method. Add the following lines to your object's **draw** method:

```
drawFace(g);
drawEyes(g);
drawSmile(g);
```

- Compile your **SmileyFace** class. If you get any compiler errors, try to determine where you made any mistakes. If you cannot figure out what is wrong, ask the lab instructor for assistance.

4.4   PUTTING IT ALL TOGETHER

- Open the file **SmileyWindow.java**.

```
import java.awt.*;
import javax.swing.*;
import java.io.*;

public class SmileyWindow {
    JFrame window;

    public SmileyWindow() {
        window = new JFrame("Smile");
        window.setDefaultCloseOperation(JFrame.EXIT_ON_CLOSE);
    }

    public void setSize(int width, int height) {
        window.setSize(width, height);
    }

    public void paint() {
        window.setVisible(true);
    }

    public static void main(String[] args) throws IOException {
        SmileyWindow me = new SmileyWindow();

        System.out.print(
            "Enter window size : ");
        BufferedReader stdin =
            new BufferedReader(new InputStreamReader(System.in));

        int size = Integer.parseInt(stdin.readLine());
```

363

```
        me.setSize(size, size);
        me.paint();
    }
}
```

- You may have noticed that the window we created is square. Until we learn to write a program that can make decisions with the **if** statement, it is easier to determine the diameter of the face using a square window.

- Compile and run the program. It should prompt you for a size and then display an empty window with width and height equal to the size which you provided as input. Do you understand how the program works?

- Now we will add our **SmileyFace** to the window. Add an instance variable named **face** of type **SmileyFace** to your program.

```
SmileyFace face;
```

- When we call our **SmileyWindow** constructor, it initializes the **JFrame** for our window and sets its default close operation to **EXIT_ON_CLOSE**. Add a line of code in the constructor to initialize the face variable by calling its default constructor.

```
face = new SmileyFace();
```

- When the window size is set in the **setSize()** method, we need to set the size of our **SmileyFace** object. We will set our **SmileyFace** diameter to ¾ths of the window width. The x position of the face will be ½ the distance remaining after the diameter is subtracted from the width of the window. The y position is the same as the x position except that we allowed 10 pixels to accommodate the window title bar. Add the following lines of code to **setSize()**:

```
// calculate size of smiley face, 3/4 of the window width
int diameter = width / 4 * 3;

int x = (width - diameter ) / 2;
int y = x + 10;
```

- Notice the first line of code:

```
int diameter = width / 4 * 3;
```

Why wouldn't we use the following?

```
int diameter = 3 / 4 * width;
```

364

If we used the preceding line of code the value for diameter would always be set to 0. Why? (*Hint: This has something to do with* `int` *arithmetic*.)

_____

_____

_____

_____

_____

- Use our calculated diameter and x and y positions to set these values in `face`. Add the following lines in your `setSize()` method following the code you just added to calculate these variables.

```
face.setDiameter(diameter);
face.setX(x);
face.setY(y);
```

- Now our final step is to call `SmileyFace.draw()`. In the `paint()` method, add the following lines of code:

```
Graphics g = window.getGraphics();
face.draw(g);
```

- We want `face` to draw itself in `window`, so we call `window.getGraphics()` to get the graphics context for `window`. We pass this graphics context to `face`.

- Compile and run the program. If it does not compile or run correctly, try to determine what the problem is. If you cannot figure it out, ask your lab instructor for assistance.

- When your program runs successfully, try entering different sizes to see if your face is drawn correctly. It is possible to enter sizes that are too small or sizes that are too large. In later chapters we will learn how to address this problem.

- Show your completed program to the lab instructor.

4.5 FINISHING UP

- Copy any files you wish to keep to your own drive.

- Delete the directory `\javalab`.

- Hand in your check-off sheet.

Congratulations! You have now finished the fourth laboratory.

CHECK-OFF SHEET: LABORATORY 4

4.1   IDENTIFICATION

Name:	
Email:	
Section:	
Date:	

4.2   CHECK-OFFS

As you complete each laboratory activity, obtain a laboratory instructor's initials. Hand in the sheet at the end of the laboratory session so that your participation in the laboratory activities can be recorded.

✓	Activity	Lab Instructor's Initials
☐	**Smiley face design**	_____
☐	**Smiley face code**	_____
☐	**Program completed**	_____

LABORATORY 5
Decisions, Decisions

Objective

As your knowledge of the Java language grows, your capacity to write more useful and more complex programs also increases. The `if` statement is a powerful tool for decision making. However, it can lead to considerable confusion if you do not fully understand its usage. This laboratory familiarizes you with the `if` statement, Boolean logic, and introduces you to program decision making.

Key Concepts

- The `if` statement
- Boolean logic
- Truth tables
- The `switch` statement
- Comparing objects using `equals()`

5.1 GETTING STARTED

- Using the procedures in the previous laboratories, create the working directory `\javalab` on the appropriate disk drive and obtain a copy of self-extracting archive `lab05.exe`. The copy should be placed in the `javalab` directory. Execute the copy to extract the files needed for this laboratory.

5.2 SYNTAX ERRORS AREN'T THE ONLY PROBLEM

In addition to syntax errors, also known as compile-time errors, there are also logic errors. Code often compiles successfully (i.e., there are no syntax errors). Does this mean that the code will work? Well, it will do *exactly* what you tell it to do, but not necessarily what you want it to do. Programmers sometimes write programs that they think *look* correct and that compile without producing any errors, but *do not* produce the intended results (i.e., there are logic errors). This situation results in frustrated users, and sometimes in users who do not know that the program is producing incorrect results.

Another source of logic errors is misunderstandings about the uses of particular language features and their effects on the flow of execution in the program (what the program does and which paths it takes when you run it). In the following exercise we will learn how to follow the logic of an `if` statement and to create tests cases to avoid unintended errors.

5.3 THE `if` STATEMENT

The `if` statement allows the programmer to make decisions. If some expression is true, one course of action is taken. If the expression is false, the course of action is skipped. The `if` statement can lead to problems. The following exercises will help you to understand the `if` statement so that you can avoid some of its troublesome pitfalls.

- Open the program `triangle.java`. This program expects as input three numbers in nondecreasing order. The numbers represent the lengths of three sides of a possible triangle. It first determines whether the user correctly entered the numbers. If the user did not, the program terminates with a message to the user. If the instructions were followed, the program determines whether the numbers correspond to the sides of a triangle, and if they do, what kind of triangle.

- Examine the program to learn how it works.

```
import java.io.*;

public class Triangle {

    public static void main(String[] args) throws IOException {

        // prompt user to type 3 numbers in nondecreasing order

        BufferedReader stdin = new BufferedReader(new
            InputStreamReader(System.in));

        System.out.println("\nPlease enter the lengths of the sides
            of your possible triangle.");
        System.out.println("The program requires that the numbers
be in
            nondecreasing order.");
        System.out.println("That is, first number <= second number
            <= third number.\n");

        System.out.print("First number: ");
        int side1 = Integer.parseInt(stdin.readLine());
```

```
        System.out.print("Second number: ");
        int side2 = Integer.parseInt(stdin.readLine());

        System.out.print("Third number: ");
        int side3 = Integer.parseInt(stdin.readLine());

        // make sure user followed our rules

        if ( (side1 > side2) || (side2 > side3) ) {

            // the user did not follow the instructions
            System.out.println("Unacceptable numbers. Program
quits.");
            return;
        }

        // check to see whether or not numbers form sides of a
triangle

        if (side1 + side2 <= side3) {
            // numbers do not form a triangle

            System.out.println("Lengths cannot represent the sides
of a triangle.");

        }
        else if (side1 == side3) {
            // numbers form a equilateral triangle

            System.out.println("Numbers represent the sides of an
equilateral
                triangle.");
        }
        else if ( (side1 == side2) || (side2 == side3) ) {
            // numbers represent an isosceles triangle

            System.out.println("Numbers represent the sides of an
isosceles
                triangle.");
        }
        else { // triangle is scalene
            System.out.println("Numbers represent the sides of a
scalene
                triangle.");
        }

    }
}
```

- What output do you expect with the inputs 5 4 9 (in that order)? What output do you expect with the inputs 4 5 9 (in that order)? Record your answers. Compile and run the program to check your understanding.

Ordering	Expected Result	Actual Result
5 4 9		
4 5 9		

- As a post laboratory exercise provide additional test inputs that cause the other output messages to be displayed (i.e., inputs that correspond to the various kinds of triangles).

- Why do you think it is important to develop a set of test inputs so that every part of a program is executed at least once?

- Close the triangle.java file.

Now we will use the if statement to help compute the value of a standard Boolean operation.

- Open the file Nand.java.

```
import java.io.*;

public class Nand {
    public static void main(String[] args) throws IOException {

        // Prompt user and read input values for p and q

        BufferedReader stdin = new BufferedReader(new
                InputStreamReader(System.in));

        System.out.print("Please enter a logical value (true,
false): ");
        boolean p =
Boolean.valueOf(stdin.readLine()).booleanValue();

        System.out.print("Please enter another logical value (true,
false): ");
        boolean q =
Boolean.valueOf(stdin.readLine()).booleanValue();
```

```
        // compute the correct value to assign to nand using if-
else-if's

        boolean nand;
        if ( (!p) && (!q) ) {
            nand = true;
        }
        else if ( (!p) && (q) ) {
            nand = true;
        }
        else if ( (p) && (!q) ) {
            nand = true;
        }
        else {  // (p) and (q)
            nand = false;
        }
        // display nand's value

        System.out.println( p + " nand " + q + " = " + nand);
    }
}
```

- Do you understand how the following line of code works?

```
boolean q = Boolean.valueOf(stdin.readLine()).booleanValue();
```

- Open the Java API and read the specifications for the methods `Boolean.valueOf()` and `Boolean.booleanValue()`. The line of code above reads a string from the standard input, `stdin.readLine()`. The string is converted to a Boolean object using `Boolean.valueOf(stdin.readLine)`. Since we want the primitive `boolean` value, not the `Boolean` object, we then convert the object to a primitive type by calling `booleanValue()`.

- This program offers one solution to the following truth table for the Boolean `nand` operation, which is the negation of the `and` operation (not (p and q)).

p	q	nand
false	false	true
false	true	true
true	false	true
true	true	false

- Using the four possible input combinations, run the program to verify its correctness.

- Observe that only the final combination—p and q both true—causes the nand result to be false. Restructure your code so that it uses a single `if` and a single `else`. (Test only whether the combination defined in the last row of the truth table is the one you have).

- Compile and run the program. Once it is correct, show it to a laboratory instructor. If you cannot determine the proper test expression, ask for help.

5.4   A SIMPLE PREDICTION

- Consider the following program from the file `Predict.java`. Then determine what the inputs need to be for the strings "1", "2", "3", "4", or "5" to be displayed.

```java
import java.io.*;

public class Predict {

    public static void main(String[] args) throws IOException
    {
        boolean p, q, r;

        System.out.println("Enter 3 logical values (true or
false):");

        BufferedReader in = new BufferedReader(new
                InputStreamReader(System.in));


        p = Boolean.valueOf(in.readLine()).booleanValue();
        q = Boolean.valueOf(in.readLine()).booleanValue();
        r = Boolean.valueOf(in.readLine()).booleanValue();

        if (p && q) {
            if (r) {
                System.out.println("1");
            }
            else {
                System.out.println("2");
            }
        }
```

```
        else if (q && r) {
            System.out.println("3");
        }
        else {
            if (p || !r) {
                System.out.println("4");
            }
            else {
                System.out.println("5");
            }
        }

    }
}
```

- Record your answers in the following table. Show two ways for "4" to be displayed. Are there others?

p	q	r	output
			1
			2
			3
			4
			4
			5

5.5   A COMMON MISTAKE

- Consider the following program. What is its output?

```
public class Mistake {
```

```
public static void main(String[] args)
{
    boolean b = false;

    if (b = false) {
        System.out.println("true");
    }
    else {
        System.out.println("false");
    }
}
```

- Record your answer in the following table.

Your Answer	Program Output

- Open the file `Mistake.java`. Run the program and record the output in the preceding table. Step through the program. What is happening in this program? Do you believe such code should compile successfully?

5.6   USING SWITCH

- Open the file `Shapes.java`. Compile and run the program. Enter several different inputs to observe how the program works

- The program's `main` method is listed below. Observe the `if-else` statement that determines which shape to draw.

```
public static void main(String[] args) throws IOException {

    System.out.print("Enter the number of sides (3-8) for your
shape: ");

    BufferedReader in = new BufferedReader(new
            InputStreamReader(System.in));

    int numSides = Integer.parseInt(in.readLine());
```

```
        Shapes myShape = new Shapes();

        if (numSides == 3) {
            myShape.createTriangle();
        } else if (numSides == 4) {
            myShape.createQuadrilateral();
        } else if (numSides == 5) {
            myShape.createPentagon();
        } else if (numSides == 6) {
            myShape.createHexagon();
        } else if (numSides == 7) {
            myShape.createHeptagon();
        } else if (numSides == 8) {
            myShape.createOctagon();
        }

        System.out.println("Your choice : " +
myShape.getDescription());
        myShape.display();
    }
```

- Convert the if-else statement in the program to a switch statement.

- Compile and run your program.

- How many test inputs do you need to ensure that your program runs correctly? In the space below, list the test inputs that you ran to test your program.

_____

_____

_____

_____

_____

_____

_____

_____

- Did you add a default line to your switch statement? Is there any reason not to add a default line? Is it always appropriate to have a default line associated with a switch statement?

- Do not close the shapes.java file, you will use it in the next section.

5.7 COMPARING OBJECTS

- This exercise uses the `Shapes.java` program from the previous section. We will modify the program to allow the user to select two shapes. Our code will compare the two `Shapes` objects it creates and tell the user if he chose the same shape twice.

- In order to compare objects, we need to create our own implementation of the `equals()` method that all objects have.

- What field of our `Shapes` class should we compare to determine if two different shapes are equal?

- The easiest way to compare `Shapes` is to compare their `description` strings. Since our code, not the user, controls the assignment of the `description` string, we can be sure that the `description` string always corresponds to the correct `Polygon` shape.

- Add the following method to your code.

```
public boolean equals(Object obj) {
    if (obj instanceof Shapes) {
        Shapes comp = (Shapes)obj;
        if (description.equals(comp.description))
            return true;
        else
            return false;
    }
    else {
        return false;
    }
}
```

- Modify your code so it prompts the user twice to choose shapes. Create two objects, `myShape` and `myShape2` based on the user's selections. An easy way to modify the code is to copy your input prompt and `switch` statement for `myShape`, paste it below and change `myShape` to `myShape2` in the pasted lines. Add the following lines of code to your main method after the objects `myShape` and `myShape2` are created.

```
if (myShape.equals(myShape2)) {
    System.out.println("You chose " +
myShape.getDescription() +
                        " twice.");
}
else {
```

```
            System.out.println("You chose : " +
myShape.getDescription() +
                               " and " +
                    myShape2.getDescription());
    }

    myShape.display(100,100);
    myShape2.display(400,100);
```

- Compile and run your program. If you are having difficulty, ask your lab instructor for assistance.

- Enter several different test cases to ensure that your program is working correctly.

5.8   FINISHING UP

- Copy any files you wish to keep to your own drive.

- Delete the directory \javalab.

- Hand in your check-off sheet.

Congratulations! You have now finished the fifth laboratory.

CHECK-OFF SHEET: LABORATORY 5

5.1   IDENTIFICATION

Name:	
Email:	
Section:	
Date:	

5.2   CHECK-OFFS

As you complete each laboratory activity, obtain a laboratory instructor's initials. Hand in the sheet at the end of the laboratory session so that your participation in the laboratory activities can be recorded.

✓	Activity	Lab Instructor's Initials
☐	**"Triangles.java"**	_____
☐	**"Nand.java"**	_____
☐	**Predictions**	_____
☐	**Mistakes**	_____
☐	`switch` **statement**	_____
☐	`equals` **method**	_____

LABORATORY 6
Looping and File Reading

Objective

In this laboratory we will explore the principal looping statements in Java—`while`, `do while` and `for`. We will also practice extracting input values from sources other than `System.in`.

Key Concepts

- Looping
- `while` statement
- `do while` statement
- `for` statement
- Common looping problems
- File stream extraction

6.1   GETTING STARTED

- Using the procedures in the introductory laboratory handout, create the working directory `\javalab` on the appropriate disk drive and obtain a copy of self-extracting archive `lab06.exe`. Place the copy in the `javalab` directory. Execute the copy to extract the files needed for this laboratory.

6.2   EXPLORING VARIOUS LOOPING CONSTRUCTS

Java provides several looping mechanisms. In this lab, we first explore the `while` statement, then the `do while` statement, and finally the `for` statement.

while

Consider the following program that displays the sum of the integers in the range 1...n, where n is a user-supplied positive value. If n is 4, then the program displays the sum of 1 + 2 + 3 + 4, which is 10. The program contains two mistakes. Can you find the mistakes?

```java
import java.io.*;

public class Sum {
    public static void main(String[] args) throws IOException {
        System.out.print("Enter a positive integer: ");

        BufferedReader in = new BufferedReader(new
                                    InputStreamReader(System.in));
        int n = Integer.parseInt(in.readLine());

        int i = 1;
        int sum = 0;

        while (i <= n) {
            sum = sum + n;
            ++i;
        }

        System.out.println("The sum from 1 to " + n + " is " +
sum);
    }
}
```

- One mistake is a failure to observe good programming practice—the user-supplied value is not verified to be positive. Determine where a modification should be made so that if a negative value is supplied, the complement of that value is used instead. The modification should notify the user that a change was made to the input. The complement is computed in the following manner:

      n = -n;

- The second mistake in the program takes place in updating sum. Identify the mistake and determine what the correct expression should be.

- Open the file named Sum.java. It should contain the preceding program.

- Determine manually the sum of the integers from 1 to n for the following values of n: 3, 5, and 10. Record your answer in the following table in the "manual" column. Run the program and record the program results in the "program output" column.

- Did you get the same answers for your manual calculations as you did from the computer program? If not, try to figure out why. If you cannot determine the reason, ask the lab instructor for help.

n	manual	program output	corrected manual	corrected program
3				
5				
10				
-5	--	--		
0	--	--		

- Correct the two mistakes in the program code. Compute the values manually using the corrected code and record your answers in the "corrected manual" column. Now run the program and record the output for the preceding values for n in the "corrected program" column. Also, manually compute the values for -5 and 0 as inputs and then run the program and record the program results.

- Let's modify the program to calculate a different sum. Rather than calculating the sum of the integers from 1 to n, let's instead calculate the sum of integers from m to n, where m and n are user-supplied values and m ≤ n .

- The program has several new characteristics:

  o It prompts for two input values m and n.

  o n does not have to be positive.

  o The value of m must be verified to be less than n. If m > n , then swap the values of m and n and tell the user about the correction.

  o Integer i, instead of taking on the values 1...n, must take on the values m...n.

- Modify sum.java so that it correctly implements the preceding changes.

- Manually determine the sum of values in the intervals `-5...-1`; `-3...3`; and `5...10`. Record your answers in the following table.

m..n	manual	program output
-5...-1		
-3...3		
5...10		
8...6		

- Compile and run the modified program to observe the output using the specified intervals. Now try the interval `8...6`. Record the program output in the preceding table.

- Does your program perform correctly? If not, try to determine why.

do while

- Modify `Sum.java` to use a `do while` loop instead of a `while` loop where the `do while` statement has the following form.

  > do *Action* ; while(*Expression*)

- Do you have to change the test expression when you convert this `while` statement to a `do while` statement? Is this always the case when you convert a `while` statement to a `do while` statement?

- Build and run the modified program, and observe the output with the intervals used previously. Record your program output in the following table.

m..n	program output
-5...-1	
-3...3	
5...10	
8...6	

386

- Does your program perform correctly? If not, try to determine why.

for

- Now, modify `sum.java` to use a `for` loop, where a `for` statement has the following form.

    `for` (*ForInit* ; *ForExpression* ; *ForUpdate*) *Action*

- For our problem the initialization step component of the `for` statement should define and initialize variable `i`. The loop test expression does not need to change. The post expression needs to increment `i` once for each updating of `sum`. The updating of `sum` should be the sole action of the `for` loop body.

- Compile and run the modified program to observe the output using the same intervals used previously. Record your program output in the following table.

m..n	program output
-5...-1	
-3...3	
5...10	
8...6	

- Does your program perform correctly? If not, try to determine why. Show all your results to your laboratory instructor.

6.3   NESTED LOOPING

- Consider the following program.

```
public class Count1 {
    public static void main(String[] args) {
```

```java
        int counter1 = 0;
        int counter2 = 0;

        for (int i = 1; i <= 10; ++i) {
            ++counter1;
        }

        for (int j = 1; j <= 15; ++j) {
            ++counter2;
        }

        System.out.println("counter1: " + counter1);
        System.out.println("counter2: " + counter2);
    }
}
```

- Determine the output of the program and record it in the following table.

Count1.java	manual	program output
counter1		
counter2		

- Open the file named Count1.java. It should contain the preceding program.

- Compile and run the program. Record the program output in the preceding table. Did you get the same answers from your manual calculations as you did from the computer program? If not, try to determine why. If you cannot determine the reason, ask your laboratory instructor to help you.

- Now consider the following program:

```java
public class Count2 {

    public static void main(String[] args) {

        int counter1 = 0;
        int counter2 = 0;

        for (int i = 1; i <= 10; ++i) {
            ++counter1;
            for (int j = 1; j <= 15; ++j) {
                ++counter2;
            }
        }

        System.out.println("counter1: " + counter1 );
```

```
            System.out.println("counter2: " + counter2 );
      }
}
```

- Determine the output of the program and record it in the following table.

Count2.java	manual	program output
counter1		
counter2		

- Open the file named Count2.java. It should contain the preceding program.

- Compile and run the program. Record the program output in the preceding table. Did you get the same answers from your manual calculations as you did from the computer program? If not, try to determine why. If you cannot determine the reason, ask for help.

- Why do Count1.java and Count2.java produce different results?

- These simple programs demonstrate the power of nested looping—with nested loops, actions can take place multiple times in meaningful ways. Show your results to the laboratory instructor.

6.4   CONCENTRIC RECTANGLE DISPLAY

The next exercise shows how loops can accomplish a significant amount of work using a small number of statements. You will be writing a program to draw a geometric picture that should resemble the following figure. The picture has five elements and each element is a series of concentric rectangles that alternate in color.

- Open the file `Rectangles.java`. As written, the function displays only three of the concentric elements. If you run this program the output will resemble the following figure.

- The initial section of the main method first defines several constants.

```
final int SIZE = 400;
final int CENTER_X = SIZE/2;
final int CENTER_Y = SIZE/2;
final int NUM_ITERATIONS = 20;
final double SCALING = 0.8;
final int OFFSET = SIZE/4;
```

- The constant `SIZE` represents the width and height of the window that contains the concentric rectangles. Constants `CENTER_X` and `CENTER_Y` represent the center coordinates of the window. `NUM_ITERATIONS` represents the number of times the rectangles will be drawn. `SCALING` represents the amount to reduce the rectangle size on each iteration. `OFFSET` represents one-quarter of the length of a side of the window. You can use `OFFSET` to help determine the centers of the concentric rectangles that abut the sides of the window.

- We next define the display window.

```
JFrame window = new JFrame("Concentricity");
window.setDefaultCloseOperation(JFrame.EXIT_ON_CLOSE);
window.setSize(SIZE, SIZE );
window.setVisible(true);
Graphics g = window.getGraphics();
```

- The concentric rectangles are displayed in `JFrame window` (whose title is "Concentricity"). The width and height of `window` are set to the constant `SIZE`.

390

The `Graphics` object `g` is the graphics context of `window` that we will use to render the rectangles.

- Next the method defines the variable `side`. The variable `side` represents the current size of a side of the rectangle being drawn. The first rectangles that are displayed have sides whose lengths are equal to the constant `SIZE`.

  ```
  int side = SIZE;
  ```

- A `for` loop occurs next in the function. The loop iterates `NUM_ITERATIONS` (20) times. In each iteration, three rectangles are drawn—one rectangle for each of the three concentric series being displayed. (Your job is to modify the code so that it also displays the other two series.)

  ```
  for (int i = 1; i <= NUM_ITERATIONS; i++)
  ```

- The first task of the `for` loop is to determine the color of the rectangles to be drawn for the current iteration. If the value of `i` is even, the rectangle is yellow; otherwise, the rectangle is blue. The color is set using the graphics context `g`.

  ```
  Color drawColor;

  if (i % 2 == 0) {
      drawColor = Color.yellow;
  }
  else {
      drawColor = Color.blue;
  }

  g.setColor(drawColor);
  ```

- The rectangles are now drawn using the method `Graphics.fillRect()`.

- The first rectangle drawn is the rectangle in the upper-left corner of `window`. Constants `CENTER_X`, `CENTER_Y`, and `OFFSET` determine the center of this rectangle. By subtracting `OFFSET` from `CENTER_X` and from `CENTER_Y`, we can indicate a rectangle closer to the origin with respect to both the x-axis and y-axis. The coordinates of the center of this rectangle are (`CENTER_X - OFFSET`, `CENTER_Y - OFFSET`). However, the method `Graphics.fillRect()` draws a rectangle given the coordinates of the top left corner of the rectangle. To find these coordinates, we subtract half of the length of the rectangle (variable `half`) from the center coordinates of the rectangle.

```
int half = side / 2;
g.fillRect(CENTER_X - OFFSET - half, CENTER_Y - OFFSET - half,
side, side);
```

- The next rectangle drawn is the rectangle from the group in the lower right corner of `window`. A positive `OFFSET` added to the window's center coordinates gives the location of the center of this rectangle. Subtracting variable `half` from these coordinates gives us the upper left corner of this rectangle.

```
g.fillRect(CENTER_X + OFFSET - half, CENTER_Y + OFFSET - half,
side, side);
```

- The final rectangle is drawn at the center of `window`. Because it is at the center, `OFFSET` is not needed.

```
g.fillRect(CENTER_X - half, CENTER_Y - half, side, side);
```

- Note that the order in which the rectangles are drawn can affect the display.

- To prepare for the next iteration, `side` is updated. In the next iteration, the program draws rectangles whose size is approximately 80 percent (the value of `SCALING`) of the size of the current rectangles.

```
side = (int)(side * SCALING);
```

- Now modify the `for` loop body to construct and draw two more rectangles per iteration. These rectangles should fill the corners of the window that have been ignored temporarily.

- Demonstrate your completed work to the laboratory instructor. Why do the rectangles from one iteration remain on the screen for the next iteration?

6.5   USING INPUT FILE STREAMS

Often we need to use a program to examine a data file. In this exercise, you will learn to use input file streams to extract data from a file. Other types of file processing will be considered in later labs.

- Open the file `Upper.java`. The program in this file counts the number of uppercase letters in the text that it extracts. As written, the program extracts its values from the standard (keyboard) input.

```
import java.io.*;

public class Upper {

    public static void main(String[] args) throws IOException {

        int numUpperCase = 0;
        int currentCharacter;
```

```
        BufferedReader in = new BufferedReader(new
                                InputStreamReader(System.in));
        currentCharacter = in.read();

        while (currentCharacter != -1) {

            if ( Character.isUpperCase((char)currentCharacter) ) {
                numUpperCase++;
            }
            currentCharacter = in.read();
        }
        System.out.println("Upper case chars: " + numUpperCase);
    }
}
```

- Examine the program to get a sense of how it accomplishes its task. Although the method `in.read()` reads a single character, it returns an `int` value. If the end of the stream has been reached, `in.read()` returns -1. When we start the loop, we determine if the stream has ended by checking to see if the value is -1. If the stream has not ended, we enter the loop where we need to cast the return value to a `char` in order pass it to the method `Character.isUpperCase()`.

- Compile and run the program. Note that the program does not issue a prompt to the user to start supplying text. Type the following text as your input. When you are finished typing the text, you need to signal the program that you are done. On most PCs, typing a line consisting solely of a CTRL-Z followed by ENTER produces the signal; other systems often use CTRL-D followed by a carriage return.

  ```
  Java is the greatest!
  This course is FANTASTIC.
  This Line Has A Lot Of Uppercase Letters
  ```

- Make sure that the answer produced by the program agrees with your expectation.

- You will now modify the program to extract values from a file rather than from standard (keyboard) input. The class `FileReader` is the input stream type for representing a file. In this example, you define and use a `FileReader` object named `reader` that represents the input file stream you need to process. Define your `FileReader` just above the current line that defines the `BufferedReader` around `System.in`. Use the file `input.txt`, which is located in the same directory as `Upper.java`.

- You will now wrap a `BufferedReader` around `reader`. Modify the `BufferedReader in` to read from `reader`, rather than `from System.in`.

- Since reading from `System.in` also uses a `BufferedReader,` you will not have to change the rest of the code.

- Open the file `input.txt` and examine its contents. Record your expectation of the program's output below.

  Expected output: _____ Actual output: _____

- Compile and run the program; record the actual output above. Make sure you understand why the program produced this output.

- Show your results to the laboratory instructor.

6.6 FLAWED LOOPING

Improper initialization statements and termination conditions often are causes of incorrect program behavior. The following example illustrates some common mistakes.

- Open the file `Fraction.java`. Examine the program to get a sense of what occurs during execution. The program attempts to compute the value 1 by summing the fraction 1/n, n times. For example, if n=3, then, ideally, the program should compute $1/3 + 1/3 + 1/3 = 1$.

```java
public class Fraction {

    public static void main(String[] args) {

        int total;        // running sum of the fraction total
        int n;            // number of fraction units
        int fraction;     // will be 1/n;
        int loopCounter;  // number of times for loop has executed
so far

        n = 2;
        fraction = 1/n;
        loopCounter = 0;

        for (total = 0; total != 1; total += fraction) {
            ++loopCounter;
        }

        System.out.println("The total is " + total);
    }
}
```

- Run the program and observe its output, or in this case, lack of output. The program contains an infinite loop. To terminate the program, if you are running a dos shell window, you may be able simply to close the shell window. If not, you may need to enter an escape sequence. On PCs this sequence is normally CTRL-ALT-DEL, which is entered by striking the DEL key while holding down the CTRL and ALT keys. A help window should appear where you can terminate the errant process. Sometimes as a result of the infinite loop, you are forced to restart the machine without saving the program. In this case you will lose unsaved modifications. As a precaution, you should always save a program before running it.

- Modify your code so you can monitor the code's calculations. Make the following additions to your code. If you are using a debugger in your lab, you do not need to modify the code. Instead watch the variables `total`, `fraction`, and `loop`.

```
BufferedReader in = new BufferedReader(new
InputStreamReader(System.in));

for (total = 0; total != 1; total += fraction) {
   ++loopCounter;
   System.out.print("total: " + total);
   System.out.print(" fraction: " + fraction);
   System.out.println("  loopCounter: " + loopCounter);
   in.readLine();
}
```

- Have your `main` method throw `IOException`, as you learned in previous labs. Add a line at the top of the code to import the Java `io` library.

- Use the command `in.readLine()` to pause between calculations.

- Monitor the output until you identify the problem.

- Correct the problem and again monitor the program to observe the behavior of the variables. The program should work correctly now. Show your results to the laboratory instructor.

- Modify `n` so that it has the value `10`. Again step through the program and observe the output. If necessary, terminate the program.

- The first time you ran the program, a mismatch occurred in the variable types representing the fraction. That error is most likely not the problem with this execution. Therefore, a different problem is occurring in the loop. The problem now is that the fraction `1/10` is not represented perfectly by the machine. As a result, the exact sum is not calculated. Try to correct or otherwise overcome this problem.

- Show your correct program output to the laboratory instructor.

6.7   FINISHING UP

- Copy any files you wish to keep to your own drive.

- Delete the directory `\javalab`.

- Hand in your check-off sheet.

Congratulations! You have now finished the sixth laboratory.

CHECK-OFF SHEET: LABORATORY 6

6.1   IDENTIFICATION

Name: Email:	
Section: 	
Date:	

6.2   CHECK-OFFS

As you complete each laboratory activity, obtain a laboratory instructor's initials. Hand in the sheet at the end of the laboratory session so that your participation in the laboratory activities can be recorded.

✓	Activity	Lab Instructor's Initials
☐	**Looping constructs**	_____
☐	**Nested looping**	_____
☐	**Rectangles**	_____
☐	**Input streams**	_____
☐	**Flawed looping**	_____

LABORATORY 7
All About Methods

Objective

Understanding methods involves learning how *parameters* are passed and how *scope* works. Misuse of parameters and misunderstanding of scope are common problems encountered by programmers—problems that often result in unexpected errors.

Overriding and *overloading* methods are powerful tools in object-oriented programming. Learning to use these techniques correctly provides you with greater skill as an object-oriented programmer.

Key Concepts

- Parameter passing
- Methods inherited from `Object`
- Overriding methods
- Overloading methods
- `static` methods
- `java.util.Random` class
- Scope and name reuse

7.1   GETTING STARTED

- Using the procedures in the introductory laboratory handout, create the working directory `\javalab` on the appropriate disk drive and obtain a copy of self-extracting archive `lab07.exe`. Place the copy in the `javalab` directory. Execute the copy, extracting the files needed for this laboratory.

7.2   FUN WITH PARAMETERS

Up to this point, your experience with methods has been limited. However, you should not underestimate their usefulness in imposing logical structure upon programs. An important part of using methods entails the understanding of parameters. Parameters enable methods to be flexible. With parameters a single method can handle a variety of related tasks—the parameters determine which tasks to do and which values to compute. Parameters have this important role because they provide the primary interface between the method to be invoked and the calling program fragment. Parameters enable programmers to control the values or objects that pass in and out of a method. Programs with methods that use parameters to share information are modular and are easy to understand.

For each of the problems in this laboratory, perform the following activities with your group.

- Read the program, but do not run it!

- Trace through it by hand and determine what the results of the program will be.

- Whenever you are asked to explain or describe something, write your answers in the space provided.

- Discuss your results with your group and come to a consensus on the answer. When you have reached a consensus, open the file containing the program and run it. The programs are named for the respective problem—for example, Problem 1 corresponds to `Problem01.java`.

- If your predetermined answer disagrees with the results produced when you run the program, go back and see why your predetermined answer is incorrect. If you cannot discover the reason, ask a laboratory instructor for assistance. Remember to obtain a check-off from the laboratory instructor for each solution.

Helpful Hint: When you try to trace parameters by hand, it is useful to draw a box for each parameter and then to keep the value in the box current. This approach enables you to see what is happening with each parameter.

7.3   PROBLEM 1

```
public class Problem01 {

    public static void f() {
    }

    public static void main(String[] args) {

        int i = 10;
        int j = 20;
```

```
        f();

        System.out.println( "main: i = " + i );
        System.out.println( "main: j = " + j );
    }
}
```

- What output is produced?

7.4 PROBLEM 2

```
public class Problem02 {

    public static void f(int i, int j) {

        System.out.println( "f: i = " + i );
        System.out.println( "f: j = " + j );
    }

    public static void main(String[] args) {
        int i = 10;
        int j = 20;

        f(i, j);

        System.out.println( "main: i = " + i );
        System.out.println( "main: j = " + j );
    }
}
```

- What output is produced?

7.5 PROBLEM 3

```
public class Problem03 {

    public static void f(int i, int j) {

        i += j;
        j += i;

        System.out.println( "f: i = " + i );
        System.out.println( "f: j = " + j );
    }

    public static void main(String[] args) {
```

```
        int i = 10;
        int j = 20;

        f(50, j);
        f(i, 50);

        System.out.println( "main: i = " + i );
        System.out.println( "main: j = " + j );
    }
}
```

- What output is produced?

7.6 PROBLEM 4

```
public class Problem04 {

    public static void f(int i, int j) {

        int temp;

        temp = i;
        i = j;
        j = temp;

        System.out.println( "f: i = " + i );
        System.out.println( "f: j = " + j );
    }

    public static void main(String[] args) {

        int a = 10;
        int b = 20;

        f(a, b);
        f(b, a);

        System.out.println( "main: a = " + a );
        System.out.println( "main: b = " + b );
    }
}
```

- What output is produced?

7.7 PROBLEM 5

```java
import java.awt.Point;

public class Problem05 {

    public static void f(Point i, Point j) {

        Point temp;

        temp = i;
        i = new Point(3,3);
        j = temp;

        System.out.println( "f: i = ( " + i.x + ", " + i.y + " )"
);
        System.out.println( "f: j = ( " + j.x + ", " + j.y + " )"
);
    }

    public static void main(String[] args) {

        Point a = new Point(1,1);
        Point b = new Point(2,2);

        System.out.println( "main: a = ( " + a.x + ", " + a.y + "
)" );
        System.out.println( "main: b = ( " + b.x + ", " + b.y + "
)" );

        f(a, b);
        f(b, a);

        System.out.println( "main: a = ( " + a.x + ", " + a.y + "
)" );
        System.out.println( "main: b = ( " + b.x + ", " + b.y + "
)" );
    }
}
```

- What output is produced?

- Why would it be illegal to change the first call of method `f()` in `main()` to `f(i, j)`?

7.8 ROBLEM 6

```java
import java.awt.Point;

public class Problem06 {

    public static void f(Point i, Point j) {

        i.move(3,3);

        System.out.println( "f: i = ( " + i.x + ", " + i.y + " )"
);
        System.out.println( "f: j = ( " + j.x + ", " + j.y + " )"
);
    }

    public static void main(String[] args) {

        Point a = new Point(1,1);
        Point b = new Point(2,2);

        System.out.println( "main: a = ( " + a.x + ", " + a.y + "
)" );
        System.out.println( "main: b = ( " + b.x + ", " + b.y + "
)" );

        f(a, b);

        System.out.println( "main: a = ( " + a.x + ", " + a.y + "
)" );
        System.out.println( "main: b = ( " + b.x + ", " + b.y + "
)" );

        f(b, a);

        System.out.println( "main: a = ( " + a.x + ", " + a.y + "
)" );
        System.out.println( "main: b = ( " + b.x + ", " + b.y + "
)" );
    }
}
```

- What output is produced?

7.9 PROBLEM 7

```java
import java.awt.Point;

public class Problem07 {

    public static void f(Point i, Point j) {

        i.move(3,3);
        j = i;
        j.move(4,4);

        System.out.println( "f: i = ( " + i.x + ", " + i.y + " )"
);
        System.out.println( "f: j = ( " + j.x + ", " + j.y + " )"
);
    }

    public static void main(String[] args) {

        Point a = new Point(1,1);
        Point b = new Point(2,2);

        System.out.println( "main: a = ( " + a.x + ", " + a.y + "
)" );
        System.out.println( "main: b = ( " + b.x + ", " + b.y + "
)" );

        f(a, b);

        System.out.println( "main: a = ( " + a.x + ", " + a.y + "
)" );
        System.out.println( "main: b = ( " + b.x + ", " + b.y + "
)" );

        f(b, a);

        System.out.println( "main: a = ( " + a.x + ", " + a.y + "
)" );
        System.out.println( "main: b = ( " + b.x + ", " + b.y + "
)" );
    }
}
```

- What output is produced?

7.10 OVERRIDING METHODS

All classes in Java ultimately descend from the standard class `object`. Every class inherits several methods from `object`. However, all classes should override the following inherited methods:

- `public String toString()`

- `public Object clone()`

- `public Boolean equals(Object v)`

In the following exercise you will create a class to represent a die (the singular of "dice") You will add the three methods listed above to the class.

- Open the file `Die.java`.

```java
import java.util.Random;

public class Die {
    private static final int NUM_FACES = 6;

    private int value;
    Random generator;

    public Die() {
        generator = new Random();
        roll();
    }

    public Die(long seed) {
        generator = new Random(seed);
        roll();
    }

    public int roll() {
        value = generator.nextInt(NUM_FACES) + 1;
        return value;
    }

    public int getValue() {
        return value;
    }

    private void setValue(int x) {
        value = x;
    }

    public String toString() {
    }
```

```
    public Object clone() {
    }

    public boolean equals(Object v) {
    }
}
```

- Why is the method `setValue()` declared `private`?

- The `java.util.Random` class generates random integers using the `nextInt()` method. To obtain more detail about the `Random` class, see the Java API. In most random number generators, you have the option of supplying a "seed," that is, a value to initialize the generator. If two generators are initialized with the same seed, they will produce the same sequence of numbers. One problem we will encounter in testing our `Die` class is that if we create two `Die` objects in the same millisecond (this is very likely if the objects are created consecutively) the dice will have the same value, because by default Java seeds the `Random` class with the clock. We will allow a constructor to take a seed value to prevent this from happening.

- Now, you will add code to override `Object`'s `toString()` method. Add code so that `toString()` returns the following (if value of die is `6`):

      Die[6]

- How do we decide if two dice are equal? Add code to implement the `equals()` method.

- Finally, add code to implement the `clone()` method. What needs to be cloned? The value of the die is obvious, but what about the random number generator?

- Open the file `DiceTester.java`.

```
import java.util.Random;

public class DiceTester {

    public static void rollTest(Die a, Die b) {
        for (int i=0; i < 10; i ++) {
            a.roll();
            b.roll();
            System.out.print( a + "   " + b);
            if (a.equals(b)) {
                System.out.print(" ** EQUAL **");
            }
            System.out.println("");
        }
    }
```

```
        }

        public static void main(String[] args) {
            Random seeder = new Random();

            Die a = new Die(seeder.nextLong());
            Die b = new Die(seeder.nextLong());

            rollTest(a, b);

            b = (Die)a.clone();
            System.out.println("\n\nCloned dice:\n------------");
            System.out.print( a + "   " + b);
            if (a.equals(b)) {
                System.out.print(" ** EQUAL **");
            }
            System.out.println("");

            System.out.println("\n\nCloned dice roll test:");
            System.out.println("----------------------");
            rollTest(a, b);
        }
    }
```

- Notice that the two dice are seeded with random values so that they are not inadvertently seeded with the same clock time (millisecond), producing the same values.

- Run DiceTester and observe the output using your Die object. Run the program a few times to make sure duplicate values on the dice are rolled. Is the output what you expected? If not, change your code so it produces the correct output.

- Do the cloned dice always roll the same value? If not, can you modify the program so that they do (*hint: use a seed*)? Decide whether cloned dice should or should not always roll the same value.

- Show your program output to the lab instructor.

- Keep the Die.java and DiceTester.java files open for use in the next exercise.

7.11 OVERLOADING METHODS

- Overloaded methods are methods with the same name, but with different parameters.

- In the file `DiceTester.java`, there is a static method `rollTest` that accepts two `Die` objects as parameters, rolls these dice ten times, and outputs the result of each roll. It also reports if the values on the dice are equal.

- Overload the `rollTest` method and create a method with the following header:

```
public static void rollTest(Die a)
```

- This method should accept one die, roll it ten times, and display the result of each roll, similar to the `rollTest(Die a, Die b)` method.

- Add the following lines to the end of the `main` method:

```
System.out.println("\n\nRoll one die:\n------------");
rollTest(a);
```

- Run the program and make sure the output is as expected.

- Show your program output to the lab instructor.

- You will notice that the `rollTest` methods in the `DiceTester.java` program are declared `static`. Since the `DiceTester` class is never instantiated, these methods cannot be run as *instance methods*. They must be run as *class methods*, that is, they are run without an instance of the class `DiceTester`. To be run as *class methods*, they must be declared `static`.

7.12 FUN WITH SCOPE

In the previous exercises, we investigated parameter passing behavior by analyzing various programs and by determining their output. Now we will perform a similar analysis to explain name reuse as it applies to some different scopes that can be provided in a program. For the next several problems, do the following:

- Read the program, but do not run it!

- Trace through it by hand and determine what the results of the program will be.

- Whenever you are asked to explain or describe something, write your answers in the space provided.

- Discuss your results with your group and come to a consensus on the answer. When you have reached a consensus, open the file containing the program and run it. The programs are named for the respective problem—for example, Problem 8 corresponds to `Problem08.java`.

- If your predetermined answer disagrees with the results produced when you run the program, go back and see why your predetermined answer is incorrect. If you cannot discover the reason, ask a laboratory instructor for assistance. Remember to obtain a check-off for each solution.

7.13 PROBLEM 8

```java
public class Problem08 {

    static int a = 0;
    static int b = 1;

    public static void f() {

        System.out.println( "a: " + a );
        System.out.println( "b: " + b );

        a = 10;
        b = 20;

    }

    public static void main(String[] args) {

        int a = 2;
        int b = 3;

        System.out.println( "a: " + a );
        System.out.println( "b: " + b );

        f();

        System.out.println( "a: " + a );
        System.out.println( "b: " + b );
```

```
        }
}
```

- What output is produced?

7.14 PROBLEM 9

```
public class Problem09 {

    static int counter = 0;

    public static void f() {
        ++counter;
    }

    public static void g() {
        int counter = 10;
        f();
        f();
    }

    public static void h() {
        f();
        g();
        f();
    }

    public static void main(String[] args) {

        f();
        System.out.println( counter );

        counter = 0;

        g();

        System.out.println( counter );

        counter = 0;

        h();

        System.out.println( counter );
    }
}
```

- What output is produced?

7.15 PROBLEM 10

```java
public class Problem10 {

    public int i = 0;

    public void f(int i) {
        System.out.println( "i: " + i );
        i = 4;
        System.out.println( "i: " + i );
        i = this.i;
        System.out.println( "i: " + i );
    }

    public static void main(String[] args) {

        Problem10 testObject = new Problem10();

        int i = 1;

        System.out.println( "i: " + i );

        testObject.f(i);

        System.out.println( "i: " + i );
        System.out.println( "i: " + testObject.i );
    }
}
```

- What output is produced?

7.16 PROBLEM 11

First determine whether the following program will compile correctly. If you believe that it will not, state why. If you believe that it will, determine its output.

```java
public class Problem11 {

    public static void f(int a) {

        System.out.println( "int a: " + a );
    }

    public static void f(char a) {
```

```
        System.out.println( "char a: " + a );
    }

    public static void main(String[] args) {

        int i = 1;
        char c = 'c';

        f(i);
        f(c);
    }
}
```

- What is your analysis (and output if any)?

- Suppose main contained the invocation f(2.5). Would the program still compile? Why or why not?

7.17 FINISHING UP

- Copy any files you wish to keep to your own drive.

- Delete the directory \javalab.

- Hand in your check-off sheet.

Congratulations! You have now finished the seventh laboratory.

CHECK-OFF SHEET: LABORATORY 7

7.1   IDENTIFICATION

Name:	
Email:	
Section:	
Date:	

7.2   CHECK-OFFS

As you complete each laboratory activity, obtain a laboratory instructor's initials. Hand in the sheet at the end of the laboratory session so that your participation in the laboratory activities can be recorded.

✓	Activity	Lab Instructor's Initials
☐	**Problems 1 - 7**	_____
☐	**Creating a die class**	_____
☐	**The rollTest method**	_____
☐	**Problems 8 - 11**	_____

LABORATORY 8
Arrays and Collections

Objective

A programmer often needs to represent a group of variables or objects together in a list. The basic Java list mechanism is the array. We will review array basics in this lab. When you use a list, you often need to be able to find values in the list. Therefore, we will review several search algorithms. Finally, since lists are so common in programming, Java provides several collection classes that implement various types of lists used by programmers. We will introduce one example of these collection classes, namely the `ArrayList`.

Key Concepts

- One-dimensional arrays
- Subscripting
- Array manipulation
- Searching techniques
- Java collections framework
- Iterators
- `ArrayList`

8.1   GETTING STARTED

- Using the procedures in the introductory laboratory handout, create the working directory `\javalab` on the appropriate disk drive and obtain a copy of self-extracting archive `lab08.exe`. Place the copy in the `javalab` directory. Execute the copy to extract the files needed for this laboratory.

8.2 ARRAY BASICS

- Open the program file `Five.java`. This program first extracts five values from the standard input stream and uses them to set the values of the elements of an array. The program then displays the values of the array. Even though the program performs its intended task, the implementation can be improved.

```java
import java.io.*;

public class Five {
    final static int LIST_SIZE = 5;

    public static void main(String[] args) throws IOException {

        int[] numbers = new int[LIST_SIZE];

        System.out.println( "Enter a list of " + LIST_SIZE + "
elements" );

        BufferedReader in = new
                BufferedReader(new InputStreamReader(System.in));

        for (int i = 0; i < 5; ++i) {
            System.out.print( "Number:   " );
            numbers[i] = Integer.parseInt(in.readLine());
        }

        System.out.println( "\n" + "The entered list is: " );
        for (int i = 0; i < 5; ++i) {
            System.out.println( "numbers[" + i + "]: " + numbers[i]
);
        }
    }
}
```

- Modify the program so that it extracts and prints eight numbers instead of five numbers. Run the program after it has been modified.

- What modifications did you make so that the program handles eight numbers? Should each modification have been necessary or should the original programmer have written the program differently? Can you suggest some guidelines for writing programs with arrays and constants? Write them down and discuss them with your lab instructor.

- Now modify the program so that it displays the minimum value in the list immediately before displaying the values in the entire list. The following screen capture illustrates the desired input/output features.

- Demonstrate to the lab instructor that your modified program works correctly.

- Modify the program further as follows: when displaying the values in the list, if the element being processed is equal to the current minimum value, display the string "minimum" at the end of the output line. Demonstrate to the lab instructor that your program works correctly.

A common error when using arrays is trying to use an out-of-bounds array index. Java automatically checks that valid array subscripts are used. If a subscript is determined to be invalid, an exception of type `ArrayIndexOutOfBoundsException` is generated. The exception will prevent your program from inappropriately accessing memory outside its allocated space. However, a good programmer ensures that the array is always sufficient to hold the intended information. A good programmer also avoids using an invalid index.

- Open the program file `Sum.java`. This program initializes two arrays `a` and `b` and produces a third array `c` whose values are the sums of the corresponding values of `a` and `b`.

```
public class Sum {
```

```java
static final int LIST_SIZE = 10;

public static void main(String[] args) {

    int a[] = { 30, 21, 19, 28, 29, 12, 54, 23, 24, 25 };

    int b[] = { 54, 54, 72, 15, 21, 28, 32, 56, 61, 33 };

    int c[] = new int[LIST_SIZE];

    int i;

    for (i = 1; i <= LIST_SIZE; ++i) {
       c[i] = a[i] + b[i];
    }

    System.out.print( "     a: { ");
    for (i = 0; i <= LIST_SIZE; ++i) {
       System.out.print( a[i] + " ");
    }
    System.out.println( "}\n" );

    System.out.print( "     b: { ");
    for(i = 0; i <= LIST_SIZE; ++i) {
       System.out.print( b[i] + " ");
    }
    System.out.println( "}\n" );

    System.out.print( "a + b: { ");
    for (i = 0; i <= LIST_SIZE; ++i) {
       System.out.print( c[i] + " ");
    }
    System.out.println( "}\n" );
  }
}
```

- In the space provided below, write down any errors you can detect in the
  program.

  _____

  _____

  _____

  _____

  _____

420

- When using a `for` loop in Java to iterate through an array, you usually allow the loop indices to range from 0 to n-1, where n is the size of the array. This design accommodates the fact that Java numbers array indices from 0 to n-1. Hence, the typical `for` loop initializes its loop control variable to zero and repeats the loop as long as the index is less than the size of the list.

- Correct the errors in the program above. Compile and execute the program. Check the sums to ensure that the program is running correctly.

8.3   SEARCHING

Often it is necessary to search a list of data to determine if a particular value is present. We will now examine two or three methods of searching for a particular value: *sequential*, *binary* and (optional) *interpolation*. Record the number of element comparisons needed to complete each search.

Sequential Search

- Open the program file `Sequential.java`. This class implements a sequential search.

```
public class Sequential {
    int[] list;
    int comparisons;

    public Sequential(int[] values) {
        comparisons = 0;
        list = values;
    }

    // if key is found, returns the index of key, else returns -1
    public int search(int key) {
        comparisons = 0;
        int index = -1;

        if (list != null) {
            boolean done = false;
            for (int i=0; i<list.length && !done; i++) {
                if (list[i] == key) {
                    done = true;
                    index = i;
```

```
        }
            comparisons++;
        }
    }

    return index;
}

    // returns true if index is a valid index, else returns false
    public boolean isValidIndex(int index) {
        return (index >= 0 && index < list.length);
    }

    // returns list value at index, if index is invalid returns -1
    // note: will not check that index is valid, must call
isValidIndex
    public int getValue(int index) {
        return list[index];
    }

    // return the number of comparisons made in most recent search
    public int getComparisons() {
        return comparisons;
    }

    // return size of list
    public int getSize() {
        return list.length;
    }
}
```

- Open the file `Searcher.java`. This file loads an array of integers from a file,
  `unsorted.dat`, and initializes a `Sequential` object with these values. It
  prompts the user for a key and uses `Sequential` to search for the key. The
  program outputs the results of the search.

```java
import java.io.*;

public class Searcher {

    static final int MAX_LIST_SIZE = 1000;
    static final String FILE_NAME = "unsorted.dat";

    // opens file named fileName, loads the values of the file
into a
    // int array and returns the array
    public int[] loadFile(String fileName) throws IOException {
        BufferedReader fileIn = new
                BufferedReader(new FileReader(fileName));
```

```
        int[] buffer = new int[MAX_LIST_SIZE];

        int counter = 0;
        boolean done = false;
        String newLine = fileIn.readLine();

        while (newLine != null && !done ) {
            newLine = newLine.trim();
            buffer[counter++] = Integer.parseInt(newLine);
            if (counter >= MAX_LIST_SIZE)
                done = true;
            newLine = fileIn.readLine();
        }

        // transfer numbers to list
        int[] list = new int[counter];
        for(int i = 0; i<counter; i++) {
            list[i] = buffer[i];
        }

        return list;
    }

    public static void main(String[] args) throws IOException {

        // load file, initialize search
        Searcher testSearch = new Searcher();
        int[] values = testSearch.loadFile(FILE_NAME);
        Sequential search = new Sequential(values);

        // prompt and search for key
        System.out.print("Enter key value: ");
        BufferedReader in = new
                BufferedReader(new InputStreamReader(System.in));
        int key = Integer.parseInt(in.readLine());
        int index = search.search(key);

        // output results
        if (!search.isValidIndex(index)) {
            System.out.println("\n*** The value " + key + " was not
found");
        }
        else {
            System.out.print("\n*** Found value ");
            System.out.println(search.getValue(index));
        }
        System.out.print("*** Number of comparisons required : ");
        System.out.println(search.getComparisons());
        System.out.print("*** to process a list of size : ");
```

423

```
            System.out.println(search.getSize());
        }
    }
```

- Run the program `Searcher` using the five suggested key values to complete the first column of the following table. Then determine the average number of values examined.

	Search Technique				
Search Key	Sequential with unsorted data	Sequential with sorted data	Modified Sequential with sorted data	Binary with sorted data	Interpolation with sorted data (optional)
559					
344					
2415					
297					
1173					
Average					

With randomly arranged data and a random key value which is present in the list, a program generally will examine about half the list to find the key value. If the key value is not present, the entire list will be examined. If we know instead that the data is ordered (sorted) already, then we can do much better in general, whether or not the key is present.

- Modify the program to use the data file `sorted.dat`. This file is the same as `unsorted.dat`, but the numbers have been sorted.

- Run the program and complete the second column of the table.

424

- How has sorting affected the average number of comparisons? Probably not at all, because the program has not been modified to take advantage of the sorting. A significant advantage can be realized if we use the fact that the data has been sorted. Now let's modify the search class to achieve this advantage.

- Because the data is sorted, we can stop searching for the key value once we find a list value that is greater than or equal to the one for which we are searching. Modify the `Sequential` class to terminate the search accordingly. Your modification should cause the loop to terminate once the key value is less than or equal to the value in the list that is being compared (`done = true`). If the key *is equal* to the current value in the list, then the `index` value should be set appropriately.

- Run `Searcher` again and complete the third column of the table.

Binary Search

The binary search described in this section is more efficient than the modified sequential search. When you search for a name in a phone book, you probably don't start at the beginning and search sequentially. You exploit the fact that the names are in sorted order to eliminate a large sections of names in a single step.

The binary search can be implemented as an iterative technique in which each iteration eliminates half of the remaining values from further consideration. The search starts with the middle list element and decides which half of the data to examine further. In the next iteration, the middle element from the half of the data values that can possibly contain the key value is determined, and from it, the range of possible positions for the key value is restricted further. The process is repeated until the search finds the key value or until the search determines that the key value is not present as indicated by the fact there are no more potential positions to consider.

- Open the file `Binary.java`.

```java
public class Binary {
    int[] list;
    int comparisons;

    public Binary(int[] values) {
        comparisons = 0;
        list = values;
    }

    // use binary search to search list for key,
    // if found return index, else return -1
    public int search(int key) {
```

```
            comparisons = 0;
            int index = -1;

            if (list != null) {
            boolean done = false;
               int left = 0;
               int right = list.length - 1;

               while (left <= right && !done) {
                   int p = (left + right) /2;
                   if (list[p] == key) {
                       comparisons+=1;
                       done = true;
                       index = p;
                   }
                   else if (list[p] < key) {
                       left = p + 1;
                       comparisons+=2;
                   }
                   else {
                       right = p - 1;
                       comparisons+=3;
                   }
               }
           }

        return index;
        }

        // returns true if index is a valid index, else returns false
        public boolean isValidIndex(int index) {
            return (index >= 0 && index < list.length);
        }

        // returns list value at index, if index is invalid returns -1
        // note: will not check that index is valid, must call
    isValidIndex
        public int getValue(int index) {
            return list[index];
        }

        // return the number of comparisons made in most recent search
        public int getComparisons() {
            return comparisons;
        }

        // return size of list
        public int getSize() {
            return list.length;
        }
    }
```

- Examine the method `search` in `Binary.java` to determine how the binary search algorithm is implemented. In particular, notice that value `p` is used as an index of the middle element of the values currently being considered.

- Modify the `Searcher` program to use a `Binary` object instead of a `Sequential` object in the `main` method to search for the key. Run the program and complete the fourth column of the table.

- Does the binary search perform more or fewer comparisons than the sequential search?

Interpolation Search (optional)

As a variation on a binary search, there is an alternative for choosing a value for `p` that sometimes is more efficient than always picking the middle element. This alternative supposes that the values in the list being processed are uniformly distributed over the interval between the leftmost and rightmost elements being considered. We can choose as the value for `p` the index of the element that is most likely to contain the key value. People typically use a technique similar to this to find a name in a phone book.

Suppose the list contains 1,000 values, and the value range is 1 … 1,000. If the key value is 4, the expected location is the fourth position. Similarly, if the list contains 1,000 elements, the value range is 1 … 2,000, and the key value is 1,500, the expected location is the 750th position in the list.

In general, if the current range of values being considered is a … b and if n is the number of values in that range, then the expected position p of the key value is

$$p = a + (n-1)\frac{key - a}{b - a}$$

This search is referred to as an *interpolation* search.

- To modify our binary search to become an interpolation search, take the following into consideration:
   - For the "middle" position p to make sense, *key* must lie within the inclusive interval a … b. If *key* does not, it cannot be in the list. This restriction requires two comparisons to be made during each iteration of the search loop to ensure that *key* is potentially in the interval.

     ```
     if (key < a || key > b) {
        done = true;
        comparisons += 2;  // cost of if test
     ```

```
    }
    else {
        comparisons +=2;  // cost of if test
```

. . .

o   The formula for *p* cannot be evaluated if *a* and *b* are the same. Why?

_____

_____

_____

_____

This restriction means that another comparison needs to be made during each iteration of the search loop to determine whether *a* and *b* are the same.

```
if (a == b) {
    done = true;
    index = left;
    comparisons++;  // cost of if test
}
else {
    comparisons++;  // cost of if test
```

. . .

If they are different, the value of *p* is determined using the preceding formula.

In the preceding code, the value of key has been determined previously to be potentially in the interval *a* ... *b*. If the if-test indicates that *a* and *b* are the same, then *a* and *b* must both equal *key*. Why?

_____

_____

_____

_____

- Open the program file `Interpolation.java`.

```java
public class Interpolation {
  int[] list;
  int comparisons;

  public Interpolation(int[] values) {
    comparisons = 0;
    list = values;
  }

  // if key is found, returns the index of key, else returns -1
  public int search(int key) {
    comparisons = 0;
    int index = -1;

    if (list != null) {
      boolean done = false;
      int left = 0;
      int right = list.length - 1;


      while (left <= right && !done) {

        int a = list[left];
        int b = list[right];

        if (key < a || key > b) {
          done = true;
          comparisons += 2;   // cost of if test
        }
        else {
          comparisons +=2;    // cost of if test
          if (a == b) {
            done = true;
            index = left;
            comparisons++;   // cost of if test
          }
          else  {
            comparisons++;    // cost of if test

            int n = right - left + 1;
            int p = Math.round(left + (n -1) *
                          ((float)(key-a) / (b - a)));

            if (list[p] == key) {
              comparisons+=1;
              done = true;
              index = p;
            }
            else if (list[p] < key) {
```

```
                        comparisons+=2;
                        left = p + 1;
                }
                else {
                        right = p - 1;
                        comparisons+=3;
                }

            }
        }
      }
    }

    return index;
  }

    . . .

}
```

- Complete the fifth column of the table. Is the interpolation search an improvement over the binary search? What would be the effect of picking p so that it is always slightly closer to the middle of the list being considered? Discuss your results with your group and then share them with your laboratory instructor.

8.4   JAVA COLLECTIONS

ArrayList

- Open the file `CollectionsGUI.java`. This simple program uses an `ArrayList` to store strings entered by the user. The contents of the `ArrayList` are displayed as the user adds or removes strings from the `ArrayList`.

- In this program, we use a `JPanel inputPanel` to hold a label, text field, and buttons. The `JPanel inputPanel` is added to the main window container `c`.

```
JPanel inputPanel = new JPanel();
inputPanel.setLayout(new FlowLayout());
inputPanel.add(new JLabel("Enter item:"));
inputPanel.add(input);
inputPanel.add(addButton);
inputPanel.add(removeButton);
inputPanel.add(clearButton);
c.add(inputPanel, BorderLayout.NORTH);
```

Nesting components inside other components is a common practice when laying out GUIs. As a `borderLayout` is set up, each region (in this case, `NORTH`) holds only one component. In order to display several different components in the NORTH region, we nest the components inside a JPanel and add the JPanel to the NORTH region.

- Most of the other concepts needed to understand the code in this program are introduced in the *GUI Interlude I* in your text. Review the code to make sure that you understand how the GUI is built.

- Review the actionPerformed method (and companion method displayList).

```java
public void actionPerformed(ActionEvent event) {
    if (event.getActionCommand() == ADD_BUTTON_TEXT) {
        String text = input.getText();
        if (!text.equals("")) {
            list.add(text);
            displayList();
            input.setText("");
        }
    }
    else if (event.getActionCommand() == CLEAR_BUTTON_TEXT) {
        list.clear();
        output.setText("");
    }
    else if (event.getActionCommand() == REMOVE_BUTTON_TEXT) {
        String text = input.getText();
        if (list.contains(text)) {
            list.remove(list.indexOf(text));
            displayList();
            input.setText("");
        }
    }
}

private void displayList() {
    output.setText("");
    if (!list.isEmpty()) {
        for(int i = 0; i<list.size(); i++) {
            output.append(String.valueOf(list.get(i)));
            output.append("\n");
        }
    }
}
```

Make sure you understand what is taking place in these methods.

431

- When comparing strings, as in the line,

  ```
  if (event.getActionCommand() == ADD_BUTTON_TEXT) {
  ```

  why isn't the `String.equals()` method used instead of `==`? Is `==` acceptable? Why or why not?

- Compile and run the program. Experiment with adding and removing strings from the `ArrayList`.

8.5 FINISHING UP

- Copy any files you wish to keep to your own drive.

- Delete the directory `\javalab`.

- Hand in your check-off sheet.

Congratulations! You have now finished the eighth laboratory.

CHECK-OFF SHEET: LABORATORY 8

8.1   IDENTIFICATION

Name:	
Email:	
Section:	
Date:	

8.2   CHECK-OFFS

As you complete each laboratory activity, obtain a laboratory instructor's initials. Hand in the sheet at the end of the laboratory session so that your participation in the laboratory activities can be recorded.

✓	Activity	Lab Instructor's Initials
☐	**Input eight numbers**	_____
☐	**Show minimum value**	_____
☐	**Avoiding an invalid index**	_____
☐	**Search results table**	_____
☐	**Collections**	_____

LABORATORY 9
Object-Oriented Concepts

Objective

In this lab we will learn about one of the distinctive characteristics of object-oriented programming—inheritance. Inheritance is the ability to define a new class based on an existing class. Inheritance facilities code reuse and good organization. However, using inheritance correctly requires a programmer to produce a good code design before any code is written. We will review inheritance hierarchies and then explore polymorphism—a powerful mechanism allowing the same code expression to invoke different methods depending on the type of the object using the code—a technique unavailable in procedural languages. Finally, we will illustrate some of these key concepts by creating a GUI based on the `Die` class we developed in Lab 7.

Key Concepts

- Inheritance

- Inheritance hierarchies

- Polymorphism

- `abstract` classes

- `protected` access

- Overriding inherited methods

- Extending `Swing` classes

- Overriding `paintComponent()`

- Proper use of `repaint()`

9.1 GETTING STARTED

- Using the procedures in the introductory laboratory handout, create the working directory \javalab on the appropriate disk drive and obtain a copy of self-extracting archive lab09.exe. Place the copy in the javalab directory. Execute the copy to extract the files needed for this laboratory.

9.2 INHERITANCE

A key feature of an object-oriented language is inheritance. *Inheritance* is the ability to define new classes using an existing class as a basis. Inheritance supports both abstraction and code reuse. For example, suppose you are going to develop classes for different kinds of bicycles. You might develop classes to represent mountain bicycles and road-racing bicycles. It may be advantageous to introduce a base class that contains the features common to all types of bicycles and then to use the base class to create specialized classes of bicycles. Furthermore, this type of hierarchical abstraction of common features helps you understand classes by isolating the features characteristic of the base class and by collecting together the features that distinguish each specialized class. For example, even if you do not know exactly what a hybrid bicycle is, because it is a bicycle, you know it must have two wheels, handlebars, and pedals.

The relationship between a hybrid bicycle and a generic bicycle is known as an *is-a* relationship—a hybrid bicycle *is a* bicycle. The relationship between a bicycle and its wheels is a *has-a* relationship—a bicycle *has a* set of wheels.

An inheritance hierarchy often is presented pictorially. For example, the inheritance hierarchy for a few of the Swing components is

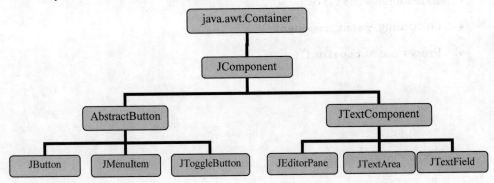

436

We see that the base class is `java.awt.Container` and that the Swing class `JComponent` is derived from `Container`. A `JButton` is a subclass of `AbstractButton` which is a subclass of `JComponent`. Likewise, a `JTextArea` *is-a* `JTextComponent` which *is-a* `JComponent` which *is-a* `Container`.

Designing an inheritance hierarchy is one of the keys to a good object-oriented design. Developing a flexible hierarchy is difficult, but in the long run, it can pay dividends by reducing both maintenance costs and future development costs.

- To get a feel for developing a hierarchy of objects based on the *is-a* relationship, develop an inheritance hierarchy for motor vehicles. For each class of motor vehicles in your hierarchy, list the attributes and behaviors of the class. Draw your motor vehicle hierarchy below.

9.3 POLYMORPHISM AND ABSTRACT CLASSES

To demonstrate polymorphism, we will design a simple program that illustrates some of its characteristics. We will design classes based on the abstract class `Fruit`.

- Open the file `Fruit.java`.

```
import java.awt.Color;

public abstract class Fruit {
    Color color;

    public void setColor(Color c) {
        color = c;
    }

    public Color getColor() {
        return color;
    }

    public abstract String getDescription();
}
```

- A class is abstract if the keyword **abstract** is included in the class heading.

- Notice the method **getDescription**. This method is an *abstract method*. The class includes no code for this method, so any instantiable class that subclasses (or extends) the class must override this method and provide code for the method.

- The methods **setColor** and **getColor** are not abstract methods. However, they are methods of the **Fruit** class so they are inherited by its subclasses. Subclasses do not have to override these methods (although they may). For simplicity, the color of the fruit is represented by a **String** (such as "**red**").

- Create four **Fruit** subclasses of your choice. We provide an example for the kiwi fruit in the file **Kiwi.java**:

```
public class Kiwi extends Fruit {

    public Kiwi() {
        setColor("brown");
    }
}
```

438

```
        public String getDescription() {
            return "New Zealand kiwi fruit";
        }
    }
```

- Open the file `FruitBasket.java`.

```
public class FruitBasket {
    static final int NUM_FRUITS = 5;

    public static void main(String[] args) {
        Fruit[] myFruit = new Fruit[NUM_FRUITS];

        myFruit[0] = new Kiwi();
        myFruit[1] =
        myFruit[2] =
        myFruit[3] =
        myFruit[4] =

        System.out.println("Fruit Basket Contents:");
        for (int i=0; i<NUM_FRUITS; i++) {
            System.out.print("A " + myFruit[i].getColor());
            System.out.println(" " + myFruit[i].getDescription());
        }
    }
}
```

- In the initialization of `myFruit` elements 1 to 4, add instantiations of your chosen fruits.

- Compile and run `FruitBasket`.

- Polymorphism allows code to invoke different methods depending on the type of object used to invoke the method.

- Show your results to the lab instructor.

9.4   EXTENDING THE DIE CLASS

In Lab 7, we developed a `Die` class that was a text-based representation of a die (singular of "dice"). In this lab we will develop graphics-based dice based on the `Die` class from chapter 7.

- Open the file `Die.java`. This is the `Die` class we developed in Lab 7.

- Review the `Die` class. To make this class graphical we simply need to add methods to allow the class to draw itself. At this point, we will address the question common to new programmers: *Do we add or extend?* Should we modify the code in the `Die` class to allow it to draw itself, or should we create a new subclass based on the `Die` class? What do you recommend? List and justify your recommendations below:

_____

_____

_____

_____

_____

_____

- In this lab, we will create a subclass of `Die` called `GraphicalDie` that extends `Die` by being able to draw itself.

- Open the file `GraphicalDie.java`. Although this class may seem complex, most of the code involves computing the locations of the dots on the die based on its size and location. First, let's examine the instance variables and class constants of the `GraphicalDie` class:

```
// class constants
private static final int DEFAULT_SIZE = 50;
private static final Color DEFAULT_DIE_COLOR = Color.white;
private static final Color DEFAULT_DOT_COLOR = Color.black;
private static final int CORNER_ARC_SIZE = 10;
private static final float DOT_SIZE_PERCENT = 0.2F;

// graphical attributes
private int size;
private Point location;
private int dotSize;
private Color dieColor;
private Color dotColor;

// computed dot locations
private int dotLeftX;
private int dotRightX;
private int dotUpperY;
private int dotLowerY;
private int dotCenterX;
private int dotCenterY;
```

- The class constants provide default values for various attributes of the die.

- The instance variables of greatest interest are the graphical attributes. These variables, `size`, `location`, `dotSize`, `dieColor`, `dotColor` define our die graphically.

- Below we provide public accessor and modifier methods for all of these variables excepted the `dotSize`, which is computed as a percentage of the die size (`DOT_SIZE_PERCENT`). The other variables, the computed dot locations, are used to draw the die. They are computed whenever the size or location of the die is modified. The user needs no knowledge of these variables, so no accessor or modifier methods are provided for them.

- Review the public modifier and accessor methods section shown here.

```
//****** PUBLIC MODIFIER AND ACCESSOR METHODS ******

    // size modifier: set the size of the die
    public void setSize(int x) {
        size = x;
        dotSize = Math.round(size * DOT_SIZE_PERCENT);
        setDotLocations();
    }

    // size accesor: get the size of the die
    public int getSize() {
        return size;
    }

    // dieColor modifier: set the color of the die
    public void setDieColor(Color c) {
        dieColor = c;
    }

    // dieColor accesor: get the color of the die
    public Color getDieColor() {
        return dieColor;
    }

    //dotColor modifier: set the color of the dots on the die
    public void setDotColor(Color c) {
        dotColor = c;
    }

    // dotColor accesor: get the color of the dots on the die
    public Color getDotColor() {
        return dotColor;
    }
```

```
// location modifier: set the location of the die
//  and the locations of the dots on the die
public void setLocation(Point p) {
    location.x = p.x;
    location.y = p.y;
    setDotLocations();
}

// location accessor: get the location of the die
public Point getLocation() {
    return (Point)location.clone();
}
```

Most of these methods are straightforward. Notice that the dot locations are computed whenever the size or location of the die is changed.

- There are several methods, such as `clone`, `toString`, and `equals`, inherited from `Object` through `Die`,. When designing our `GraphicalDie` class, we need to decide when two dice are equal. Are they equal when the values are the same, or are they equal when the values and all the graphical attributes are the same? In our program we did not override `Die`'s `equal` method, because we decided that two dice are equal when their values are equal. Was this reasonable?

- Using the variables, `size`, `location`, `dotSize`, `dieColor`, and `dotColor` that define our die graphically, override the `clone()` method from `Die`. Be sure to use the accessor and modifier methods. If you do not, the dot locations will not be computed. This is one reason why it is important to use modifier methods rather than accessing instance variables directly. Also, make sure that you clone the `Die` object variables in addition to the `GraphicalDie` instance variables.

```
//******* OVERRIDDEN METHOD INHERITED FROM DIE/OBJECT *******

public Object clone() {
}

public String toString() {
}
```

- Now provide code to override the `toString` method. Compile your code and check for any syntax errors.

- Review the draw method of the `GraphicalDie` class.

```
//******* PUBLIC DRAW METHOD *******
```

```
// draw the die using the graphics context g
public void draw(Graphics g) {
    // draw the die
    g.setColor(dieColor);
    g.fillRoundRect(location.x, location.y,size, size,
                    CORNER_ARC_SIZE, CORNER_ARC_SIZE);

    // draw a border around the die
    g.setColor(dotColor);
    g.drawRoundRect(location.x, location.y, size, size,
                    CORNER_ARC_SIZE,CORNER_ARC_SIZE);

    // draw dots
    int value = getValue();
    if (value == 1 || value == 3 || value == 5)
        drawCenterDot(g);
    if (value >= 2)
        drawUpperLeftLowerRightDots(g);
    if (value >= 4)
        drawLowerLeftUpperRightDots(g);
    if (value == 6)
        drawSideDots(g);
}
```

The method draws a rounded rectangle to represent a die, draws a border around the die, then determines which dots to draw, and draws the appropriate dots.

- There are several accessory methods used by the **draw** method to draw the dots on the die.

```
// draw the center die dot
protected void drawCenterDot(Graphics g) {
    g.fillOval(dotCenterX, dotCenterY, dotSize, dotSize);
}

// draw the upper left and lower right die dots
protected void drawUpperLeftLowerRightDots(Graphics g) {
    // upper left
    g.fillOval(dotLeftX, dotUpperY, dotSize, dotSize);

    // lower right
    g.fillOval(dotRightX, dotLowerY, dotSize, dotSize);
}

// draw the lower left and upper right die dots
protected void drawLowerLeftUpperRightDots(Graphics g) {
    // lower left
    g.fillOval(dotLeftX, dotLowerY, dotSize, dotSize);
```

```
                     // upper right
                     g.fillOval(dotRightX, dotUpperY, dotSize, dotSize);    }

                 // draw the side (center) dots
                 protected void drawSideDots(Graphics g) {
                     // side left
                     g.fillOval(dotLeftX, dotCenterY, dotSize, dotSize);

                     // side right
                     g.fillOval(dotRightX, dotCenterY, dotSize, dotSize);
                 }
```

- All of these methods are declared `protected`. If, in the future, we subclass
  (extend) `GraphicalDie` to create a die that displays eight dots, we can still call
  these accessory methods to display the various dots because the accessory
  methods are `protected`. We would add another accessory method to draw the
  top middle and bottom middle dots. If these methods were `private`, we would
  not be able to access them in our subclass. We would need to write code to
  draw all the dots.

9.5   DESIGNING A GUI USING INHERITANCE

For our program, we want to display two dice in a window. We will provide a ROLL
button that will "roll" the dice. When the dice are rolled, the graphical image of the
dice will update automatically.

JPanel subclass

- How do we draw two dice? The method for drawing items in Java is to
  subclass a `JPanel` object and override its `drawComponent` method to draw the
  items. This `JPanel` subclass then is added to a `JFrame` to be displayed. Open
  the file `DicePanel.java`.

```
import java.awt.*;
```

```
import javax.swing.*;
import java.util.Random;

public class DicePanel extends JPanel {
    GraphicalDie firstDie;
    GraphicalDie secondDie;

    // class constants
    private static final int DIE_SIZE = 70;
    private static final int X_OFFSET = 40;
    private static final int Y_OFFSET = 30;

    public DicePanel(int windowWidth) {
        super();

        // construct dice

        // seed the dice with random numbers so they won't
generally
        // generate identical values when rolled
        Random seeder = new Random();
        firstDie = new GraphicalDie(seeder.nextLong());
        secondDie = new GraphicalDie(seeder.nextLong());

        // set dice size
        firstDie.setSize(DIE_SIZE);
        secondDie.setSize(DIE_SIZE);

        // set dice locations based on window width
        int firstDieX = windowWidth/2 - X_OFFSET - DIE_SIZE;
        int secondDieX = windowWidth/2 + X_OFFSET;
        int diceY = Y_OFFSET;
        firstDie.setLocation(new Point(firstDieX, diceY));
        secondDie.setLocation(new Point(secondDieX, diceY));
    }

    public void rollDice() {

    }

    public void paintComponent(Graphics g) {

    }
}
```

- Notice that `DicePanel` is a subclass of `JPanel`. `DicePanel` has two instance variables to reference the two dice it will display, `firstDie` and `secondDie`.

445

- Let's review the constructor. The first line is a call to `super()`. This calls `JPanel`'s constructor. Is this explicit call necessary? If we delete this line, will Java call it anyway?

- Next the constructor constructs the dice and sets their size and locations (relative to the window width, passed as a parameter to the constructor). Make sure you understand the code before proceeding.

- Implement the `rollDice` and `paintComponent` methods. The correct implementation should be only two lines long for each method.

- Compile your code and check for syntax errors.

JFrame subclass

- We will now design the primary GUI that will display the panel and the ROLL button. Open the file `DiceGUI.java`.

```java
import java.awt.event.*;
import javax.swing.*;
import java.awt.*;

public class DiceGUI extends JFrame implements ActionListener {
    // class constants
    private static final int WINDOW_WIDTH = 350;
    private static final int WINDOW_HEIGHT = 200;
    private static final BorderLayout LAYOUT_STYLE = new
BorderLayout();

    //instance variables
    private JButton rollButton;
    private DicePanel diceDrawArea;

    //DiceGUI(): constructor
    public DiceGUI() {
        super("Dice");

        // configure GUI
        setSize(WINDOW_WIDTH, WINDOW_HEIGHT);
        setDefaultCloseOperation(JFrame.EXIT_ON_CLOSE);

        //initialize instance variables
        rollButton = new JButton("Roll");
        diceDrawArea = new DicePanel(WINDOW_WIDTH);

        //register event listener
        rollButton.addActionListener(this);

        // add components to container
```

```
        Container c = getContentPane();
        c.setLayout(LAYOUT_STYLE);

        c.add(diceDrawArea, BorderLayout.CENTER);
        c.add(rollButton, BorderLayout.SOUTH);
    }

    // actionPerformed(): roll button action event handler
    public void actionPerformed(ActionEvent e) {

    }

    //main() : application entry poinht
    public static void main(String[] args) {

    }
}
```

- **DiceGUI** is a subclass of **Jframe**. It implements **ActionListener**. A class can extend only one class, but it may implement one or more interfaces.

- Review the constructor. Notice the call to **super("Dice")**. This calls **JFrame**'s constructor with the parameter **"Dice."** This call sets the window title to **"Dice."**

- The rest of the constructor code is straightforward. A ROLL button is created using **this** as an **actionListener**. The ROLL button and a **DicePanel** are added to the **DiceGUI**.

- We will now add code to the **actionPerformed** and **main** methods. First, what do we want to happen when the ROLL button is pressed? We want the dice to roll. Add the following line to the **actionPerformed** method:

    ```
    diceDrawArea.rollDice();
    ```

- To run our program, we need to instantiate a **DiceGUI** object and call its **show** method. Add code to the **main** method to accomplish this.

- Compile and run **DiceGUI**.

- Click the ROLL button several times. Does anything happen?

- Try this experiment. Notice the values displayed on the dice. Press the ROLL button a few times.

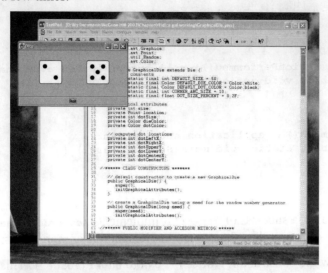

Cover the dice window with another window.

Select the dice window to give it focus.

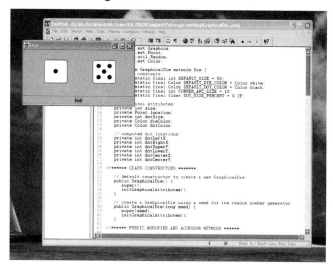

The values of the dice have changed! The dice were being rolled when the ROLL button was pressed, but the window was not redrawn. The window was forced to be redrawn when it was uncovered, which is why the values were updated.

- When the dice window regained focus, the windowing system determined that part of the window needed to be redisplayed and the window's `repaint` method was called automatically. The `repaint` method calls the `JPanel` method `paintComponent`—which you overrode in your `DicePanel` class with instructions to draw the dice.

- To force a window to be redrawn, call its `repaint` method yourself. Modify your `actionPerformed` method to as follows.

```
public void actionPerformed(ActionEvent e) {
   diceDrawArea.rollDice();
   repaint();
}
```

- You should note, however, that *you never directly call* `paintComponent`. To accommodate task scheduling considerations, *you must call* `paintComponent` *indirectly* through the `repaint` method.

- Compile and run your program. Show the working program to your lab instructor.

9.6   FINISHING UP

- Copy any files you wish to keep to your own drive.

- Delete the directory \javalab.

- Hand in your check-off sheet.

Congratulations! You have now finished the ninth laboratory.

CHECK-OFF SHEET: LABORATORY 9

9.1   IDENTIFICATION

Name:	
Email:	
Section:	
Date:	

9.2   CHECK-OFFS

As you complete each laboratory activity, obtain a laboratory instructor's initials. Hand in the sheet at the end of the laboratory session so that your participation in the laboratory activities can be recorded.

✓	Activity	Lab Instructor's Initials
☐	**Inheritance hierarchy**	_____
☐	**Fruits**	_____
☐	**Graphical die program**	_____

LABORATORY 10
Exceptions

Objective

Learning how to catch and handle exceptions allows you, as a programmer, to produce robust code. In this laboratory, you will become acquainted with some common exceptions that a beginning programmer encounters and handles. You will learn how the exceptions are generated, and how to "catch" them. As part of learning to "catch" exceptions, we will review the dynamics of `try-catch` blocks, paying special attention to the details of exception propagation.

Key Concepts

- `Throwable` class hierarchy
- Throwing exceptions
- Exception propagation
- `try-catch` blocks
- Subclassing exceptions
- `finally`

10.1 GETTING STARTED

- Using the procedures in the introductory laboratory handout, create the working directory `\javalab` on the appropriate disk drive and obtain a copy of self-extracting archive `lab10.exe`. Place the copy in the `javalab` directory. Execute the copy to extract the files needed for this laboratory.

10.2 THE JAVA API ON EXCEPTIONS

In this section and in the next, you will become familiar with some of the common exceptions that you are likely to encounter as a beginning programmer.

- Open the Java API specification. Find the specification for `java.lang.Throwable`. All exceptions descend from this class.

- In the diagram of the `Throwable` class hierarchy shown below, put the following seven exceptions in their correct places. Use the API specification to determine class descendancy. Note that this is only a small selection of the classes available in the hierarchy.

  o `java.lang.NumberFormatException`

  o `java.lang.ArrayIndexOutOfBoundsException`

  o `java.lang.StringIndexOutOfBoundsException`

  o `java.lang.NegativeArraySizeException`

  o `java.lang.NullPointerException`

  o `java.lang.ArithmeticException`

  o `java.io.FileNotFoundException`

A Selection of Classes in the `Throwable` Class Hierarchy

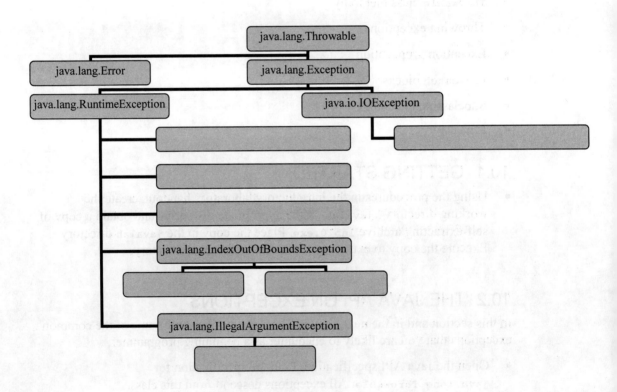

10.3 GENERATING EXCEPTIONS

- Open `ExceptionGenerator.java`.

```java
public class ExceptionGenerator {

    public static void main(String[] args) {

        try {

            // Enter your code here
            int b = Integer.parseInt("1.34");

        }
        catch (Exception e) {
            System.out.println("Caught Exception 'e'");
            System.out.println("--------------------");
            System.out.println(e);
        }
    }
}
```

- For each of the seven common exceptions listed above, modify `ExceptionGenerator` so that it generates the specified exception. Enter the code in the space provided. If you need help determining how to generate the exception, look up the exception description in the Java API specification. The first one is completed for you on the following page.

NumberFormatException

Program output:

```
Caught Exception 'e'
--------------------
java.lang.NumberFormatException: 1.34
```

- Code that produces this exception:

```java
int b = Integer.parseInt("1.34");
```

455

ArrayIndexOutOfBoundsException

Program output:

```
Caught Exception 'e'
--------------------
java.lang.ArrayIndexOutOfBoundsException
```

- Code that produces this exception:

StringIndexOutOfBoundsException

Program output:

```
Caught Exception 'e'
--------------------
java.lang.StringIndexOutOfBoundsException: String index out of
range: 10
```

- Code that produces this exception:

456

NegativeArraySizeException

Program output:

```
Caught Exception 'e'
--------------------
java.lang.NegativeArraySizeException
```

- Code that produces this exception:

NullPointerException

Program output:

```
Caught Exception 'e'
--------------------
java.lang.NullPointerException
```

- Code that produces this exception:

ArithmeticException

Program output:

```
Caught Exception 'e'
--------------------
java.lang.ArithmeticException: / by zero
```

- Code that produces this exception:

FileNotFoundException

Program output:

```
Caught Exception 'e'
--------------------
java.io.FileNotFoundException: file.dat (The system cannot find
the file specified)
```

- Code that produces this exception:

10.4 UNDERSTANDING PROPAGATION

- Open the file `TestException.java`.

```
public class TestException extends Exception {
    public TestException() {
    }

    public TestException(String s) {
        super(s);
    }
}
```

- The class `TestException` is a custom exception that we created to use in the following demo programs. To create your own exceptions, you simply subclass an `Exception` in the `Exception` class hierarchy.

For each of the problems in this section, carry out the following activities with your group.

- Read the program, but do not run it!

- Trace through the program by hand and determine what the results of running the program will be.

- Whereever you are asked to explain or describe something, write down your answers in the space provided.

- Discuss your results with your group and come to a consensus. When you have reached a consensus, open the file containing the program and run it. The programs are named for the respective problem—for example, Demo01 corresponds to `Demo01.java`.

- If your predetermined answer disagrees with the results produced when you ran the program, go back and determine why your predetermined answer is incorrect. If you cannot discover the reason, ask a laboratory instructor for assistance. Remember to obtain a check-off for each solution.

- ## Demo01

```java
public class Demo01 {
    public void a() throws TestException {
        System.out.println("Entering a()");
        b();
        System.out.println("Exiting a()");
    }

    public void b() throws TestException {
        System.out.println("Entering b()");
        c();
        System.out.println("Exiting b()");
    }

    public void c() throws TestException {
        System.out.println("Entering c()");
        throw new TestException("thrown by c");
    }

    public static void main(String[] args) throws TestException {
        Demo01 test = new Demo01();

        System.out.println("Entering main()");
        test.a();
        System.out.println("Exiting main()");
    }
}
```

Enter the expected output here:

Demo02

```java
public class Demo02 {
    public void a() throws TestException {
        System.out.println("Entering a()");
        b();
        System.out.println("Exiting a()");
    }

    public void b() throws TestException {
        System.out.println("Entering b()");
        c();
        System.out.println("Exiting b()");
    }

    public void c() throws TestException {
        System.out.println("Entering c()");
        throw new TestException("thrown by c");
    }

    public static void main(String[] args) {
        Demo02 test = new Demo02();

        System.out.println("Entering main()");

        try {
            test.a();
        }
        catch (TestException e) {
            System.out.println("\nCaught TestException!\n");
        }

        System.out.println("Exiting main()");
    }
}
```

- Enter the expected output here:

Demo03

```java
public class Demo03 {
    public void a() {
        System.out.println("Entering a()");

        try {
            b();
        }
        catch (TestException e) {
            System.out.println("\nCaught TestException!\n");
        }

        System.out.println("Exiting a()");
    }

    public void b() throws TestException {
        System.out.println("Entering b()");
        c();
        System.out.println("Exiting b()");
    }

    public void c() throws TestException {
        System.out.println("Entering c()");
        throw new TestException("thrown by c");
    }

    public static void main(String[] args) {
        Demo03 test = new Demo03();

        System.out.println("Entering main()");
        test.a();
        System.out.println("Exiting main()");
    }
}
```

- Enter the expected output here:

462

Demo04

```java
public class Demo04 {
    public void a() {
        System.out.println("Entering a()");
        b();
        System.out.println("Exiting a()");
    }

    public void b() {
        System.out.println("Entering b()");

        try {
            c();
        }
        catch (TestException e) {
            System.out.println("\nCaught TestException!\n");
            return;
        }

        System.out.println("Exiting b()");
    }

    public void c() throws TestException {
        System.out.println("Entering c()");
        throw new TestException("thrown by c");
    }

    public static void main(String[] args) {
        Demo04 test = new Demo04();

        System.out.println("Entering main()");
        test.a();
        System.out.println("Exiting main()");
    }
}
```

- Enter the expected output here:

Demo05

```java
public class Demo05 {
    public void a() {
        System.out.println("Entering a()");
        b();
        System.out.println("Exiting a()");
    }

    public void b() {
        System.out.println("Entering b()");

        try {
            c();
        }
        catch (TestException e) {
            System.out.println("\nCaught TestException!\n");
            return;
        }
        finally {
            System.out.println("Exiting b()");
        }
    }

    public void c() throws TestException {
        System.out.println("Entering c()");
        throw new TestException("thrown by c");
    }

    public static void main(String[] args) {
        Demo05 test = new Demo05();

        System.out.println("Entering main()");
        test.a();
        System.out.println("Exiting main()");
    }
}
```

- Enter the expected output here:

- What is the difference between the output of Demo4 and the output of Demo5?

- Why do these programs produce different results?

Demo06

```java
public class Demo06 {
    public void a() {
        System.out.println("Entering a()");

        try {
            b();
        }
        catch (TestException e) {
            System.out.println("\nCaught TestException!\n");
        }

        System.out.println("Exiting a()");
    }

    public void b() throws TestException {
        System.out.println("Entering b()");

        try {
            c();
        }
        catch (TestException e) {
            System.out.println("\nCaught TestException!\n");
            throw e;
        }
        finally {
            System.out.println("Exiting b()");
        }
    }

    public void c() throws TestException {
        System.out.println("Entering c()");
        throw new TestException("thrown by c");
    }
```

```
    public static void main(String[] args) {
        Demo06 test = new Demo06();

        System.out.println("Entering main()");
        test.a();
        System.out.println("Exiting main()");
    }
}
```

- Enter the expected output here:

10.5 FINISHING UP

- Copy any files you wish to keep to your own drive.

- Delete the directory \javalab.

- Hand in your check-off sheet.

Congratulations! You have now finished the tenth laboratory.

CHECK-OFF SHEET: LABORATORY 10

10.1 IDENTIFICATION

Name: Email:	
Section: 	
Date:	

10.2 CHECK-OFFS

As you complete each laboratory activity, obtain a laboratory instructor's initials. Hand in the sheet at the end of the laboratory session so that your participation in the laboratory activities can be recorded.

✓	Activity	Lab Instructor's Initials
☐	**Throwable class hierarchy**	_____
☐	**Exception generation**	_____
☐	**Demo01 – Demo06**	_____

LABORATORY 11
Recursion

Objective

In this lab, we will explore recursion, an elegant and powerful approach to problem solving. While recursion often simplifies programming steps, the approach is not always intuitive for programmers who are not used to thinking "recursively." This lab will help you develop your ability to think "recursively."

Key Concepts

- Using activation records to trace recursion
- Mutual recursion
- Recursive binary search

11.1 GETTING STARTED

- Using the procedures in the introductory laboratory handout, create the working directory \javalab on the appropriate disk drive and obtain a copy of self-extracting archive lab11.exe. Place the copy in the javalab directory. Execute the copy to extract the files needed for this laboratory.

11.2 TRACING RECURSION USING ACTIVATION RECORDS

A Greatest Common Denominator (GCD) is the largest number that will factor into each of two numbers. For example, the GCD of 15 and 10 is 5. The code to find a GCD is elegant when programmed using recursion. We will trace through the code several times using activation records to understand how the recursion for GCD works.

- Open the file MyMath.java.

```
public class MyMath {

    public static int GCD(int value1, int value2) {
        if (value2 % value1 == 0) {
            return value1;
        }
```

```
        else {
            return GCD(value2, value1 % value2);
        }
    }
}
```

- We have created a static method GCD to find the GCD of two integer parameters, value1 and value2. As you can observe, the code to find the GCD is only a few lines long.

- Now open the file FindGCD.java.

```
public class FindGCD {

    public static void main(String[] args) {
        if (args.length == 2) {
            int value1 = 0, value2 = 0;

            try {
                value1 = Integer.parseInt(args[0]);
                value2 = Integer.parseInt(args[1]);
            }
            catch (NumberFormatException e) {
                System.out.println("Invalid number format");
                return;
            }

            System.out.println(MyMath.GCD(value1, value2));
        }
        else {
            System.out.println("Invalid arguments");
        }
    }
}
```

- The program FindGCD computes the GCD from command line arguments. The majority of the code for this short program makes sure that the user enters valid command line arguments. The computation (and output) of the GCD consists of the single line:

```
System.out.println(MyMath.GCD(value1, value2));
```

- To compute the GCD for the numbers 52 and 117, compile both files. At the command line enter:

```
c:\javalab>java FindGCD 52 117
```

The output should be 13.

- Now we will use activation records trace the recursion using the numbers `52` and `117`. The test condition for each recursive call is

  ```
  value2 % value1 == 0
  ```

  Remember that the percent sign (%) stands for `mod`, *that is the modulus, or remainder left over after* `value1` *is divided into* `value2`.

  If the test condition is true, `value1` is returned as the GCD and all method calls are exited. If the test condition is false, then new values for the parameters are computed and the method is called again. The new values are

  ```
  GCD(value2, value1 % value2)
  ```

- In the diagram below, compute and enter the values for the parameters `value1` and `value2` after each recursive call of GCD.

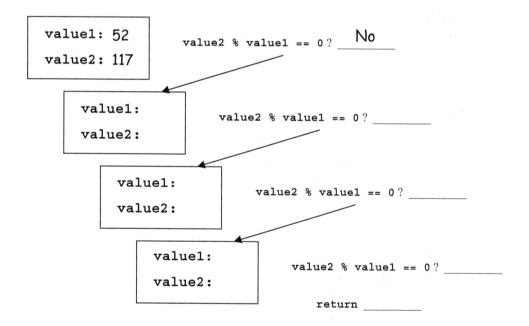

- If you are having difficulty determining the values of the parameters, modify the `GCD` method to output the values of its parameters after each call.

471

- In the space below, draw the activation records for the following command line input:

```
c:\javalab>java FindGCD 646 798
```

11.3 MUTUAL RECURSION

In this exercise we run a program that uses *mutual recursion*. With mutual recursion, instead of one method calling itself repeatedly, two or more methods call each other recursively. For example, method A might call method B which calls method A which calls method B and so on until a base case is reached.

The program models a game involving two players, "a" and "b" who start the game holding 12 tokens each. The players take turns. On his turn, if player "a" has an even number of tokens he must give a fifth of his tokens to player "b." Otherwise, player "a" discards 2 tokens and player "b" discards 1 token. On player "b"'s turn, if player "b" has an even number of tokens, he must discard 3 tokens and player "a" must discard 2 tokens. Otherwise, player "b" gives a third of his tokens to player "a." The game continues until a player has no tokens at the start of his turn. It is possible for a player to hold a negative number of tokens.

- Open the file `PointlessGame.java`. Review the code to understand how the code implements the game.

```java
public class PointlessGame {
    private int count = 0;
    private int aCount = 0;
    private int bCount = 0;

    private int aTokens = 12;
    private int bTokens = 12;

    private void a() {
        count++;
        aCount++;
```

472

```java
        if (aTokens <= 0) {
            return;
        }

        if (aTokens % 2 == 0) {
            int fifth = aTokens / 5;
            aTokens -= fifth;
            bTokens += fifth;
        }
        else {
            aTokens -= 2;
            bTokens -= 1;
        }

        b();
    }

    private void b() {
        count++;
        bCount++;

        if (bTokens <= 0) {
            return;
        }

        if (bTokens % 2 == 0) {
            aTokens -= 2;
            bTokens -= 3;
        }
        else {
            int aThird = bTokens / 3;
            aTokens += aThird;
            bTokens -= aThird;
        }

        a();

    }

    public void run() {
        a();
    }

    public static void main (String[] args) {
        PointlessGame test = new PointlessGame();

        test.run();

        System.out.println("Done. Total method calls : " +
test.count);
        System.out.println("\ta method calls : " + test.aCount);
```

```
System.out.println("\tb method calls : " + test.bCount);
System.out.println("\ta tokens : " + test.aTokens);
System.out.println("\tb tokens : " + test.bTokens);
    }
}
```

- A *base case* is a case which can be solved without recursion. What is the *base case* for method a?

  _____

- What is the *base case* for method b?

  _____

- What do you expect the output of the program to be? Write your answer in the space below. You may also use the space to draw activation records for each method call.

- Compile and run the program. Does your expected output match the actual output? If not, try to determine why. It may help to add lines in the code to output the values of the variables after each method call.

- Show your program output to the lab instructor.

11.4 THE ONE-QUESTION RECURSIVE BINARY SEARCH

The binary search presented in the text asks two questions. First it asks if the midpoint element is the element being sought. If so, the search ends. Otherwise, it asks if the element being sought is lexically less than the midpoint element. This two-question approach is slightly more efficient when the element being sought is present in the list. When the element is not present in the list, it is slightly more efficient to ask just the second question, namely, is the element being sought lexically less than the midpoint element? When the list is reduced to just one element, a single comparison is made to determine if this is the element being sought. In this exercise, you will modify the two-question approach code described in the text to become the one question approach.

- Open the file `BinarySearch.java`.

```java
public class BinarySearch {

    private static int search(int value, int[] numbers, int first,
                              int last) {
        if (first > last) {
            return -1;
        }
        else {
            int mid = (first + last) / 2;
            if (value == numbers[mid]) {
                return mid;
            }
            else {
                if (value < numbers[mid]) {
                    return search(value, numbers, first, mid-1);
                }
                else {
                    return search(value, numbers, mid+1, last);
                }
            }
        }
    }

    public static int find(int value, int[] numbers) {
        return search(value, numbers, 0, numbers.length-1);
    }
}
```

- We have simplified the textbook's binary search by changing the search list to an array of integers. The logic of the code is the same.

- Open the file `TestBinarySearch.java`. This program uses the file `sorted.dat` to provide a sorted list of 5000 `int` values for our binary search. Compile and run the program. Using the values in the table below as input, write the index of each value in the "Two question search" column, if the values are found. Write "not found" if the value is not found.

Value	Index	
	Two question search	One question search
38		
1027		
1367		
7509		
9981		

- Which lines of code in `BinarySearch` ask the question, *is the midpoint element the element being sought*? Write the lines in the space below.

- Which lines of code above ask the question, *is the element being sought lexically less than the midpoint element*? Write the lines of code in the space below.

- Modify the `BinarySearch` code so that it does not ask the first question, *is the midpoint element the element being sought*? Instead, modify the code to wait until there is only one element in the list and then ask the question, *is this the element being sought*?

476

- Compile and run your modified program. Using the values in the table above as inputs, fill in the "One question search" column with the index values returned by the program. If the answers in both columns are identical, show your table and modified code to the lab instructor. If they are not, try to determine why and then fix your code.

- The major time-saving step in your modified code is the elimination of the line of code that compares the search value to the value of the midpoint element.

```
if (value == numbers[mid])
        . . .
```

While this step does not appear to be time-consuming because it is simply comparing two `int`'s, it can be a major time consumer when objects instead of primitive types are compared; the comparison of objects is more complex.

11.5 FINISHING UP

- Copy any files you wish to keep to your own drive.

- Delete the directory `\javalab`.

- Hand in your check-off sheet.

Congratulations! You have now finished the eleventh laboratory.

CHECK-OFF SHEET: LABORATORY 11

11.1 IDENTIFICATION

Name:	
Email:	
Section:	
Date:	

11.2 CHECK-OFFS

As you complete each laboratory activity, obtain a laboratory instructor's initials. Hand in the sheet at the end of the laboratory session so that your participation in the laboratory activities can be recorded.

✓	Activity	Lab Instructor's Initials
☐	**GCD activation records**	_____
☐	**Mutual recursion**	_____
☐	**One question binary search**	_____

LABORATORY 12
Threads

Objective

In our final lab, we will study multiple flows of control. Java allows programmers to run several processes concurrently using *threads*. Our exploration of threads will acquaint us with the `Timer` and `TimerTask` standard classes. We will conclude the lab by exploring Swing-based animation using threads.

Key Concepts

- `Timer` class

- `TimerTask` class

- Fixed-rate vs. fixed-delay scheduling

- Swing-based animation

- Creating tasks at runtime

12.1 GETTING STARTED

- Using the procedures in the introductory laboratory handout, create the working directory `\javalab` on the appropriate disk drive and obtain a copy of self-extracting archive `lab12.exe`. Place the copy in the `javalab` directory. Execute the copy to extract the files needed for this laboratory.

12.2 EXPLORING THE `Timer` AND `TimerTask` CLASSES

- Open the Java API specification and locate the description of the `java.util.Timer` class.

- Read the description of the class. Does this class offer real-time guarantees of scheduling? That is, if you create a clock, are you guaranteed that it will be updated exactly once every second? Do you understand why? Write your explanation below. Ask a lab instructor for assistance if you do not understand the class description completely.

_____

_____

_____

_____

- Read the description for the following `Timer` method

  ```
  public void schedule(TimerTask task, long delay, long period)
  ```

- For what kinds of tasks is this scheduling method suited?

  _____

  _____

- Next read the description for the `Timer` method

  ```
  public void scheduleAtFixedRate(TimerTask task, long delay,
  long period)
  ```

- For what kinds of tasks is this scheduling method suited?

  _____

  _____

  _____

- Now, find the Java API specification for the class `java.util.TimerTask`.
- Review the specification. What method should you override when you subclass this class?

  _____

- How is this method called?

  _____

  _____

- Review your answers with the lab instructor.

12.3 UPDATING THE `SimpleClock` APPLICATION

- Open the file `SimpleClock.java`. This program is introduced in the text.

- Compile and run the `SimpleClock` application.

- Now, try an experiment. Cover up the `SimpleClock` with another window. Alternately give focus to each window. You will notice that sometimes, when the `SimpleClock` window is given focus, it is blank. This is because the window is updated every second. If the window is covered, essentially erasing the display, and then uncovered before it is scheduled to be updated, it remains blank until the update.

Original display

Covering the window

The display before it is updated

- We will learn how to avoid this problem by subclassing **JPanel** and by creating a panel that knows how to redraw itself on demand instead of waiting to be updated.

- Let's start by creating a **ClockPanel**. Open the file **ClockPanel.java**.

```
import javax.swing.JPanel;
import java.util.Date;
import java.awt.Graphics;
import java.awt.Color;

public class ClockPanel extends JPanel {

    public ClockPanel() {
        setBackground(Color.white);
    }

    public void paintComponent(Graphics g) {
        super.paintComponent(g);

        Date time = new Date();
        g.setColor(Color.blue);
        g.drawString(time.toString(), 10, 20);
    }
}
```

- Let's review the code. First the constructor sets the background color to white.

- Then the method **paintComponent(Graphics g)** method tells our subclassed component how to draw itself. This is the method you must override when you subclass a Swing component. Notice the call to

    ```
    super.paintComponent(g);
    ```

Among other tasks, a JPanel knows how to draw its background. If this line is removed from your code, your ClockPanel's background will not be rendered correctly. It is important to call JPanel's paintComponent method whenever you subclass it.

- The rest of our code in paintComponent is straightforward. A Date object is created. It is drawn on the ClockPanel at the coordinate (10, 20) in the color blue.

- Now we need a JFrame to hold and to display our panel. Open the file ExtendedClock.java.

```
import javax.swing.JFrame;
import java.awt.*;

public class ExtendedClock extends JFrame {
    ClockPanel clockDisplay;

    public ExtendedClock() {

        setDefaultCloseOperation(JFrame.EXIT_ON_CLOSE);
        setSize(200, 60);

        clockDisplay = new ClockPanel();

        getContentPane().add(clockDisplay);
    }


    public static void main(String[] args) {
        new ExtendedClock().show();
    }
}
```

- Review the code and make sure you understand how it works. Then compile and run ExtendedClock.java and observe the output.

- How does the behavior of this application differ from the behavior of SimpleClock.java?

- What happens if you cover the ExtendedClock window with another window, and then return focus to the ExtendedClock window?

- You should have observed that the ExtendedClock window updates the time only when the operating system indicates that it needs to be updated.

- Let's create a `TimerTask` class that will cause the `ExtendedClock` to be updated every second. Open the file `ClockTask.java`.

```
import java.util.TimerTask;
import javax.swing.JPanel;

public class ClockTask extends TimerTask {
    ClockPanel clock;

    public ClockTask(ClockPanel clockDisplay) {
        clock = clockDisplay;
    }

    public void run() {
        clock.repaint();
    }
}
```

- We have created a `TimerTask` subclass that, when run, asks the `ClockPanel` to redraw itself by calling its `repaint()` method. We introduced the `repaint()` method in Lab 9 when we created our `GraphicalDie` class. Remember, that *you never call* `paintComponent` *directly*. To accommodate task scheduling considerations, *you must call* `paintComponent` *indirectly* through the `repaint` method.

- Now we need to add a timer to the `ExtendedClock` class to schedule our `ClockTask`.

- In the `ExtendedClock` class, add a line to import the `java.util.Timer` class.

- Now add a class variable named `timer` of type `Timer` to the `ExtendedClock` class. Add a line of code to instantiate the object.

- From your research in the previous exercise, which `Timer` method should be called to schedule the `ClockTask`?

```
      timer.schedule(new ClockTask(clockDisplay), 0, 1000);
```
or
```
      timer.scheduleAtFixedRate(new ClockTask(clockDisplay), 0,
1000);
```

Add the appropriate line to the end of your constructor's code.

- Make sure you understand how the code works. Then compile and run the `ExtendedClock` application.

- Using the alternating window focus technique you used with the `SimpleClock` application at the beginning of this section, can you ever make your `ExtendedClock` appear blank when it gains focus? Why or why not?

- In the `SimpleClock` application from the text, `drawString` is called to draw a blank string to erase the old time before the new time is drawn. Is there an equivalent erasure in our `ExtendedClock` application? Do you know why this is the case?

- Discuss your answers to these questions with the lab instructor and show your program to him or her.

12.4 FIREFLY SCHEDULING DEMO

Anyone who has visited rural or quiet suburban areas in the eastern United States during the summertime is familiar with an insect referred to as a "firefly" or "lightening bug." These flying beetles have an ability to "light up" an area on their abdomens. On dark nights, large numbers of these insects rival fireworks. If you have not seen fireflies in action, you will have to content yourself with the simulation program we will develop in this section.

- Let's start by designing a class to represent a firefly. Make a list below of things a firefly does that would be useful in our simulation. Also include a list of attributes our fireflies should have.

_____

_____

_____

_____

_____

_____

_____

- Open the file `FireFly.java`.

```
import java.awt.Color;
import java.awt.Graphics;
import java.util.Random;
```

```java
public class FireFly {
    private Random generator;
    private int x;
    private int y;
    private boolean lit;
    private int boundsWidth;
    private int boundsHeight;

    private static final int SIZE = 6;
    private static final Color COLOR = Color.yellow;
    private static final int maxXStep = 20;
    private static final int maxYStep = 20;

    public FireFly  (int areaWidth, int areaHeight) {
        setBounds(areaWidth, areaHeight);

        generator = new Random();

        x = generator.nextInt(boundsWidth);
        y = generator.nextInt(boundsHeight);

        turnOn();
    }

    public boolean isLit() {
        return lit;
    }

    public void turnOn() {
        lit = true;
    }

    public void turnOff() {
        lit = false;
    }

    public void setBounds(int width, int height) {
        boundsWidth = width;
        boundsHeight = height;
    }

    public void move() {
        // determine if positive or negative x movement
        int xOffset = generator.nextInt(maxXStep);
        if (generator.nextBoolean()) {
            x += xOffset;
        }
        else {
            x -= xOffset;
        }
```

```
        // determine if positive or negative y movement
        int yOffset = generator.nextInt(maxYStep);
        if (generator.nextBoolean()) {
            y += yOffset;
        }
        else {
            y -= yOffset;
        }
    }

    public void draw(Graphics g) {
        if (lit) {
            g.setColor(COLOR);
            g.fillArc(x, y, SIZE, SIZE, 0, 360);
        }
    }
}
```

- Let's review the code. In the following spaces, describe what each collection of methods does.

```
public FireFly(int areaWidth, int areaHeight)
```

```
public boolean isLit()
public void turnOn()
public void turnOff()
```

```
public void move()
```

```
public void draw(Graphics g) {
```

- There is another method,

  ```
  public void setBounds(int width, int height)
  ```

  This method is used to indicate the area where the firefly is created and moves about.

- We now have a class that can create a firefly, move it, turn its abdominal light on and off causing it to "blink," and is able to draw itself. Now let's create a panel that will display our fireflies.

- Open the file `FireFlyPanel.java`.

```java
import javax.swing.JPanel;
import java.util.ArrayList;
import java.awt.*;

public class FireFlyPanel extends JPanel {
    ArrayList flies;

    public FireFlyPanel() {
        setBackground(Color.black);

        flies = new ArrayList();
    }

    public void addFireFly() {
        FireFly newFly = new FireFly(this.getWidth(),
this.getHeight());
        flies.add(newFly);
    }

    public void paintComponent(Graphics g) {
        super.paintComponent(g);

        for (int i = 0; i < flies.size(); i++) {
            FireFly current = (FireFly)flies.get(i);
            current.draw(g);
        }
    }
}
```

- Review the code for our `FireFlyPanel`. Do you understand how the code works? A black panel will display 0 to an unlimited (theoretically) number of fireflies. It has the ability to add fireflies as needed.

- Now, we need to create a `JFrame` to display our panel. Open the file `FireFlies.java`.

```java
import javax.swing.*;
import java.awt.*;
import java.awt.event.*;

public class FireFlies extends JFrame implements ActionListener {
    FireFlyPanel flyPanel;
    JButton addFireFlyButton;

    public FireFlies() {
        // set up JFrame
        setDefaultCloseOperation(JFrame.EXIT_ON_CLOSE);
        setSize(600, 400);

        // create flyPanel
        flyPanel = new FireFlyPanel();

        // create button, register action listener
        addFireFlyButton = new JButton("Add A Firefly");
        addFireFlyButton.addActionListener(this);

        // add components to content pane
        Container c = getContentPane();
        c.add(flyPanel, BorderLayout.CENTER);
        c.add(addFireFlyButton, BorderLayout.SOUTH);
    }

    public void actionPerformed(ActionEvent e) {
        flyPanel.addFireFly();
        flyPanel.repaint();
    }

    public static void main(String[] args) {
        new FireFlies().show();
    }
}
```

- Using the techniques we learned in Lab 9 while designing our graphical dice program, we have created a frame that displays our `FireFlyPanel` along with a `JButton` we can use to add more fireflies to our display. If you do not understand how our `JFrame` subclass implements `ActionListener`, turn back to Lab 9 and review the graphical dice sections.

- Compile and run `FireFlies.java`. Experiment with the program. Does the window redraw itself correctly when another window covers it?

- Have you noticed that the program really is not a good simulation because our fireflies neither move nor blink on and off? Let's now add some animation to our program.

- Open the file `FireFlyTask.java`.

```java
import java.util.TimerTask;

public class FireFlyTask extends TimerTask {
    FireFly myFly;
    FireFlyPanel display;

    public FireFlyTask(FireFly fly, FireFlyPanel panel) {
        myFly = fly;
        display = panel;
    }

    public void run() {
        myFly.move();
        if (myFly.isLit()) {
            myFly.turnOff();
        }
        else {
            myFly.turnOn();
        }
        display.repaint();
    }
}
```

- In your own words, describe what the `run` method does:

- Why is the constructor passed references to a `FireFly` object and to a `FireFlyPanel` object?

- With regard to the `repaint()` call in the `run` method, if there are multiple tasks calling `repaint()` all at the same time, Java's sophisticated task scheduling thread will group these `repaint()` calls into one call instead of issuing multiple method calls. This is one important reason to call `repaint()` rather than `paintComponent()`. This method also is more sophisticated than "blacking out" the old location and redrawing the object in its new location, as sometimes is done.

- Now that we have a task that can move and blink a firefly, let's add a `Timer` object to control the tasks. In your `FireFlyPanel`, add a line to import `java.util.Timer`. Next, add a class variable named `flyController` of type `Timer`. Instantiate `flyController` in the `FireFlyPanel` constructor.

- Our fireflies behave in a very simple manner. We will schedule each firefly to move and to turn on or off every second after being instantiated. Add the following line of code at the bottom of the `addFireFly` method code.

  ```
  flyController.schedule(new FireFlyTask(newFly, this), 0, 1000);
  ```

- Why is the `schedule` method called instead of the `scheduleAtFixedRate` method?

- Compile and run your program. Add one firefly. Observe its behavior. Add another, and observe its behavior. Do the fireflies blink at the same time? Why or why not? Experiment with adding more fireflies.

- Experiment with the window rendering. Cover part of the window with another. Cover the entire window with another window and then uncover it. Does the animation continue as expected?

- You will notice that some of the fireflies eventually leave the screen. What do you think is the best way to handle these individual fireflies? Should you call the `TimerTask.cancel()` method? Why or why not?

- Modify the code to implement your handling of these "lost" fireflies. Show your code modifications to the lab instructor and demonstrate your program to him or her.

12.5 FINISHING UP

- Copy any files you wish to keep to your own drive.

- Delete the directory \javalab.

- Hand in your check-off sheet.

Congratulations! You have now finished the twelfth and final laboratory.

CHECK-OFF SHEET: LABORATORY 12

12.1 IDENTIFICATION

Name: Email:	
Section:	
Date:	

12.2 CHECK-OFFS

As you complete each laboratory activity, obtain a laboratory instructor's initials. Hand in the sheet at the end of the laboratory session so that your participation in the laboratory activities can be recorded.

✓	Activity	Lab Instructor's Initials
☐	**Exploring the API specs**	_____
☐	**ExtendedClock application**	_____
☐	**Firefly simulation**	_____